# FROM JICAMA TO JACKFRUIT

**ISI** Mark A. Boyer and Shareen Hertel, Series Editors

International Studies Intensives (ISI) is a book series that springs from the desire to keep students engaged in the world around them. ISI books pack a lot of information into a small space—they are meant to offer an intensive introduction to subjects often left out of the curriculum. ISI books are relatively short, visually attractive, and affordably priced.

### Titles in the Series

*The Rules of the Game: A Primer on International Relations,* Mark R. Amstutz

*Development Redefined: How the Market Met Its Match,* Robin Broad and John Cavanagh

*Protecting the Global Environment,* Gary C. Bryner

*A Tale of Two Quagmires: Iraq, Vietnam, and the Hard Lessons of War,* Kenneth J. Campbell

*Celebrity Diplomacy,* Andrew F. Cooper

*Global Health in the 21st Century: The Globalization of Disease and Wellness,* Debra L. DeLaet and David E. DeLaet

*Terminate Terrorism: Framing, Gaming, and Negotiating Conflicts,* Karen A. Feste

*Watching Human Rights: The 101 Best Films,* Mark Gibney

*The Global Classroom: An Essential Guide to Study Abroad,* Jeffrey S. Lantis and Jessica DuPlaga

*Democratic Uprisings in the New Middle East: Youth, Technology, Human Rights, and US Foreign Policy,* Mahmood Monshipouri

*Sixteen Million One: Understanding Civil War,* Patrick M. Regan

*People Count! Networked Individuals in Global Politics,* James N. Rosenau

*Paradoxes of Power: US Foreign Policy in a Changing World,* David Skidmore

*Global Democracy and the World Social Forums,* Jackie Smith and Marina Karides et al.

*From Jicama to Jackfruit: The Global Political Economy of Food,* Kimberly Weir

*Governing the World? Addressing "Problems without Passports,"* Thomas G. Weiss

### Forthcoming in the Series

*Violence Against Women in the Law,* David L. Richards and Jillienne Haglund

*The New Warfare: Rethinking Rules for an Unruly World,* J. Martin Rochester

*Global Democracy and the World Social Forums, Second Edition,* Jackie Smith and Marina Karides et al.

*International Relations as Negotiation,* Brian R. Urlacher

*Myth and Reality in International Relations,* Jonathan Wilkenfeld

*Spirits Talking: Conversations on Right and Wrong in the Affairs of States,* Stephen D. Wrage

# FROM JICAMA TO JACKFRUIT

## THE GLOBAL POLITICAL ECONOMY OF FOOD

*Kimberly A. Weir*

**Paradigm Publishers**

Boulder • London

Copyright © 2014 Paradigm Publishers

Published in the United States by Paradigm Publishers, 5589 Arapahoe Avenue, Boulder, CO 80303 USA.

Paradigm Publishers is the trade name of Birkenkamp & Company, LLC, Dean Birkenkamp, President and Publisher.

Library of Congress Cataloging-in-Publication Data

Weir, Kimberly A.
  From jicama to jackfruit : the global political economy of food / Kimberly A. Weir.
    pages cm — (International studies intensives)
  Includes bibliographical references and index.
  ISBN 978-1-59451-931-4 (pbk. : alk. paper)
  ISBN 978-1-61205-657-9 (consumer ebook)
  1. Food supply—Economic aspects. 2. Food supply—Political aspects. 3. Food industry and trade—Economic aspects. 4. Food industry and trade—Political aspects. 5. Food policy. I. Title.
  HD9000.6.W42 2014
  338.1'9—dc23

                                                                                    2013046473

Printed and bound in the United States of America on acid-free paper that meets the standards of the American National Standard for Permanence of Paper for Printed Library Materials.

Designed and Typeset by Straight Creek Bookmakers.

18 17 16 15 14   1 2 3 4 5

*For my mom. Thanks for everything, Joan.*

# CONTENTS

# PREFACE AND ACKNOWLEDGMENTS

When I first taught a class on the politics of food, I never imagined it would develop into a regular course, let alone a book. As the class developed, so did my thinking and teaching approaches, many of which have found their way into this book. I wanted to bring the history of food together with contemporary issues in its production, distribution, and consumption. I also wanted to relate the everyday matter of food with the more exotic (and sometimes arcane) elements of international political economy. What resulted is a book with the following features that I hope professors and students alike will find helpful and engaging:

- Two introductory chapters presenting key concepts and background to food politics and international political economy (IPE).
- Five central chapters, each devoted to a particular food selected for its illustration of a particular aspect of IPE. These chapters are consistently structured to present an introduction to the food, a brief history of it, matters related to production, and issues surrounding the food in the global system.
- A final concluding chapter that sums up the connections between food and the global economy.
- Each chapter includes a conclusion and chapter questions to stimulate thought and discussion.

- Many chapters include tables and figures with data on food issues around the world. Student exercises included draw on these data.
- All chapters include two different kinds of special box inserts: "New-to-You Food," describing some out-of-the-ordinary foodstuffs that are becoming mainstay parts of diets around the world, and "Recipe Boxes," describing challenges to common food practices or assumptions—providing recipes for rethinking what we eat.

I am grateful to the many students who have taken my food class over the years; their interest has allowed me to keep teaching this really fascinating topic, inspiring me to make it something more. I feel fortunate that the board of editors for this series was willing to take a chance on such a different approach to international political economy. I am also grateful to the anonymous reviewers for helping me see the forest for the trees. Without the support of my managing editor, Jennifer Knerr, this book never would have made it into print. I certainly appreciate all the support of my family, friends, and colleagues (especially my office mates, Quincy, Sally, Buffy, Bertram, and Ernie), but most of all, I am grateful to Michael K., my most favorite person.

# CHAPTER 1

―∞∞∞―

## FOOD AND YOU

### *The Evolution of Abundance*

What did you have for breakfast? Did you ever stop to think about all of the people and steps involved in how your banana, cereal, or energy bar got to your table or into your backpack? If you skipped breakfast, did you not have the time or inclination to eat or could you or your family not afford food?

Many of us take food for granted, both in terms of availability and production. Although the media regularly bombards consumers with information about "how many carbs" or "how much fat" the stuff we eat packs, most of us don't consider the politics and policies behind the growing, harvesting, technology, processing, transport, packaging, trade, marketing, or sale of what we consume. Food production, however, is a politically entrenched issue that rallies interest groups, incites riots, and occasionally provokes trade wars.

After a few times teaching an international relations course I developed and called "The Politics of Food," I discovered that each of the following food items offers particular insight into specific areas of the global economy and highlights various transnational issues. Following the trade of spices reveals the evolution of the international monetary system and the economic disparities that have emerged. The production of cocoa offers insight into the tensions arising from the global trade of a product that heavily relies on

1

child labor and into the countries that rely on this cash crop. The explosive demand for soybeans provides a means to explore how the need for international investment draws multinational corporations to developing economies, which is in turn fostering a global food-production model. The harvesting of tomatoes uncovers an ugly side of food production that depends on exploited migrant workers and land degradation. Fishing for tuna brings into question sustainable food production using public goods that can only be saved through international organizations.

Each of these food items allows for broad consideration of economic policies, capitalism, colonization, globalization, interdependence, and development. These topics also offer a means to examine the roles of multinational corporations and international organizations, global economic disparities, human rights and labor concerns, difficulties over cooperation, and sustainable development issues. But before exploring what these particular food items reveal about the global political economy, this chapter starts by having you complete an exercise to get a better idea of your eating habits. Completing this exercise will help you see how your own food choices fit into the greater scheme of an increasingly globalized food system. After giving you a better sense of your place in the global food chain, the chapter examines the implications of the increasing abundance of food options for producers and consumers.

## YOUR PLACE IN THE FOOD CHAIN

As the world increasingly becomes more globalized and interdependent, the kinds of choices humans make both define and dictate political policies. When we peel a banana, rarely do we think about the banana workers in Honduras. When we eat a candy bar, most of us don't try to piece together where Hershey's or Nestlé bought the cacao, milk, or sugar. Although aware that convenience and time often take precedence over cost and nutrition, we are less aware of the global implications of choosing fast food over a home-cooked meal. Our goal is to unwrap the consequences of a diet increasingly supplied by a global food system and how this phenomenon is intertwined with the global economy.

Considering what you eat provides a frame of reference for understanding the global food system. By completing Exercise 1.1, you should get a better sense of your own eating habits and food choices and the factors that shape them. College students often lead hectic lives, relying on caffeine to pull an all-nighter, mindlessly popping sugar-filled candy at the computer, eating a bag of potato chips in the car on the way from school to work, or caving into the temptation to order out for pizza. What used to be the "freshman ten" is now the "freshman fifteen." Yet, as students—and consumers—are barraged with junk food and try to keep up with the fast-paced world around them, societal factors pressure young women and men to be thin and look radiant, resulting in self-esteem issues and often eating disorders. What does this have to do with the global food system? Food manufacturers work hard to get consumers to buy their stuff—to find the next "killer" food, the next Pop-Tarts or Lunchables with such a huge impact that it creates a new product category.[1] The term "killer" is more appropriate than first realized when coined, since snack foods are among the main contributors to the increase in diseases like obesity and type 2 diabetes that threaten mortality.

Well aware of the habits of consumers, food companies regularly develop more convenient foods or "energy" drinks targeted at students, in the same way they entice kids with "fun" foods (think green ketchup) while allowing mothers to reconcile convenience with nutrition by telling them that Pop-Tarts have some nutritional value if made with whole grains. Billions of dollars are spent on marketing food products specifically to teenagers and children. Consider the number of food commercials aired during cartoons (or during any television show, for that matter, bombarding consumers with mouth-watering images). Restaurants use the same strategies to bring customers through their doors—or up to their drive-thru windows. Coffee shops advertise socially conscious beans to assuage consumer guilt over paying $4 for a latte. The choices people make with their wallets help to determine what is produced and where, as well as products' availability and success. These companies, in turn, impact what and how much a person eats.

The food choices Americans, Europeans, and even people in developing countries face have evolved along with economic interdependence and interconnectedness, largely spurred most recently by policies adopted by the United States following the Great Depression and World War II. In the 1930s, the United States adopted a food-security policy, built around agriculture subsidies, with the objective of ensuring that the massive food shortages prevalent during the dust bowl era would never again plague the country. The same policies were instituted in western European countries, including Great

## Exercise: You Are What You Eat

### PART I

To get a better sense of what you eat, keep a food diary for three days. For each day, log the following:

- Everything you eat and drink during a meal, along with any snacks you have.
- The time of day of each meal (breakfast, lunch, dinner, snack, brunch, etc.).
- How long it takes you to eat your meal or snack.
- Where you eat your meal and with whom, if anyone.
- The number of calories you consume on each day. Calculate this using the calorie information on your food packages and the Nutritional Food Database calorie guide (http://www.calorieking.com/foods/?partner=ghf). You can also track your meals using the online menu planner offered by the US Department of Agriculture (USDA) (https://www.supertracker.usda.gov/default.aspx).

### PART II

Complete the following questions based on your three-day food diary:

1. The US government first offered nutrition guidelines in 1894. The United States Department of Agriculture updated these recommendations a number of times until it got into a rut with the "Basic Four," which persisted from 1956 until 1992. The "Food Guide Pyramid," introduced in 1992, increased the proportion of grains, vegetables, and fruits to the amount of protein and dairy. Although revised to become "MyPyramid" in 1995, the model remained essentially the same—just with a much more confusing design. The adoption of "MyPlate" coincided with First Lady Michelle Obama's "Let's Move" initiative to create awareness about the rise in childhood obesity in America. Even though the portions did not change from those recommended in MyPyramid, MyPlate offers a better visual representation of what proportion of foods should make up a meal, making it simple enough for even kids to get a sense of what to eat.
2. Consider the USDA's MyPlate (http://www.choosemyplate.gov/downloads/mini_poster_English_final.pdf) and indicate whether your diet meets the minimum recommendations per day for each of its food groups:
   - Fruit: 2 cups
   - Vegetable: 2.5 cups

- Grains: 6 ounces
- Dairy: 3 cups
- Protein foods (meats, beans and peas, and seeds and nuts): 5.5 ounces

3. How many meals did you have each day? What constitutes a meal for you?
4. How many meals did you have with someone else? How many times did you eat on the run?
5. How much of your food was ready-made? This includes pop-in-the-microwave or -oven foods, takeout foods, nutrient bars (like Clif Bars or PowerBars), and so on.
6. Were the days you kept your food diary typical for you, or were they radically different for some reason?
7. Did you find yourself making different food choices because you were keeping track of what you ate?
8. What have you learned about your eating habits from this exercise?

## PART III

The USDA's Foreign Agricultural Service details in pie charts the calorie intake of people in six different regions of the world (the United States, the European Union, sub-Saharan Africa, North Africa, Latin America, and developing Asia). Check out the calorie intake charts for the different regions of the world at http://www.sallymundo.com/kimberly/food/fas.html and compare how food intake in these regions differs from your own dietary choices. Although based on information from 1995 to 1997, these statistics still provide a useful tool for comparing your diet to that of the average US citizen as well as to those of people across the world.

Referring to your food diary, answer the following:

1. Indicate the total number of calories you consumed for each of the three days and the average for those days.
2. How does the number of calories you consumed compare to the averages for people in each of the six groups throughout the world?
3. Compare the diets of Americans and Europeans. What is the main difference?
4. Compare the US pie chart to that for sub-Saharan African. What is the main difference? What is the reason for this difference?
5. Most people's diets in the global south are still plant based, with about two-thirds of calories coming in the form of cereal grains, including rice, wheat, or maize, and starchy vegetables and legumes, like potatoes, beans, yucca, taro, and cassava. Approximately how many of your calories came from cereal grains and starchy vegetables and legumes?

Britain, France, and Germany, as well as in Japan, following World War II. During the Cold War, Western countries increased grain production to use food aid as a foreign policy tool to sway developing countries as well as to justify continued support to domestic farmers.[2] A longer-term consequence of this policy to encourage more grain production was an oversupply of grains that eventually glutted the market. The surplus of corn, in particular, led agribusiness in the United States to find alternative uses for the grain. High-fructose corn syrup first started replacing more expensive cane sugar in the 1980s, then became a popular additive in any number of unsuspecting places as a way to enhance food flavor. The concern for US reliance on foreign fossil fuels also led researchers to find ways to use corn as a biofuel.

In 1900, about 40 percent of the US population worked in the farming industry.[3] By 2009, farmers constituted less than 1 percent of the population.[4] This shift was the result of more efficient farm equipment that freed up labor to move into other industries. The development of chemical fertilizers and pesticides, along with the consolidation of farms into larger lots, vastly increased production. Yet, at the same time, the going rate for commodities has remained steady over time, despite the need to invest more in farming technology. In order to compete with the constant prices of their commodities, farmers were forced to increase their output with upgraded technology and bigger fields or to abandon farming all together. Farmers can only compete in today's market by increasing production because the price paid for corn, wheat, or beef does not match the increased cost to produce these commodities (called "price inelasticity" in economic terms). To stay in business, farmers must regularly upgrade to the latest technology and/or increase field size through land rental or purchase to grow more crops or fatter livestock in order to remain competitive, subjecting them to what is called the "treadmill effect."[5]

A popular misconception is that big businesses own much of the farmland that produces crops in the United States. Although nonfamily farms are gaining more of the market, families still own and operate over 80 percent of US farms.[6] The differences lie in small-scale versus large-scale production and output. As apparent in Figure 1.1, since 1989, small family farms have been squeezed out of production by large-scale family and nonfamily farms. Note that of those farmers who received government subsidies, 75 percent of the support went to non-family-owned and very large family-owned farms.[7] Figure 1.2 shows that profitability by farm type is increasingly favoring large-scale and nonfamily farms. In 2007, despite only constituting 12 percent of all farms, large-scale and nonfamily farms accounted for 84 percent of the value of US agricultural production.[8] Because farming on a bigger scale facilitates increased production and therefore greater profits, smaller farms find it difficult to match how much they need in profits to compete.

Also during the Cold War era, the United States promoted development of its own corporations by encouraging foreign direct investment in allied countries rebuilding after World War II. After saturating these markets, corporations sought out new markets to invest their capital. Rather than exporting its product, for example, Coca-Cola found it much more cost-effective to build plants or buy existing soft drink–producing factories abroad. The strategy worked well for this and other companies. By providing jobs in overseas production plants, corporations increased the buying power of local consumers. In order to compete, local companies created similar soft drink and snack products. The need to branch out also pushed companies to increase distribution in rural areas of developing countries and to network with grocers and deliverers to secure routes and access to stores. The consequence

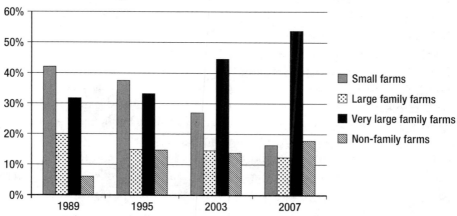

**Figure 1.1 Farm Trends in the United States.**

*Sources:* USDA, for data made available for 1989, 1995, 2003: http://www.ers.usda.gov /publications/EIB12/EIB12c.pdf p. 8; 2007 data from http://ers.usda.gov/Publications /EIB66/EIB66.pdf page v.
Farm sizes: Small = sales between $0–$250,000; Large-scale family= <$250,000 in sales; Non-family = no sales limits. The report does not differentiate income differences between large and very large family-owned farms, even though the data it provides is broken down.

**Figure 1.2 Operating Profit Margins for US Farms.**

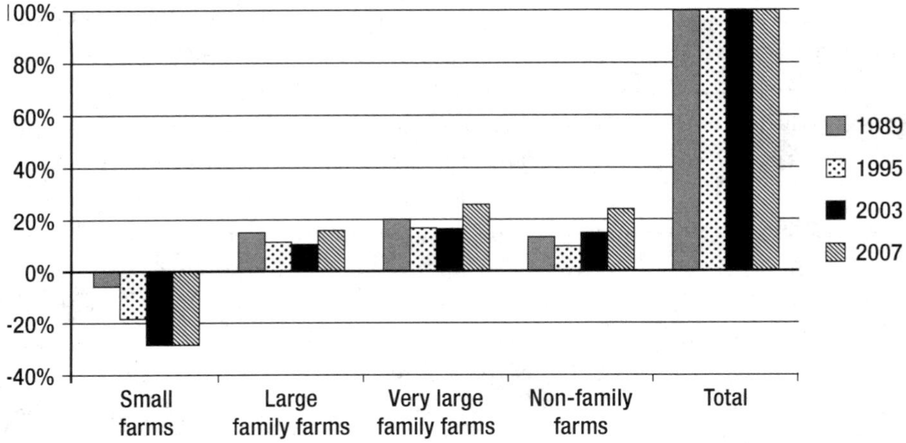

Sources: USDA, for data made available for 1989, 1995, 2003: http://www.ers.usda.gov /publications/EIB12/EIB12c.pdf p 8 ; 2007 data from http://ers.usda.gov/Publications/EIB66 /EIB66.pdf page v.
Farm sizes: Small = sales between $0–$250,000; Large-scale family= <$250,000 in sales; Non-family = no sales limits. The report does not differentiate income differences between large and very large family-owned farms, even though the data it provides is broken down.

of supplying poorer people with low-cost, convenient processed foods is an increase in the number of obese people in developing countries.

As grocery and food conglomerates gain market control, they have more power over producers, largely as a result of Walmart's business strategies and success.[9] If farmers want to continue to sell their commodities, they need to keep production costs low yet produce the fattest animals, most uniform, unblemished produce, and heartiest grain. The increase in large-scale and nonfamily farms reflects the effect that large corporations have on agribusiness. Farmers rarely find the opportunity to add value to products like corn, beef, or lettuce in the way food manufacturers can because marketing requires deep pockets. Basic food items sold by corporations are increasingly becoming branded, such as Cuties clementines, PureHeart mini watermelons, Texas Rio Star grapefruit, and Everybody's Nuts pistachios. These same companies increase their profit margins when they add value to basic commodities. PepsiCo processes oats into Quaker oatmeal, and General Mills makes them into Cheerios. This manufacturing process, even if it just entails packaging oats in a container or adding more ingredients, allows corporations to sell goods at a much higher price. Both of these advantages give corporations leverage over farmers to determine the price they are willing to pay for commodities. In the same way farmers compete to sell their goods, food manufacturers must contend with grocery retailers if they are to make a profit. These producers pay a premium to retailers for shelf space and placement or to be featured at the end of an aisle. Basically farmers are at the mercy of food manufacturers and grocers, while food manufacturers are at the mercy of the grocery retailers, who sit at the top of the food chain.[10] They, in turn, are pitted against each other to offer the most value for the lowest prices.

### Greater Competition = Bigger Waistlines

In order to compete with other corporations for grocery sales, food giants found creative ways to charge more for basic food items like pasta, dairy, breads, and cereals. Processing foods with sugar, sodium, and chemicals allowed food companies to "add value," justifying increasing the cost of an item. Processing foods, however, also adds calorie density. Take popcorn, for example. A portion of three tablespoons of popcorn kernels popped in one teaspoon of vegetable oil costs about seven cents to make and has 135 calories. A bag of microwave popcorn is at least fourteen times more expensive and serves up easily double the calories, but it's much tastier, right? Food manufacturers have added value to the product to give consumers a reason to buy more than just a bag of kernels to pop the old-fashioned way, on a stove in a pan that has to be washed, instead of in a disposable bag for two minutes in a microwave. But that added value in convenience and flavor is paid out in cost and calories (and excess packaging that is detrimental to the environment).

Inherently no food is bad, but preparation matters. Replacing a home-cooked dinner of baked chicken, steamed rice, and buttered broccoli with the much more convenient Tyson's breaded chicken (ready to eat in just ten minutes!), Rice-A-Roni, and Bird's Eye lightly sauced cheesy broccoli adds more calories, sodium, and, yes, even sugar. Just stopping at KFC to pick up a bucket of chicken, with sides of mashed potatoes, gravy, biscuits, and coleslaw, may prove even more convenient but involves a huge health trade-off.

Another factor to keep in mind is that most foods, if not eaten in moderation, can pack on some serious pounds. Snack foods and soft drinks are usually sold in multiple-portion packages. Another way to add value is to sell bigger packages because cost decreases as volume increases. Plus it is easier to get someone to pay ninety-nine cents for a bigger bag of potato chips (usually 2.5 ounces), as opposed to a smaller bag with just one portion (1 ounce) for fifty cents, because even though it costs more, the larger package is the better deal. The problem is that people tend to eat more than one serving when presented with a multiserving snack, increasing the likelihood of overconsumption.[11]

The desire for processed foods, coupled with the convenience they offer, creates countless marketing options for food manufacturers: single-size servings, prepackaged individual lunches, complete dinners, family-size portions, and many "just-add-meat" vegetable, potato, rice, or pasta meal starters. This move to a diet of processed foods has increased American waistlines, serving up millions of unhappy people who turn to the weight-loss industry for a quick fix. Value-added processed foods have engendered a huge market for no-fat, low-fat, reduced-fat, low-sodium, and even no-calorie foods, introducing any number of other "healthy" alternative (and, yes, processed) foods. Corporations such as Kraft Foods take advantage of having gotten people hooked on macaroni and cheese, Lunchables, and Philadelphia cream cheese by introducing health-conscious options like Nabisco 100 Calorie Packs and Lean Cuisine, Healthy Choice, Weight Watchers, and South Beach products.

Restaurants compete in a similar way to entice consumers: by offering greater quantity at a lower price. Restaurant chains offering fast food or even sit-down service have increased serving sizes. McDonald's Dollar Menu, Burger King's BK Breakfast Value Menu, 7-Eleven's Big Gulp, Olive Garden's all-you-can-eat soup and salad bowls, and Red Robin's Bottomless Steak Fries are all attempts by food corporations to draw people in to get more for less. Similarly, portion sizes have increased significantly over the last few decades. What once was considered a large soda at a fast-food restaurant is now a "regular." Plates of pasta can weigh in at one pound, with burgers registering in at over one thousand calories each! Endless baskets of tortilla chips with salsa or bread and butter can add a lot of calories to a meal, but they make people feel like they are getting more for their money. Bigger servings of French fries, pasta, or potato chips and burgers, steaks, or chicken do not cost a restaurant a whole lot more, but the retailer can charge much more for a platter full of food than for one with portion sizes closer to the national standards for servings, and consumers will be more satisfied with the bigger portion.

# FOOD AVAILABILITY

Due to technological advances in agriculture and transportation, global north countries have a much greater capacity to produce more food on less land. Corporations take advantage of lower commodity prices to offer consumers greater access to less expensive foods and more product choices. Take the banana: this most widely consumed fruit in the United States is not indigenous to the continental states and was introduced only in the late nineteenth century. In fact, preparation directions were initially included with the tropical fruit, in much the same way that unusual items like cherimoya, Buddha's hand, or jicama found in the produce section of the supermarket often have a sticker with instructions. In Central America, corporate plantations formed, improving farming techniques, developing railway lines, and improving shipping methods to make this tropical fruit a commonly consumed food by the 1920s.

The growing desire for exotic foods, driven by a larger number of immigrant communities, travel abroad, and food shows on television, led supermarkets to meet the demand with more international foods, sometimes devoting entire aisles to these new and strange choices. To try something different, check out the Asian section for pad thai or soba noodles. If you're in the mood for something from south of the border, head to the Latino section for tacos, salsa, and refried beans, or try quinoa, a staple food of the Andes. If you're craving Indian food, pick up some aloo palak, channa masala, pappadums, and chutney, and you've got a meal. Stores provide a seemingly endless variety of ready-to-eat meals and prepared sauces, offering authentic-tasting cuisine.

Rising concerns for how produce is grown and how processed foods are made give grocers another niche market to tap with organic and "alternative" foods. Recognizing the potential for adding value to foods, conglomerates see dollar signs because the people seeking healthier foods are likely to be more affluent with more disposable income. Sometimes conglomerates create their own brands, cashing in because they can justify charging higher prices for these specialty products. Kraft's Back to Nature organic chocolate chip cookies, made with fair trade chocolate, sell for $4.99 for a 9.5 ounce box, whereas Nabisco's Chips Ahoy! retail at $3.49 for a 15.25 ounce package. (Note that Nabisco also appeals to the weight-loss crowd with its SnackWell's line, making a tidy profit with less for more.) If a small company manages to get its foot—and food—into a grocery chain and proves successful, chances are it will either have to merge with another company to remain competitive (consider the Hain–Celestial Seasonings relationship) or be sold outright to a conglomerate (in the way that Boca, the maker of veggie burgers, is now a subsidiary of Kraft Foods).

Consumers' concerns about what goes into processed foods and, therefore, what they are putting into their bodies, along with their social concerns for the treatment of farm laborers and animals, have pushed many grocery chains to stock products that could once only be found in health food stores. Food retailers found it worth their while to devote coveted shelf space to organic, natural, and even fair trade/ethically traded foods. Entire grocery chains, like Trader Joe's and the aptly named Whole Foods, have sprung up, appealing to enough customers to base their entire inventory on these products. Consumers tend, however, to overlook the fact that processed food is still processed, so cookies containing organic wheat or made with unbleached cane juice sugar don't necessarily have fewer calories or constitute a healthful dietary choice.

## HEALTH IMPLICATIONS OF A GLOBAL FOOD SUPPLY

The human body is slow to evolve. As a result, humans crave the fats and sugars our ancestors were programmed to seek out for sustenance. Because sugar and fat are not only readily available but also low-cost, these cravings are easily satisfied for those living in wealthier countries and increasingly so for people in developing parts of the world. As sugar and fat are both very enticing to the palate and very calorie dense, it is easy to consume more than the small portions necessary for the body. Products like potato chips, candy, and soft drinks, which are filled with sugar, fat, or both, are considered "empty calories" because, despite their calorie density, they are not filling, and refined sugars are quickly metabolized. In excess, these sugars can wreak havoc on the body's insulin levels, potentially leading over time to type 2 diabetes. Increased food availability at lower prices, coupled with a more sedentary lifestyle, has led to greater numbers of overweight or obese adults. The World Health Organization estimates that more than 1 billion adults are overweight, with at least 300 million of them considered obese, and has labeled this epidemic "globesity."[12]

Unlike our ancestors, who had to work hard for their survival, hunting and gathering food or working on farms, people in advanced industrialized countries (and increasingly in emerging economies) lead considerably more sedentary lifestyles. Americans expend fewer calories on average than even a few decades ago. With about 36 percent of US adults (that's more than one in three) considered obese, it is no surprise that in reaction to the fast-paced lifestyle fueled by fast foods, a "slow-food" movement has emerged, attempting to reshape people's understanding of how their eating habits impact their bodies as well as the planet.[13]

In addition to the 36 percent of adult Americans the Centers for Disease Control and Prevention (CDC) estimates are obese, an additional 33 percent of the adult population is overweight.[14] In effect, an astonishing 69 percent of the adult population aged twenty years or older is overweight or obese in the United States. This epidemic, without question, complicates health care in America. Perhaps not surprisingly, children are not immune to this problem either. Since the late 1970s, obesity rates among children and teenagers have risen by over 10 percent.[15] The CDC has tracked body mass index trends in the United States since 1985, when no state exceeded an average of 14 percent of obese adults.[16] Ten years later, 1995 was the first year data was available for all states. At that time, no state average exceeded the 15 to 19 percent category, but within a decade, the numbers had changed drastically. Figure 1.3 shows that since 2010 more than 92 percent of all US states averaged obesity rates of 15 percent or more.

By 2009, Colorado was the only state that averaged less than 20 percent adult obesity, with nine states weighing in at 30 percent or more. By the next year, even Coloradans had crossed the line of obesity, with all states' adults steadily gaining weight. By 2014, Colorado had been superseded by Montana as the least obese state. That seven of the states with the largest obese adult population in 2011 are among the poorest in the country is not a coincidence.[17] Not only does a healthier diet require more time and effort than one based on processed, prepared foods, but "a calorie-dense diet costs $3.52 a day compared with $36.32 a day for a low-calorie diet."[18] As a result, poorer people fill their grocery carts with inexpensive, calorie-dense foods like sugar-coated cereals, white bread, Ramen noodles, American cheese, and less-lean meats; they buy little produce or whole-grain food as these are more expensive per calorie and require more preparation.

In response to these alarming statistics, Americans have organized to pressure schools and government to enact policies, ranging from the proposed

## Recipe Box

### Calorie Consumption

After you complete the food diary exercise, try this. To determine how many calories you eat on average, multiple your weight by thirteen. For example, if you weigh 150 pounds and lead a moderately active lifestyle, you consume about 1,950 calories a day. For athletes, multiply bodyweight by fifteen to determine average calorie consumption. Does your calculation accurately reflect your food diary entries? If not, why do you think that's the case? If you are interested in losing weight, to find out how many calories you need to eat to lose one pound per week, calculate your recommended calorie intake at http://www.vegan-weight-loss.com/recommended-calorie-intake.html. For a more sophisticated analysis of weight management, check out the Body Weight Simulator at http://bwsimulator.niddk.nih.gov.

**Figure 1.3 Adult Obesity Rates in the United States.**

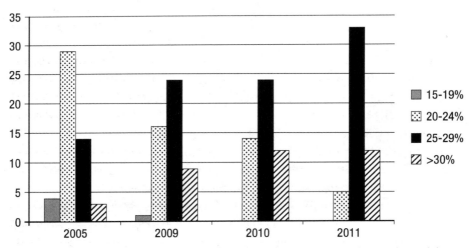

Legend:
- 15-19%
- 20-24%
- 25-29%
- >30%

Source: Center for Disease Control and Prevention, http://www.cdc.gov/obesity/data/adult.html#Prevalence
Percentages are for adults who are obese. In 2010 and 2011, there were no states below the 15–19 percent range.

ban of cupcakes at elementary school birthday parties to imposition of a "Twinkie tax" and removal of soft drink machines from schools and school premises. Elected officials, who have to deal with health-care costs, also have an interest in reducing waistlines, and a "fat tax" on sugary drinks (similar to the "sin tax" levied on tobacco and alcohol products) could increase their operating budgets. New York State proposed a penny-an-ounce tax on sugar beverages, but it was dropped. New York City went so far as to ban the sale of supersized sugar soft drinks because of policymakers' concerns about rising disease and related health-care costs. A coalition of civil rights groups and the beverage industry appealed the decision, and the ban was overturned. Other cities and countries have tried passing similar regulations, only to have them overturned or to find them unenforceable; for instance, the Danes just crossed over to Germany to buy the cheaper high-fat foods their government was trying to limit by imposing a tax, which the Danish government eventually just abolished.

Unhealthy citizens cost governments lots of money. Costs vary from country to country and report to report. The CDC cites estimates of about $147 billion in medical costs for obese Americans in 2008 versus just $39 billion in 2003.[19] With changes to state responsibility due to US government health-care reforms, Arizona toyed with fining Medicaid recipients $50 a year if they failed to follow the diet regime prescribed by their doctor.[20] In Japan, the government has resorted to extreme measures to steer its population away from an increasing trend toward obesity. In 2008, a national law was passed requiring doctors to measure the waistlines of patients (ages forty to seventy-four) during their annual physicals.[21] If found to be *metabo* (overweight), Japanese have three months to lose weight on their own to reduce their waistline to the maximum 33.5 inches (men) or 35.4 inches (women). Failure to do so results in required dietary counseling. If the government does not reach its goal of reducing waistlines by 2015, it will impose fines on companies and local governments for failure to successfully address the *metabo* problem.

Europeans are not immune to globesity either. Although Europeans are on the whole more resistant to weight gain because they tend to walk and cycle more than their US, Canadian, and Australian counterparts, the trend is changing.[22] Obesity rates have tripled over the last twenty years, with 50 percent of adults and 20 percent of children overweight and one-third of them considered obese.[23] New Zealand boasts one of the highest obesity rates among the rich countries, with about one-third of its population considered obese, leading the government to begin denying work visas to applicants who do not have "an acceptable standard of health" to reduce additional health-care costs.[24] In Great Britain, almost 25 percent of the adult population is considered obese, making it the third most obese country in the world.[25] Although weight problems are more often associated with people in wealthier parts of the world, of the 300 million obese adults worldwide, more than one-third live in developing countries.[26] Mexico ranks second in the world—higher than all the other rich countries except the United States—with its 24 percent obesity among adults.[27] Obesity surprisingly exists in places associated with malnutrition, like India, where it is becoming problematic and introducing cardiovascular disease and type 2 diabetes, the same diseases prevalent in the global north. At the same time, 42.5 percent of children suffer from malnutrition, and death from diarrhea is commonplace.[28]

Arab countries in the Middle East and North Africa face a similar situation, with malnourished poor juxtaposed against overfed wealthy. Children suffer from stunted growth, and pregnant women suffer from anemia, while obesity rates for adults range from 25 percent in Lebanon to a high of 43 percent in Saudi Arabia.[29] Diabetes prevalence in the United Arab Emirates exceeds that in the United States, with almost 20 percent of the population afflicted with type 2 diabetes and another 27 percent likely to develop it.[30] The irony is that even though people suffer from malnutrition, they can also be obese. Bedouins in these countries are relatively poor, but even they are susceptible to overeating. And though these statistics for obesity in the Middle East and North Africa are staggering, impoverished islanders in Oceania suffer higher rates of death associated with obesity than anyone else in the world—even people in rich countries.[31]

The phenomenon of overweight, undernourished people stems from changes in food consumption and availability. People throughout the world have differing views on a dietary increase of fat and sugar.[32] Whereas people in wealthier countries increasingly struggle to limit their intake of fat (particularly from animals) and sugar, those in the developing countries strive to eat more foods with these ingredients because this transition away from a poverty-based diet of plant-based staple foods not only provides more variety but also indicates affluence. As income in developing countries increases, intake of fat and sugar also rises. Even when people experience economic hardships, once they transition to including a wider variety of foods in their diet, people will not revert to their former eating habits.[33] As socioeconomic standards rise in developing countries, people have more buying power, giving them greater access to fast and junk foods. Corporations have a greater incentive to tap these markets, using the same strategies that have profited them in the global north, including adding value to products. As they move into more countries, securing delivery routes and making distribution agreements with local grocers to sell soft drinks, candy, and snacks, as well as prepared, processed foods, the globesity problem will only escalate, as has proven the case in China, where one-fifth of the population is now either overweight or obese.[34] Although the percentages are relatively low in comparison to world averages, the concern lies in how quickly the rates have increased, particularly among children. A chubby baby is seen as a happy baby because of a shift in eating habits that mirror the global north.

The evolution of abundance thus affects people around the world. More people have access to food, but what they are choosing or can afford to eat is contributing to globesity and the diseases associated with obesity. A number of factors explored in the upcoming chapters explain the evolution of the global food supply chain that now challenges human health and well-being.

## ON THE MENU

Now that you have a better sense of where you fit in the global food system and the implications of your and others' dietary choices, Chapter 2 lays the foundation for understanding international political economy and examines the key themes and concepts used throughout the subsequent chapters. Chapters 3 through 7 focus on a particular food item in order to explain the components that make up the global political economy and to highlight an issue prevalent in that part of the system. Chapter 3's examination of the spice trade reveals how the international monetary system works by showing how the trade in nutmeg, cinnamon, peppercorn, and cloves helped to establish global currency exchange. Chapter 4 focuses on the production of cocoa beans as a way to demonstrate how the dynamics of trade and production established during European colonization affect production in the

---

**New-to-You Food: Cassava**

*Manihot esculenta* is known by many names around the world: to the Latin Americans, it is yuca; to the Filipinos, it's *kamoteng kahoy*; to the Africans, it's cassava. Although yuca might sound familiar to gardeners, this plant is not related to yucca, a prominent shrub with spiky green leaves that grows quite tall and bears white flowers. Perhaps the most familiar name to people in the global north is tapioca, the name used by the Indians. Their use of tapioca, however, extends far beyond what likely comes to mind for most people in the United States and Europe: tapioca pudding. Tapioca makes an appearance in more foods than most people realize, as a hidden ingredient that acts as a thickening agent, but to many people around the world, this root is a staple food.

Cassava is indigenous to Brazil but traveled across Latin America before the Europeans had even visited the New World. Since slave traders transported it across the Atlantic in the seventeenth century, cassava has been a staple food in sub-Saharan Africa. Europeans dismissed the root as a slave food, in the same way they frowned upon peanuts, which were also transported to Africa through the slave trade. Only because of the popularity of peanut butter in America have Europeans started to embrace it, though they tend to prefer hazelnuts in chocolate over Americans' beloved peanut-chocolate combination made famous by Reese's Peanut Butter Cups. Cassava, however, has not caught on in the same way, limiting most cassava consumption to domestic production in developing countries.

Cassava, as it is most often called in English, can be boiled, braised, grilled, fried, ground into flour, mashed into a dough, or squeezed to make beverages. In Southeast Asia, dense savory and sweet cakes are popular. In various parts of Latin America, cassava is prepared in any number of ways, including as fried bread, tortillas, and yuca chips (like potato chips). The root is vital to many people in West and Central Africa, who process it into flour to make *fu-fu*, a doughy

---

global food system. Chapter 5 focuses on soybean production in Brazil and builds on the previous chapter by examining how the exponential growth of multinational corporations has shaped the modern food system. Chapter 6 considers two connected international political economy issues: the role of migrant labor in the production of fresh tomatoes is inextricably linked to environmental issues. Chapter 7, on tuna, examines a different environmental aspect of the global food supply. Finding a way to protect this fish with wide migration patterns has proven very difficult because conservation is contingent upon international cooperation. The final chapter offers a comprehensive recap of the book's key themes and concepts by tying the individual food items together.

ball dipped into soups and sauces. Squeezed cassava is made into an assortment of alcoholic beverages served in bars across Africa and South America.

Although the starchy root provides a good source of carbohydrates and a few vitamins and minerals, it must be eaten in combination with other foods because a diet based mostly on cassava does not offer the necessary dietary proteins and fats. In poorer parts of the world, malnutrition is more prevalent in communities dependent on cassava. Yet these communities rely on cassava because it grows so well in nutrient-deficient and dry soil. Even during droughts, the root will produce food. Another significant feature of the plant is that it can be harvested on an as-needed basis, which is useful because the roots do not last long after they are extracted from the ground. Not only does cassava provide an important food source to people in developing countries, but young cassava stalks are fed to livestock because the part that grows above ground is a good source of protein and fiber.

For the many people in the world without refrigeration, cassava is highly perishable, so it is stored between layers of its leaves and soil after it is dug out of the ground. Nigeria is the world's largest producer of the plant, but exports earn the country very little as demand in the global north for fresh cassava is comparatively low. Thailand, however, grows cassava and processes it into tapioca flour, a key agricultural export for the country.

The leaves and root cannot be eaten without being washed and then cooked, soaked, or fermented to eliminate toxicity. The skin covering the inner pulpy part of the root is poisonous. The sweet variety of the plant contains less acid, requiring less work because the tough outer skin does not have to be removed before cooking. The laborious task of removing the skin of the bitter variety is necessary before cooking, however, to make it safe to eat. Certainly relying on the sweet variety would make life easier for the (almost exclusively) women who prepare food in developing countries; the bitter variety is widely grown, however, because the toxic skin helps to keep away rodents and insects that threaten crops.

## CHAPTER QUESTIONS

1. How does the "treadmill effect" describe changes in the US agriculture industry?
2. How do food manufacturers "add value" to their products to make a profit? What impact has this had on consumers' health?
3. What factors contribute to rising rates of obesity in the global north? What about in the global south?
4. For years, there was the talk of a "Twinkie tax." Now some states, like New York, have actually passed a sugar tax and banned supersized sugar soft drinks. Is this the answer to reducing consumption?

# CHAPTER 2

~∞~

# THE FOOD CHAIN

## The Political and Economic Nature of Food

Cooking contestants on the Food Channel who are presented with some spices, cocoa, soy, tomatoes, and tuna might be challenged to create one satisfying dish. Although these foods may seem to have little in common, they actually intersect on a number of issues in the global food supply chain. As each chapter in this book examines an individual food commodity, collectively they offer a broader picture for understanding the key factors and actors that shape global food-system dynamics.

This chapter discusses the recurring themes and some common international political economy concepts that appear throughout the book, as well as the layout of each of the food chapters. Three overarching themes link the food items. Colonization, the global economic divide, and globalization impact the global food supply, raising a number of transnational issues. The structure of the international monetary system creates issues for spice farmers. The cocoa bean trade has led to the use of child slave labor. The rise of soybean production is largely due to the interests of multinational corporations (MNCs), determining which countries will benefit—or not—from their investments. Tomato production heavily depends on immigrant labor. The threat of extinction of some tuna species is directly related to countries' inability to preserve the common good. Each of these food items discusses a few particular aspects of the global political economy, but they are also connected in systemic ways.

## KEY THEMES

A number of themes recur throughout this book that help to explain global food issues. Colonization, a global economic divide, the neoliberal economic model, and globalization have significantly impacted human security. Examining relationships between countries, corporations, people, and institutions uncovers the political and economic factors that influence food dynamics. Understanding these key themes is an important starting point.

### Colonization

The migration of human beings has interconnected people throughout the world. Early migrants and explorers took seeds, spices, livestock, and recipes with them as they moved across the globe. Although territorial conquest has occurred throughout history, the Europeans left an indelible mark on the world when they claimed distant lands as their own, colonizing the globe. European exploration stemmed largely from a desire to find the famed "Spice Islands" that supplied the pricey imports of peppercorn, cinnamon, cloves, and nutmeg. Their desire to control this trade led governments to sponsor expeditions that eventually ended with the Europeans conquering the lands they encountered. This domination involved settling Europeans in the colonies not only to administer them but also to spread their culture to "civilize" the "barbarians."

Colonization impacted food dynamics in irrevocable ways when the Europeans encountered territories lush with unfamiliar flora and fauna. Exports of foods from the colonies to Europe helped to fill the coffers of the monarchies as well as the newly formed trading companies. As they tasted new foods, explorers sent seeds and edibles back to their kings and queens. Some of these, like chocolate and tomatoes, proved very tasty. Others, like quinoa, did not appeal and so never reached Europe. Foods the explorers disliked tended to be associated with indigenous peoples and came to be considered foods of the poor.

Colonization has played a significant role in all of the food items discussed in this book. The desire to control the source of spices led to establishment of the international monetary system. Meeting the needs of cocoa demand in Europe laid the foundation for a trade network that gives the former colonial empires an advantage over their erstwhile colonies. Colonization helped to establish the multinational corporations that dominate the global food exchange, including soy production. Dependence on immigrant labor for tomato production is rooted in the global economic divide inherited from colonization. Although tuna is not globally popular as a result of European colonization, its popularity in Japan stems from the American presence there after World War II. Each of these food items is intricately intertwined with the global food system.

## Global Economic Divide

The dynamics established during colonization have continued to impact the world by laying the foundation for a global economic divide. Europeans gained the advantage through exploitation of their colonies to promote their own development and to support the Industrial Revolution. American colonization of the indigenous peoples on the North American continent was comparable to European domination. Americans essentially colonized westward, eventually controlling a territory rivaling the whole continent of Europe in land area. Prosperity was fueled not only by gains in land and natural resources but by the immigrants who hoped to take advantage of these opportunities. These factors allowed the United States to keep pace with development in the colonial empires through the twentieth century. Following the world wars, many colonies gained their independence, then found it difficult to develop because, as colonies established to supply European countries with raw materials and agricultural goods, they had not industrialized during the Industrial Revolution. This disadvantage became more apparent during the Cold War, so that when the ideological battle between the East and West ended, the global economic divide between countries became more apparent—so much so as that the world is generally split between the global north (GN) and the global south (GS). That most of the former colonies are GS countries is not a coincidence.

The GN consists mostly of countries situated north of the equator with advanced industrialized economies. These include the United States and

Canada, western European countries, Australia and New Zealand, and a few East Asian countries; there are about thirty in all, comprising about 17 percent of the countries in the world. The GS includes the approximately 160 developing countries in the world but is by no means homogenous. Vast economic differences result in a variety of categories. At the higher end of the GS, the "emerging economies" include the more industrially advanced and rapidly growing countries, such as China, Mexico, India, and Brazil. Other countries, such as Ghana, Egypt, and Sri Lanka, have higher growth potential than those considered "least developed countries," but they still face steeper development challenges than the better-situated emerging economies. Because of diversity in their level of development, GS is used throughout the book to discuss developing countries collectively.

This division of countries is intertwined with food politics. Unlike GN countries, GS countries rely for trade more heavily on natural resources and unprocessed agricultural products grown for export, called cash crops, than on manufactured goods, processed foods, and services. Having undergone industrialization gives the GN an advantage in manufacturing products, hence an economic advantage. A few problems have emerged as a result of the global economic divide. First, GS countries have been caught in a vicious cycle of growing crops that do not offer much return and divert resources away from meeting nutritional needs at home.

A second problem resulting from the GN-GS economic divide is that countries have different interests regarding governing food issues. These differences make implementing and enforcing global food policies regarding human rights and the environment difficult because cooperation is necessary if the policies are to be effective. Establishing and monitoring protective labor laws in the tomato industry and preserving tuna from extinction are in all countries' best interests. Tensions between not only the countries but others with an economic stake, including MNCs, complicate global governance— that is, the attempt to create a global level of authority that holds countries and other actors, such as MNCs, organizations, and leaders, accountable to an international set of rules and norms.

A third, perhaps unexpected issue to arise from the global economic divide involves health trends. Greater access to inexpensive, processed foods has increased obesity and the risk of disease not only in the GN but also in emerging economies, like India, where access to processed and fast foods has rendered people with rising incomes more prone to these health problems. As more people in the GS have greater buying power to improve their quality of life, they are also becoming burdened with the health issues endemic to developed countries.

## Neoliberal Economic Model

Interconnectedness and globalization are symbiotically tied to the world's political and economic dynamics. Neoliberals influence the global economy by pushing for a free market with minimal government intervention in economic policies. Governments enact policies that help to advance their interests in foreign relations, which include measures that protect domestic jobs that produce goods and services. Tariffs and nontariff barriers (NTBs) are two ways that countries protect their domestic markets. Tariffs are taxes on imported goods. NTBs include a variety of policies, such as quotas, or limits, on imports of a particular type or from a specific country. Another NTB regularly discussed throughout the book is the subsidy, which is money or support, such as insurance, given by a government to a producer. The neoliberal push for more countries to open their economic borders, embrace political policies that favor reduced protectionist measures such as tariffs and quotas, and privatize companies is a double-edged sword. The more people immerse in the global economy, the greater their potential to achieve a better standard of living, but with the trade-off of greater subjection to competition and exploitation.

Free market forces draw criticism from labor unions, human rights advocates, small business owners, and environmentalists, who believe that the institutions that promote neoliberal policies, including MNCs, the World Trade Organization (WTO), the International Monetary Fund, and the World Bank, only care about the bottom line. In the process, these global institutions invariably make some people's lives tougher by relocating jobs, subjecting workers to abusive labor conditions, and neglecting the environment. Neoliberals counter that, over time, breaking down economic barriers will improve the quality of life of more people as more people are brought into market capitalism.

The neoliberal economic model thrives on global trade. Capitalism taps raw materials to fuel manufacturing, feeds on competition between businesses to offer the best product at the lowest price, requires an affordable labor supply, and depends on a large consumer market. Investment is a necessary component of capitalism in order to finance production. An inventor might have an ingenious idea, but without financial backing or a company willing to take a risk on a new product, the idea might never materialize. Businesses strive to tap into global resources, labor, and consumers in order to minimize overhead and maximize their market presence in as many places as possible. That Coca-Cola reentered Burma-Myanmar after the United States ended over twenty years of economic sanctions against that country was a strategy to secure the consumer market to increase its global profit margin. This global trade is the hallmark of successful corporations.

Government policies do not always facilitate global trade to the extent that MNCs would like. One approach a government might take is to try to manipulate its currency to take advantage of global economic conditions. As governments seek to protect the interests of their citizens, these policies interfere with the objectives of the free market. Trade is directly affected by the tariffs and NTBs countries adopt. Tariffs interfere with neoliberalism because they limit foreign competition in a domestic market, thereby reducing consumers' options, possibly resulting in an inferior product at a greater cost.

Policies enacted to protect the health and safety of workers, consumers, and even the environment are sometimes deemed NTBs because, although they protect workers and consumers, they ostensibly protect domestic jobs. Setting

## Recipe Box

### The Disappearing Big Mac

Although not surprisingly a popular item in the beef-loving country of Argentina, the Big Mac mysteriously disappeared from McDonald's menus in 2012.[1] The famous sandwich is definitely a favorite of nationals, but because its price was so low, comparatively, the company removed it from the menu to lure customers to choose other, pricier value meals, such as that including the Angus Bacon Burger (US$9.90) or the Quarter Pounder with Cheese (US$7.60). At US$4.40, the Big Mac value meal costs much less. Speculation about the reason for the cost discrepancy is that the Argentinian government is trying to make its peso appear less inflated than it really is. Because the restaurant would rather have customers opt for the more expensive menu items, keeping the Big Mac off the brightly lit menu behind the counter just seemed like good business sense. When asked why the Big Mac had disappeared, McDonald's issued an official statement claiming that it was just a marketing strategy to promote new products, like its Triple Mac.

1. "Argentina's Big Mac Attack," *International Herald Tribune*, November 24, 2011, http://latitude.blogs.nytimes.com/2011/11/24/argentinas-big-mac-attack.

quotas or other parameters—such as imposing specific sanitation regulations or requiring specific fishing equipment—on imported goods can be construed as a way to minimize foreign competition in particular sectors. Regardless of their intent, neoliberals argue, any policies that limit free trade only serve to minimize the efficiency of the consumer market. Limiting government interference in economic exchange, on the other hand, will increase the standard of living of more people over time. The problem is that countries' short-term interests tend to trump long-term interests and dictate policies, making global cooperation more difficult. GS countries are less able to focus on longer-term development strategies when they struggle to meet the daily needs of their citizens. Governments have nevertheless created any number of global institutions in an attempt to discourage countries from using tariffs and implementing NTBs.

## Globalization

Technological advances have more recently moved people into closer physical and cyber proximity. Globalization involves increasing economic, political, and social connections between people around the world. Although the debate over when globalization really began and what it constitutes continues, the phenomenon has nonetheless contributed to the push toward a globalized food system. One implication of globalization is that people around the world have greater exposure to different foods due to increased contact and interaction of individuals. Chinese immigrants in Africa and South America have influenced food choices and cuisines on those continents. (What traveler would expect to find Brazilian restaurants in Beijing and Chinese cuisine in São Paolo?) Similarly, sushi bars have made their way into some of the most unexpected cities in the GS, like Accra, Ghana, whereas Middle Eastern restaurants have found their way to Mexico City.

Globalization has also had an impact on food availability. Foodstuffs have been bartered and traded for millennia, with the spices mentioned above among the most extensively exchanged. More recently, from small specialty shops to conglomerates, businesses have exposed consumers to a larger variety of food items. MNCs have indeed worked diligently to infiltrate as many markets as possible to increase their brand recognition. Pepsi established such a strong market presence in Chiapas, Mexico, that the Tzotzil Indians use the soft drink in their religious ceremonies.[1] The currently evolving system, with companies like Pepsi penetrating deeper into rural GS regions, is based on a shrinking number of multinational corporations squeezing suppliers to produce more for less and pushing producers and farmers to find creative ways to cut costs yet still compete and make a profit.[2] International grocery conglomerates like Walmart (American), Carrefour (French), and Metro AG (German), along with Kroger (the largest grocery retailer worldwide but with stores only in the United States), push the world's top food processors—Nestlé, Tyson, Pepsi, and Kraft Foods—to lower prices while simultaneously generating greater quantity and better quality. These same grocery corporations pressure farmers to grow more meat and produce for less, threatening to take their business elsewhere if farmers cannot supply beef, lettuce, corn, or almonds at prices they are willing to pay.

Corporations have also facilitated greater food production with more sophisticated, efficient farm equipment, food-processing production lines, and agrochemicals. Get on a plane and arrive at the most remote location in the world within a day or two. Go online and order products made in just about any part of the world. People, as a result of travel and media, have increased demands for the exotic things they see around the world. As food retailers compete for business, they increasingly offer these exotic foods to attract customers.

## Recipe Box

### One Restaurant, 119 Countries

Although Subway has more restaurants around the world, McDonald's has made its way into more countries, largely through its strategy of catering to local tastes. In India, where cows are sacred animals, McDonald's sells the Chicken Maharaja Mac, which is essentially a Big Mac with chicken rather than beef patties. Another favorite that appeals to the Indian palate is the Big Spicy Paneer Wrap. Because fish is a huge part of Japanese diets, the Shrimp Thousand-Island Wrap and Shrimp Filet-O are sold right alongside many items that appear on an American menu. Although it caused a huge stir in Fez, Morocco, when it built a restaurant resembling a mosque, McDonald's remains quite popular, selling the McArabia (beef patties on a flatbread) but reserving the Shogun Burger (a pork patty with teriyaki sauce and cabbage) for its Hong Kong menu. In its attempt to attract the refined palates of the French, the chain introduced its Recette au Bleu, a burger on ciabatta topped with blue cheese. And though criticized as contributing to the increasing weight of Americans, McDonald's also makes a fair profit selling enormous sandwiches in other countries as well, such as the Double Filet-o-Fish and Double Quarter Pounder in Egypt.

Exotic foods, however, are native foods for some people. Consider what it would be like to move to another country and find that breakfast was miso soup, rice, and fresh vegetables (a typical Japanese breakfast), lunch was plantains and beans (a typical Central American lunch), and dinner was goat kabobs and *ful medames* (a typical Egyptian dinner). Even though these might be palatable, over time a person would long for a less exotic meal made from familiar foods. Have you ever considered why there are so many fresh produce markets in places like New York City, Toronto, London, and Paris selling what might seem like unusual foods? These businesses started because immigrants to new places went where they could get produce that they missed, along with other ethnic foods. Interconnectedness is not just the result of migration. The food system has become increasingly interdependent over time, with increasing numbers of people relying on globally produced and processed foods.

### Transnational Issues

In addition to discussing the specific food items in a historical context, along with the main themes common throughout, each food chapter also explores the key transnational issues, or issues that transcend national borders, that arise as a result of an interconnected global food system. Because transnational issues are not confined within a particular country's political borders, they require cooperation among a variety of actors, including businesses, organizations, communities, and people—in the capacity not only of voters but, even more importantly, of consumers. On one side are those causing the issue; on the other side are those affected by it. Without buy-in from each side, issues will not be effectively resolved.

Transnational issues cannot be separated easily into neat political, economic, sociocultural, and environmental categories; they cross too many boundaries. Issues of currency exchange and buying power, exchange of goods, and human-security issues involving labor, migration, farming conditions, wages and benefits, land ownership, health concerns, land usage, transgenic (genetically modified) seeds, and global common goods overlap between chapters as easily as they transcend categorization.

The formation of international organizations is a response by governments and citizens to address transnational issues and, in the case of food politics, the increasing shift toward a global food supply chain. The need to

---

### New-to-You Food: Jackfruit

With bark that has long been used to dye Buddhist monks' robes in South and Southeast Asia, the jackfruit tree has been offering substantive nutrition for more than a millennium. Whereas Americans waste as much as 40 percent of their food, people in countries such as India sort through dumps to collect rotting jackfruit to salvage for dinner.[1] The fruit has been a staple food in diets in these tropical regions due in part, no doubt, to the fact that one jackfruit can weigh up to eighty pounds. That the fruit is packed with vitamins A and C, calcium, iron, and antioxidants is another reason the food is a dietary staple. In addition to nutrition, the plant offers many additional benefits. Its leaves, seeds, roots, and latex (its milky fluid) have medicinal uses. The hardwood tree also supplies excellent lumber. Some claim that the fruit is even a cure for hangovers.

Unlike many other fruits that grow on branches, jackfruit grows directly on the limbs of the tree. This form of growth accommodates unusually huge fruit. Jackfruit has a hard, prickly exterior with a fleshy, yellowish interior. Beneath the outer shell, the flesh is organized in sets of pods that grow around seeds. Young jackfruit has to be cooked before being eaten and tastes like—you guessed it— chicken. The ripe fruit can be eaten raw or cooked and has a taste that resembles pineapple. (I personally think ripe jackfruit smells like iced tea.) Oddly mimicking meat in its texture and consistency, jackfruit is used as a substitute in developing countries by people who cannot afford meat. In Malaysia, for example, jackfruit is canned and sold as "vegetable meat." Its meat-like quality has increased its popularity in the global north among vegetarians and the health conscious, as the texture makes it a good meat substitute for barbequing and in Southeast Asian cuisine. Increased global travel has exposed tourists to jackfruit, and global transportation of goods has facilitated its export to global south countries to satisfy the taste buds of travelers when they return home.

---

coordinate policies has pushed governments to work through intergovernmental organizations (IGOs). Where citizens feel governments and their institutions fail to adequately address the effects of the global food system, they form nongovernmental organizations (NGOs) to try to make changes that governments cannot or will not make.

**Intergovernmental organizations** Changes in food-system dynamics have led governments to become more reliant on using existing IGOs, such as the United Nations and its many agencies, or creating new ones to address these increasingly transnational issues. Because transnational issues do not recognize political borders, cooperation among countries is necessary to solve them. Governments work through IGOs to create international laws in an

The name jackfruit comes from the Malay word *chakka*, which the Portuguese explorers heard as *jaca*, hence the English name "jackfruit." Although jackfruit has been a key source of nutrition for people in Asia, transplanting the tree to Brazil has caused problems.[2] When a nonindigenous species is introduced into another ecological system, the outcome can be devastating (as discussed in Chapter 7 with the introduction of lionfish to the Atlantic coast). Jackfruit is considered an invasive species in the Brazilian rain forest because of its causal chain of damage. The Portuguese first introduced the tree in the Tijuca National Park in the 1800s as the conditions there resembled those of its native tropical origins. This exotic species proved problematic, however, because jackfruit became a food source for small animals. After eating the fruit, they subsequently spread the seeds across greater areas, leading to an increased jackfruit population that competes with native trees.[3] Marmoset and coati populations have burgeoned because of this added food source, affecting the native bird populations, whose eggs they eat. The Brazilians now face the challenge of reducing the spread of the invasive jackfruit species without harming the mammal populations that have become dependent on jackfruit as a food source.

1. "Food Waste Is Overwhelming: Here Are Five Things People Are Doing about It," NPR, August 22, 2012, http://www.npr.org/blogs/thesalt/2012/08/22/159825659/theres-too-much-food-waste-but-here-are-five-things-people-are-doing-about-it.

2. Real de Abreu, Rodolfo Cesar, and Pablo José Francisco Pena Rodrigues, "Exotic Tree *Artocarpus heterophyllus (Moraceae)* Invades the Brazilian Atlantic Rainforest," *Rodriguésia* 61, no. 4 (2010): 677–688.

3. Mileri, Milena, et al. 2012. "Removal of Seeds of Exotic Jackfruit Trees (*Artocarpus heterophyllus, Moraceae*) in Native Forest Areas with Predominance of Jackfruit Trees in the Duas Bocas Biological Reserve, Southeastern Brazil," *International Journal of Ecosystem* 2, no. 5: 93–98.

attempt to set norms and rules to govern their relations. Any organization whose membership comprises countries is considered an IGO. The World Trade Organization, the International Monetary Fund, the World Bank, the International Labor Organization (ILO), the International Pepper Community, the International Cocoa Initiative, and regional fisheries management organizations are IGOs discussed in the following chapters.

Two IGOs deserve highlighting. The World Trade Organization was created to replace the General Agreement on Tariffs and Trade (GATT), which brought countries together in 1947 to promote free trade policies by reducing import taxes. The WTO is a significant advancement over GATT because the WTO has a formal dispute mechanism in place. Countries can submit complaints to the WTO about member policies they feel violate international trade law. Through its dispute settlement, the WTO procedurally rules on and enforces its decisions. US agricultural policy was found to violate free trade policies by unfairly giving advantages to American farmers. The WTO ruled that until the United States changed its domestic policy regarding farmer subsidies, the country would have to compensate Brazil for its losses. The United States has an incentive to abide by the WTO's ruling because the government feels the long-term benefits of trade cooperation outweigh the short-term penalty for violating international laws that it feels make trading more mutually beneficial.

Another significant IGO worth discussing is the International Labor Organization, formed to address international standards for the treatment of laborers. The ILO is unique in that, although it is an agency of the United Nations, making it intergovernmental, employers and unions also participate in policy making. Because developing countries feel that cheap labor is one advantage they have over GN countries, and because all countries want to maintain control over setting minimum wages, the ILO faces difficulties in implementing meaningful and enforceable labor standards. The organization has identified Worst Forms of Child Labor as egregious abuse of children used in forced, hazardous, or trafficked labor, but it has confronted many problems in eliminating the exploitation of child labor.

**Nongovernmental organizations** Transnational issues have also given rise not only to consumer concerns about the quality and safety of the products they eat but also social concerns about who produces the food and what effect consumption is having on the planet. NGOs form to give people a way to come together to raise awareness and institute change regarding issues they feel their governments do not sufficiently address. Most NGOs focus on a broad array of issues that pertain to a general topic. They differ from IGOs in two ways. First, they are formed by private citizens to raise awareness about issues and pressure governments and IGOs to address injustices. Although they might receive financial or other support from governments, they act independently of them. Second, NGOs are not exclusively organized at the international level but rather can be formed by people to address anything from very broad global issues to local grassroots issues.

Fair trade organizations are often international NGOs that seek to promote social equity for workers and farmers producing goods for export. The global demand for chocolate has increased awareness about the role of child slave labor on cocoa plantations. Fair trade NGOs are involved in working to improve farming conditions and wages in producing countries. National and local NGOs are often referred to as "nonprofits." The Coalition of Immokalee Workers is one example of a grassroots organization formed to address human rights issues for tomato workers in Florida. To resolve human rights issues, the NGO confronts labor, immigration, and human-trafficking laws.

## CONCLUSION

Each of the next five chapters examines a particular food item as it relates to the global food supply. Each starts with an introduction to the food item, identifying its origins, uses, and rise in popularity. This section includes a brief history of how the food spread from its native location to become part of the global food supply chain. An understanding of the food item and its history lays the necessary foundation for the next section, which considers production. This part of each chapter examines the role of government, corporations, and farmers or fishers involved in supplying consumers. The last section of each chapter considers the transnational issues that have emerged from the production and consumption of the food in relation to the global food chain. The effects of the global food system involve an interconnected array of political, economic, social, and environmental issues resulting from increased interaction and interdependence in a worldwide food chain.

Examining global food production offers a way to explain how the global political economy works. Chapter 3 begins with the international monetary system by focusing on how the trade of nutmeg, cinnamon, peppercorn, and cloves helped to establish global currency exchange. Other than sliding a plastic card or digging out cash, consumers don't think much about the exchange taking place when they buy groceries. Even when traveling abroad, tourists go to an ATM machine or exchange service for the pounds, euros, or dinars needed to sample the local cuisine. As people increasingly moved away from a system of barter to one of large-scale trade, they needed to find a reliable way to accept payment for goods without being shortchanged. The creation of the gold standard resulted as a way to accommodate that need. Examining the spice trade helps to show how that system evolved and reveals the implications of currency value and exchange.

When they discovered cacao in the form of the Aztec drink *chocolatl*, the Spanish conquistadors weren't very fond of it but recognized that it gave the natives energy and was a high-value commodity: just one bean could trade for two rabbits. The Spaniards consequently sought to control the cocoa trade, winning over European taste buds by adding sugar to hot chocolate. After exhausting the land in their Central American holdings, the Spanish relocated to South America and the Caribbean, where they subsequently lost their monopoly. West Africa now exports the majority of the world's cocoa beans only because the Europeans transported cocoa trees to their African colonies. Chapter 4 focuses on the immeasurable impact and residual effect colonization has had on cocoa production. Reliance on cash crops in West African producing countries has undermined development. The use of children, particularly trafficking in child slave labor, led to public outcries in the early 2000s that have tasked importing and exporting countries, multinational corporations, and international organizations with eliminating Worst Forms of Child Labor by committing to ethically traded cocoa beans.

Soybeans offer insight into a variety of issues facing human demands on the global food system. Although Chapter 5 largely focuses on production in Brazil, the role that MNCs play in the world supply chain of soybeans becomes apparent. The aging and subsidy-dependent US agribusiness competes with the emerging South American and Chinese markets. Increased demands by emerging economies for meat, coupled with the meat-centric diets of developed countries, strain the world's food supply. Efforts to increase production push scientists to develop faster-growing, insect- and weather-resistant crops through genetically modified, transgenic seeds as well as alternative fuels using grains to supply America's humongous appetite for energy.

Tomatoes take center stage in Chapter 6, which considers international migrant labor issues, as well as the environmental consequences of tampering with nature for large-scale food production. Even though the tomatoes in the produce section of the local grocery store rarely taste like those fresh out of the summer garden, people in the global north nevertheless have access to fresh tomatoes year-round. Increased interconnectedness leads to transportation of produce across countries—oceans, even—to stock grocery store produce cases with fresh tomatoes. But this availability comes at the cost of migrant work abuses and environmental degradation, raising questions about buying organic foods, the "locavore" movement, and sustainable development. Without immigrant, migrant laborers to pick them, tomatoes would rot on the vine. The threat of unpronounceable chemicals scares consumers into thinking that eating conventional rather than organic tomatoes opens them up to the possibility of growing a third arm. At the same time, relying on domestically produced tomatoes, as well as organic and local produce, overlooks the impact these consumer choices have on the environment and sustainable development. As none of these issues are as simple as the media makes them out to be, Chapter 6 delves into the complex perishable-foods market to consider its effect on the global food supply.

Tuna, a fish with wide migration patterns, offers one of the best cases to consider how economic interests collide with efforts to protect species from extinction and the ecosystem from irrevocable damage. International cooperation is necessary to conserve tuna, but fishers, corporations, and even states are at odds when devising policies. Protecting the tuna population involves monitoring international waters and controlling ports of entry for fishing vessels. With the increasing popularity of Japanese sushi bars, the Atlantic and southern varieties of bluefin tuna (used for sashimi) are under threat of extinction. Even the Atlantic yellowfin tuna has been put on the endangered species list because of increased consumption. Chapter 7 considers the implications of the growing taste for Japanese food for the global trade of tuna and the tensions that arise over fishing rights, territorial waters, and sustainable development.

In addition to reconsidering the common themes that connect very different food items, the concluding chapter offers some food for thought about the future of food. What are the future trends in an increasingly globalized food supply chain? How has colonization affected food production? Will self-interested sovereign states be able to find a way to reconcile their differences over international policies to address human and environmental issues? Where do multinational corporations fit into the equation? These questions arise out of the shift in food production. Examining its relationship with the global political economy can shed some light on why these issues have emerged and what direction the world is taking.

## CHAPTER QUESTIONS

1. How did colonization lay the foundation for the current global food system?

2. How does the neoliberal economic model facilitate the global food system?
3. How does globalization impact food availability?
4. How do IGOs and NGOs help to address transnational food issues?

# CHAPTER 3

---

## SPICES

### *The Evolution of the International Monetary System*

Demand for peppercorn, cinnamon, nutmeg, and cloves—literally worth their weight in gold because of the high cost of importing them—was the primary reason the Europeans set out to find the mythical "Spice Islands." Muslim and Turkish traders controlled access to these luxuries, and prices were high because goods changed hands numerous times before they hit the European market. The Europeans believed the famed Spice Islands to be the source of these exotic spices. In actuality, they grew in a wide region spanning Sri Lanka, the eastern coast of India, and the islands in the Molucca Sea that make up modern-day Indonesia.

European countries wanted to turn a profit from the highly lucrative spice trade. Exploration was a necessity to gain control of the supply of exotic spices, which were in high demand and had both economic and social value. Christopher Columbus set out to find the Spice Islands in the late fifteenth century but instead ended up in the Caribbean. The various spices he found there were so different from what was available in Europe that Columbus thought he had in fact found the Spice Islands and discovered a shorter route to the East Indies. It wasn't until a few years later, when Vasco da Gama

---

### Recipe Box

**Spice Trader for a Day**

Become Abu Al-Qazzaz to experience life as a Muslim spice trader in the fourteenth century. In the computer simulation at Spice Trade (http://www .spicetrade.org), Abu navigates the streets of Baghdad to build a spice business, encountering the trials and travails of European encroachment into the business. This game offers a more personal look at the effect of increased European competition with Muslim traders.

---

found a route around Africa, that the Europeans actually found the source of the exotic spices.

As with cocoa beans during the time of Aztec and Inca rule, spices were a form of exchange because they held an immediate, usable value in a way that metals in the Americas did not. The indigenous Indians, who were surrounded by land with abundant gold and silver, placed a much higher value on the labor-intensive, rarer cocoa bean. For this same reason, exotic spices were highly valued by the Europeans, driving them to find and control the source of the supply.

Once the Europeans gained sea access to the source, control of the spice trade shifted hands, eventually pushing the Muslim merchants out of the picture. The Portuguese were the first to enter the spice trade, followed by the Dutch, who came to monopolize the trade through their Dutch East India Company (Vereenigde Oost-Indische Compagnie). By the early eighteenth century, the British and French had moved in on the Dutch by creating their own East India trading companies and globally expanded their empires. Eventually spices became so readily available in Europe that they lost their exotic appeal, making them affordable to commoners.

The European demand for spices considerably increased the flow of goods between Europe and Asia. As a result, the spice trade laid the foundation for the modern international monetary system. This exchange created the first global trade networks by generating a demand for trade standardized through a new monetary system of currency, commercial credit, and even early corporations.[1] The world currency established by the Spaniards, circulation of the guilder, pound, and franc through the Dutch, British, and French East India Companies, and finally British economic hegemony laid the foundation for economic divide between the global north (GN) and the global south (GS) that prevails to this day.

Using the spice trade to examine the evolution of the international monetary system, this chapter considers the key spices that drove explorers to search for the source. The chapter begins with an introduction to the four spices that helped to change history: peppercorn, cinnamon, nutmeg, and clove. A brief history of the spice trade lays the foundation for discussing European entrance into the supply chain. The chapter's second part examines the Europeans' control of production and how the international monetary system evolved from their intervention. The third section considers the effects of the neoliberal economic model on modern-day spice production in the global food system.

## INTRODUCING THE SPICES

### Piper nigrum

Peppercorn (also referred to as pepper) is considered the "king of spices." Traded from India for over four thousand years, peppercorn was, and is, in the greatest demand. Black peppercorn is the most popular, followed by the white and green varieties. These very tiny fruits are removed from the stem, dried, and either ground into flakes or put whole into a peppermill for freshly ground pepper. And though pink peppercorn is often included in pepper mills, these berries come from an entirely different plant. Peppercorn originated on the Malabar Coast in Southeast India. Pepper was highly valued because of the piquant seasoning it provided when ground over food, a flavor not produced by any European spices.

Pepper was so highly valued that before any currency system was established, Europeans used it like cash in exchange for goods and services. To get an idea of the value of peppercorns in medieval times, pepper sold for four shillings per pound. Considering that five shillings could buy one hundred flasks of beer, pepper was a rather expensive item.[2] Peppercorn represented a steadier currency standard because coins contained variable amounts of precious metal. When, in the first century, Alaric I the Goth and later Attila the Hun overtook Rome, they are said to have demanded pepper as part of Rome's ransom. Tributes to royalty were commonly paid in pepper, as was rent. Debt could be paid off with the seasoning, while government officials regularly accepted bribes of just a few peppercorns. Because pepper was shipped from the Middle East by sea, sailors and dockworkers were prohibited from wearing clothing with pockets or cuffs when transporting the spice. Shippers knew the worth of just one peppercorn and realized how easily workers could conceal the spice in their clothing.

In terms of both volume exported and sales, peppercorn remains the king, with demand continuing to increase. In order to help stabilize what can be a volatile commodity price, the International Pepper Community was established under the United Nations in 1972. It is the only spice for which an intergovernmental organization formed to regulate trade. Although Vietnam is now by far the leading exporter of pepper, farmers off the Malabar Coast of India produce superior varieties.

## Cinnamomum zeylanicum

Frequently what is sold as cinnamon is really cassia, a similar-tasting spice. Both come from the inner bark of the plant, which is cut, dried, and made into sticks. Cinnamon originates in Sri Lanka, which is why some cinnamon is labeled "Ceylon cinnamon" to distinguish the superior, authentic spice from cassia, a lesser variety that originated in China. Once the British and French realized cinnamon would grow well in any tropical climate, they transplanted it to their colonies. Sri Lanka remains by far the world's largest exporter of cinnamon, though the spice makes up a small percentage of the country's exports in comparison to tea and coconut production.

## Myristica fragrans

The nutmeg tree, native to the Banda Islands (part of Indonesia), produces two valuable spices. The seed is referred to as nutmeg, whereas its outer protective layer is the source of mace. Although primarily associated with self-defense spray, mace was also a highly prized seasoning that is still used today to heighten flavor in many cream-based dishes. Nutmeg is most desirable in its whole-seed form because, once ground, it quickly loses its flavor.

Before the Europeans gained control of the flow of nutmeg to the continent in 1393, Germans paid the equivalent of "seven fat oxen" for one pound of the spice.[3] During the seventeenth and eighteenth centuries, aristocrats bought fancy nutmeg graters that often contained a compartment for the seeds to show off their wealth. Nutmeg graters from the Victorian era remain rare, expensive collectibles. Indonesia, Grenada, and India account for the bulk of the world's supply of nutmeg and mace, with Indonesia alone accounting for 75 percent of the world's share of the two spices.[4] Although demand for nutmeg and mace continues to grow, it is far overshadowed by that for pepper.

### *Syzygium aromaticum*

The spice clove comes from a tree native to a few islands in the Molucca Sea, now part of Indonesia. Cloves are the dried buds of the tree's flowers. Rarely eaten whole, they are usually ground into a powder used to enhance the flavor of meats; they are often used whole in pickling. Clove was another of the spices in high demand among Europeans. Worldwide demand for clove has reached a plateau, and Indonesia, Madagascar, and Tanzania are the largest producers. In Southeast Asia cloves are sold packed in betel leaves for chewing, while clove, or "kretek," cigarettes are popular in Indonesia.

Cloves made the headlines in 2009 when Indonesia filed a grievance with the World Trade Organization (WTO) over the ban of clove cigarette imports into the United States. In 2012, the WTO ruled that the US ban on clove cigarettes was a discriminatory policy, giving the United States an unfair competitive advantage over Indonesia for similar products (i.e., tobacco cigarettes) in its domestic market.[5] The clove cigarette market earns more than $15 million each year.[6]

## A BRIEF HISTORY OF THE SPICE TRADE

It is unlikely that Europeans give much thought anymore to the spices that fill their cupboards, though the products their ancestors sought to find and control have unquestionably influenced European cuisines. In the Netherlands, nutmeg is a commonly used spice because the Dutch East India Company controlled the supply to Europe in the seventeenth century. Curry dishes, which are seasoned with cinnamon, cloves, and peppercorn, are common in Great Britain because of British colonization of India in the eighteenth century. Soufflés would not be the same without freshly grated nutmeg, made readily available by the trees the French transplanted to their colonies. Because people in developed countries tend to take spices for granted, a brief look at the spices that changed history is worthwhile.

In the Middle Ages, the spices a family served at a meal reflected its social status. The amount and variety of spices adorning a meat platter indicated wealth, as well as intense flavor. This seventeenth-century English recipe, "To Bake Beef like Red Deer," instructs the cook as follows:

> Take a pound of Beef, and slice it thin, and half a pint of good wine Vinegar, some three Cloves, and Mace above an ounce, three Nutmegs, pound them altogether, Pepper and Salt according to your direction, and a little Sugar, mix these together, take a pound and half of Suet, shred and beat it small in a morter, then lay a row of Suet, a row of Beef, strow your spices between every lain, then your Vinegar, so doe till you have laid in all, then make it up, but first beat it close with a rowling pin, then presse it a day before you put it in your past.[7]

The ability to prepare this recipe indicated that a household was certainly well-off. Being able to buy spices like nutmeg signaled both wealth and social status. In addition to being used in cooking, spices were also valued as medicinal remedies. Doctors prescribed spices for a variety of ailments, ranging from gout to plague.

During the Middle Ages, Arab merchants served as the middlemen for spices moving from South and Southeast Asia to Europe. Having gotten a taste for it during the Crusades, Europeans began to demand cinnamon. Spice merchants took advantage of the fact that because the source was unknown to the Europeans, these exotic flavorings became elevated to luxury status, putting them in high demand. Through an intricate trade network, spices could change hands multiple times—each time for a higher price. By the time they reached Europe, prices would have at least doubled.[8] So long as they could hide

> ### Recipe Box
>
> ### Recipe Box: Nuts for Nutmeg in the Netherlands
>
> Domination of Southeast Asian spice-producing countries by the Dutch permanently affected their taste buds. Nutmeg, cinnamon, and cloves remain staples in Dutch cooking, in dishes as different as Dutch meatballs, **kruidnoten** cookies, and **borstplaat**, a fondant candy. What spices are predominant in the foods you eat? What has influenced your food preferences? If you have traveled abroad, do you now enjoy spices that you had never before eaten?

the source, Arab traders were able to control access. Stories abounded, cloaking the various spices' origins in order to control their supply. Trade routes moved spices from India to the Sinai Peninsula, with traders being certain to create an air of mystery around the source of their luxury goods. From the tenth to the fifteenth centuries, Genoa and Venice dominated the market as the central point of import from the Turks and Arabs. The Italians secured a monopoly over the spice trade because they were the entry port for goods from the Far East and controlled the overland Spice Road's entry into central and western Europe. This control over nutmeg, cinnamon, peppercorn, cloves, and other exotic spices forced those paying high prices to engage in exploration to find the source of these luxury goods. A desire for direct access to cinnamon, specifically, motivated the Portuguese to set out for the East.

Prior to having an established, globally accepted currency, Europeans needed something appealing to support their indulgence. The problem was that they had little of interest to trade besides red coral and Italian glass. To overcome this difficulty, the Venetians and Genoese bought humans from eastern Europe to exchange for spices with Muslim traders, who used the slaves as soldiers to expand their empire.[9]

*Enter the Europeans*

Some argue that Vasco da Gama's 1498 Portuguese expedition to find the Spice Islands marked the beginning of the modern age because it found a direct trade route to Asia where Europeans encountered thriving commerce and "cosmopolitan" intellectuals.[10] Without question the Europeans—and the people they encountered—were irrevocably changed by their global exploration. Driven by their desire to control the spice trade, the Europeans ultimately colonized the world.

The Portuguese and Spanish were among the first to set sail. Within a century, the Dutch, British, and French followed. That the Portuguese headed east, whereas the Spaniards headed west, is no accident. Their routes were the result of a hemispheric separation established by the Treaty of Tordesillas, by which, in the fifteenth century, the Catholic Church split the globe between the two powers. The first to reach the mystical Spice Islands was Vasco da Gama who, by 1512, was able to claim territory in Asia for Portugal. With the exception of the Portuguese explorer Pedro Cabral, who was blown onto the shores of Brazil on an Atlantic current during his attempt to retrace da Gama's route to the Spice Islands, Portugal's colonies were limited to the Eastern Hemisphere. (Brazil, incidentally, fell east of the line established by the church, so it was rightly within Portugal's territory.)

The Spanish crown was willing to foot the bill for Christopher Columbus's trip to find an alternate, presumably shorter, route to the Spice Islands because cloves were worth their weight in gold. Even though Columbus landed upon many other riches, his failure to reach the Spice Islands was a disappointment. Because Spain was confined under the Treaty of Tordesillas to the Western Hemisphere, the Spanish were later willing to support Ferdinand Magellan's expedition to find an Atlantic route to the Spice Islands. Magellan was successful, finding a route to the prized Spice Islands via the Pacific Ocean. Because cloves were in such high demand in Europe, a ship filled with twenty-six tons of the spice that returned from the expedition in 1522 covered the entire cost of Magellan's expedition.[11]

The key to dominating the spice trade laid in controlling Ceylon (modern-day Sri Lanka). The island was not only the key producer of cinnamon but, more importantly, a strategic port for access to the Malacca Strait, which lead to an abundance of spice-producing islands in the Molucca Sea. The Portuguese made a deal in 1518 with the king who controlled the port in

Ceylon to build a military outpost on the island, allowing them to control the cinnamon supply. To control clove and nutmeg supplies, the Portuguese forcibly took control of the islands in the Molucca Sea, considered the choke point of all spices heading west.[12] To keep prices high by limiting supply, the Portuguese allowed nutmeg to be grown on just two islands.[13] They were not able, however, to limit the supply of spices on other Spice Islands, as yet unknown to them, which prevented them from entirely cutting out the Muslim traders to gain a monopoly.

## PRODUCTION

Because it was not the custom among Muslims merchants to carry weapons, they were vulnerable to the Portuguese explorers, who were willing to use firepower to gain control. Prior to European arrival in South and Southeast Asia, spice producers realized that adopting Islam eased transactions with Middle Eastern buyers because religious law made weapons unnecessary. The spice trade is the primary reason why pockets of Islamic populations live along the Indian Ocean trade route (such as in India and Sri Lanka) and why Indonesia is an Islamic country, as so many of the spice-producing islands make up the country.

Like the Italians during the Middle Ages who resorted to selling slaves to the Muslims due to a lack of enticing goods for barter, the Renaissance-era Spaniards and Portuguese had few items of interest for trade in America and Asia. The Spanish and Portuguese explorers thus exploited the advantage they did have, gunpowder, which gave the conquistadors and traders the upper hand over the indigenous peoples, who only had rudimentary weapons. That the Muslims did not rely on weapons allowed the Portuguese to wrest control of the spice trade from the natives more easily.

Using force to control people generates the potential for rebellion, which is exactly what arose in 1570 when the clove growers revolted against the Portuguese. This revolution helped to move the spice trade away from the Portuguese by integrating the Dutch East India Company, established in 1602, into the trade.[14] Recognizing that failure to secure all spice sources led to the downfall of the Portuguese, the Dutch were determined to gain a solid monopoly over the spice trade. Taking advantage of the clove growers' rebellion, the Dutch moved to cut off supplies to the Muslim merchants to secure a monopoly. To that end, the Dutch company centralized the growth of clove, nutmeg, and cinnamon trees in certain areas, destroying all other known sources and regularly killing any saplings that grew from seeds carried to other areas by the wind or by birds. Because nutmeg itself is the seed of the plant, the Dutch needed a way to sell the seeds but prevent them from germinating, which could undermine their monopoly. By dipping the nutmeg in a lime solution, they prevented entrepreneurial people from starting crops.

The Dutch proved a formidable force, willing to quash uprisings in the Molucca Sea islands by mobilizing soldiers to coerce and even kill the natives. The Dutch East India Company colonized the spice-producing areas, fortifying their presence by importing prisoners and slaves to work in the industry. Dutch treatment of the indigenous laborers in the Spice Islands set the model later used for establishing and operating sugar plantations in the Caribbean. Dominance in the region helped to establish the Dutch guilder as an accepted currency for financial transactions. The Dutch spice trade monopoly lasted well into the seventeenth century, until the advent of increased competition from the British and French, who sought to expand their empires. Due to the increased supply of spices, the Dutch destroyed surplus stocks of nutmeg and cinnamon warehoused in Amsterdam to artificially maintain higher prices.

Although the Dutch East India Company was the first to establish its presence in South and Southeast Asia, the British East India Company had actually been chartered two years earlier. The British were able to take control of one of the Spice Islands, calling it Rum, but ended up selling it to the Dutch in exchange for New Amsterdam (modern-day Manhattan Island in New York City). The British East India Company's biggest asset was its holdings in India and, later, Ceylon, which the Dutch ceded to them after their loss in the Fourth Anglo-Dutch War. As they increased their presence in the region, the British chipped away at the Dutch monopoly.

The French broke into the spice trade with their own East India Company half a century later. Although France established a number of settlements, its influence in the spice-producing region was limited in comparison to that of the Dutch and English. Both the British and the French sought to increase spice supplies by smuggling seeds out of the Spice Islands and transplanting them to their African and Caribbean colonies. The British were particularly interested in nutmeg, as it was a lesser crop in the regions they controlled, yet, like cloves, was worth its weight in gold. The trees transplanted in the

British colony of Grenada thrived in the tropical climate, while the French successfully grew nutmeg and cloves in Mauritius and Zanzibar. By the time these plants began to compete with producers in Asia, however, the Dutch monopoly was already in decline. As more Europeans became familiar with the sources of exotic spices, tastes changed, and supplies became more abundant, the allure of spices faded, making them accessible to commoners.

### The International Monetary System Is Born

Without question, the desire to enter the spice trade motivated European exploration. Control of spices increased Europeans' economic power as these commodities were highly valued. Because they were traded as money, these commodities were what economists refer to as commodity money, wherein an item's value lies in its usability. Commodity money differs from payments for most transactions in the modern world, which are based on representative money in the form of currency or, increasingly, a plastic card, which is accepted as payment for goods and services. Just as gold and silver were of value because they could be melted down to make both useful tools and elaborate ornaments that accorded status to the bearer, peppercorns were also of value because of the huge demand for the spice. A landlord had an incentive to accept pepper as payment for rent (hence the term "peppercorn rent," which is still in use today) because the commodity could be used as a form of currency to buy goods.

Any number of problems arise through reliance on commodity money. One issue that affects using commodities for payment is the durability of the good. Spices are dried, giving them a longer shelf life than many other food items, but over time they lose their potency. Similarly, the quality of the good may vary considerably. True cinnamon from Sri Lanka is of a much higher quality than cassia, which is often sold as cinnamon. The issue of portability also makes commodity money less appealing. Paying the rent in a few peppercorns is very different from hauling around a ton of it to buy a plot of land. And commodity money really only holds its value when demand exceeds supply. When the European aristocrats were showcasing their nutmeg in decorative grinders, the spice was far more valuable than when the British and French started flooding the market, driving down prices. The need for representative money grew out of more than these problems, however; as more and more people encountered one another, differences in what their respective societies valued made transactions more difficult, if not impossible, especially on a large scale.

Although it could not claim territory in Asia, through its Western Hemisphere claims Spain established trade ties between the Americas and the East. Spain's far-reaching empire and newfound access to Asia put it in position to establish the first world currency. Due to currency reform in Spain in 1497, the government minted new silver coins referred to as "pieces of eight." Access to silver in the Americas allowed Spain to mint more "Spanish dollars." Because it was minted at a specific weight in grams, the Spanish dollar became a trusted currency in the early sixteenth century.[15]

Not until the late eighteenth century did the piece of eight enter regular circulation worldwide, making it what is considered the first global currency.[16] The piece of eight was in fact considered legal tender in the United States until 1857 and provided the basis for the US dollar and the Mexican peso. Until the Spanish dollar set the foundation for a global monetary system, whereby currency in and of itself carried value, the Europeans had little of interest to trade.

As the Europeans discovered more precious metals in the Americas, British and French exploration resulted in extensive colonial holdings. Their global reach enabled them to create a reliance on their minted pound sterling and franc as accepted means of exchange, challenging the Spanish piece of eight as the sole world currency. Because they were hand pressed, however, coins were susceptible to "clipping" (having their edges trimmed to harvest melts for melting into more coins), which made traders reluctant to accept coins that might be worth less than supposed.[17] Another problem was that, in lean times or under thrifty rulers, such as Henry VIII, the government might mix in other metals, reducing the gold or silver content and thereby making the coins less valuable.

### A Cheat-Proof Currency Gives Birth to the Gold Standard

Not until Charles II attempted to introduce a new system, whereby coins were uniformly machine pressed and inscribed around the edges, did trade in coins become more trusted. Sir Isaac Newton went one step further in securing the British currency by determining the exact ratio of gold to the pound sterling based on the one-guinea coin, a gold coin put into circulation after England colonized West Africa and secured the Gold Coast. By 1816,

Great Britain had established the gold standard, which essentially gave value to a currency by fixing it to gold and thereby normalized the exchange of currencies between countries.

Two important innovations developed with the creation of the gold standard. One was the use of a "unit of account" for exchange. Rather than relying on commodity money with inherent value, exchange under the gold standard used representative money. Even though most representative money has little inherent value, its worth is determined by its face value. With the exception of a few coins circulating that were considered legal tender, the global economy adopted the gold standard.

A second innovation brought by the shift to the gold standard was a system to determine the face value of exchangeable representative money, most often referred to as currency. Under the gold standard system, paper notes were only worth the face value that could be backed by gold. Newton's conversion rate equating £1 to 113.0016 grains of gold made it possible to determine exactly the precise exchange value of the Dutch guilder, French franc, and Spanish real. Establishing an exact value for currency is important because that currency could be exchanged outside a country and still hold a consistent value. This system allowed Dutch and British traders, for example, to exchange goods with payment in either country's currency, with its worth backed by gold.

By 1870, the Europeans had recognized the economic dominance of the British and moved to the gold standard, whereby countries accepted one another's currencies as payment for goods and services. This system remained in place until the start of World War I, when the British struggled to maintain the value of its currency in relation to grains of gold. Not until the United States filled the void left by the British did the gold standard resume, this time based on the value of the US dollar in relation to ounces of gold. By the late 1960s, its role as the free world's central banker under the gold standard was creating excessive economic pressures for the United States. In a move to free the country of this burden, President Richard Nixon ended the gold standard in 1971, moving the world to a system of fiat currency. Rather than having a face value backed by a certain amount of gold, fiat money is guaranteed only by the word of a government about its value as legal tender for exchange.

Even though the world moved from spice as commodity money to the gold standard to fiat currency, the spice trade had established European dominance. The United States was able to capitalize on European advances and an isolationist policy, followed by the dissolution of the colonial empires through the United Nations' principle of self-determination following World War II. The end of the Cold War determined capitalism to be the winner in the global clash between superpowers. Most of the world's countries, now constituting the global south, were first colonies and then pawns during the global bipolar power struggle.

## THE ISSUES

The European creation of the international monetary system and US hegemony in the west during the Cold War helped to establish a foundation that continues to favor GN economic dominance. The colonies were set up to support European growth and industrialization by providing raw materials and foodstuffs. Controlling the spice trade helped to expand the European empires and establish global monetary dominance. The United States picked up where the Europeans left off following World War II to advance its own agenda. Acting as the central banker for the world allowed America to extend its monetary reach, making the US dollar a highly sought currency. Japan's relationship with the United States following World War II also helped to institute the yen as a dominant currency in East Asia.

Although the GN countries were able to diversify production to move away from dependence on agricultural commodities for export earnings, GS countries are still heavily reliant on cash crops, with a higher percentage of the workforce in the agriculture sector. Under colonial rule, colonies were set up for the production of raw materials and foodstuffs needed to fuel industrialization and earn cash for the empire. After countries gained their independence through decolonization, these countries continued to exploit the cash crops they grew for the empire. Their land was already designated for growing particular crops, and there remained an international demand for the products. Farmers retained the knowledge of how to grow spices, as well as the coffee, cacao, and tea also grown on colonial plantations. Because they needed to make money, they continued to grow what they had under colonialism.

Growing cash crops will earn farmers more money than growing subsistence crops to eat and feed their livestock. Spices, cocoa, and soybeans are in global demand. Although farmers can make money growing cassava, yams, and

### New-to-You Food: Coca

Like many spices, the herb coca has been used for millennia for its flavor as well as its medicinal properties. It's the ingredient that helped to build the Coca-Cola empire and even inspired half of its name. First and foremost, however, coca is associated with the almost globally illegalized narcotic cocaine. The production and trade of this controlled substance has the unfortunate consequence of stigmatizing the use of coca leaves, which is really no different from the eating of poppy seeds, which are also used to produce heroin. The illegal drug trade aside, coca is a cash crop for Peru and Bolivia, which export the leaves, mostly for medical uses. In the United States, Coca-Cola remains the only manufacturer permitted by the government to import coca leaves for nonmedicinal purposes.[1]

The coca plant is native to the Andes region of South America. For millennia, coca has been an integral part of the culture and history of the region. Many religious ceremonies involve the use of coca leaves for offerings and decoration. People of the region also use crushed leaves in some traditional foods. The mild boost provided by chewing raw coca leaves helped the Incas build their empire. Coca is packed with nutrients, including calcium, several vitamins, and even protein. The plant has also traditionally been used for its medical benefits, including to suppress hunger, minimize pain, and treat altitude sickness.

Coca leaves are classified in the same drug category as cocaine, making possession of them illegal in most countries. Even in some Andean countries, such as Chile, the use of coca leaves is illegal, despite being part of the country's history. In the producing countries of Bolivia and Peru, it is perfectly legal to buy and sell coca products. Travelers arriving in the high-elevation areas of these countries are greeted with—and encouraged to drink—cups of coca tea to help adjust to the altitude change. Even though one might be tempted to take home coca cookies and candies for friends and family to sample, however, returning with these seemingly harmless and quite tasty treats could land a person in prison for transporting illegal drugs.

---

1. "How Coca-Cola Obtains Its Coca," *New York Times*, July 1, 1988, http://www.nytimes.com/1988/07/01/business/how-coca-cola-obtains-its-coca.html.

other staple crops to sell domestically, or possibly regionally, countries push farmers to grow cash crops because they need the money earned from selling exports. Although some countries, such as Brazil, have managed to effectively exploit agribusiness on a large scale as a way to fund industrialization, others have not managed to shift to large-scale agribusiness and continue to rely on small farm production. Although only about 15 percent of Brazilians are engaged in farming, more than 50 percent of the population of India is still agrarian, and the country struggles to feed its own people.[18]

Colonization and GN hegemony over the international monetary system have impacted global relations in the spice industry in three key ways. First, the introduction of fiat currency has increased market volatility of traded currencies, particularly for developing countries. Due to market volatility in prices of commodities, like spices grown as cash crops, GS farmers face greater risk of getting caught in a debt cycle. Second, reliance on cash crops also makes GS countries more vulnerable when weather and natural disasters ruin crops. Third, the neoliberal economic model pushes countries to open their borders, which results in increased competition.

### Market Volatility

Many GS countries only won their independence about ten years before the gold standard was abandoned in 1971. When the United States delinked the dollar, abandoning the gold standard, the capitalist world lost its central banker. Many developing countries experienced economic hardships due to the shift from the stability-inducing fixed rate of exchange to the more volatile floating exchange rate system. Without pegging their currency to a stronger currency (such as Belize pegging its dollar to the US dollar), fledgling economies are subjected to greater market volatility. By pegging to a more stable currency, however, a government has to follow the standard set by the central bank to which it has tied its currency. Times of global financial crisis, like the most recent in 2008, can lead to market volatility because of currency fluctuation. Although concentrated in Europe and the United States, the recession had a worldwide impact because changes in a large economy or region have a ripple effect.

Market volatility affects farmers of cash crops in two ways. The first has to do with the change in the value of their currency due to monetary-system stability. Because currencies are bought and sold, like any other commodity, they can gain or lose value overnight. Currency speculation increases monetary-system instability, rendering the more fragile GS economies vulnerable. A second way producers are affected involves price volatility. Changes in the value of their currency can make their exports more or less expensive, affecting the amount of a good they can sell and the earnings they receive.

**Currency speculation** Speculators hedge their bets on whether the value of a currency will go up or down, and then buy or sell accordingly. This means that people in countries with less stable currencies can go to bed with $1,000 in a bank account and wake up with $750 because traders quickly sold off their currency. They did not actually lose $250; rather, their purchasing power parity decreased because the value of their country's currency dropped. Purchasing power parity is an indicator of how much one currency can buy relative to another. When purchasing power decreases due to speculators' sales, people need more money to buy the same goods because the value of their currency has decreased while the price of goods has stayed the same. Speculation also happens with commodities. An attempt to add some stability to the trade of spices led to the creation of the World Spice Congress in 1990. Representatives from countries and businesses alike met to work toward stabilizing spice prices as well as improving production and ease of trade.

There are concerns about hedging bets on future spice prices as they rise and fall erratically. The combined effects of currency and commodity speculation can be devastating. Changes in currency value can also result in interest rate fluctuations. A rise in interest rates can affect the farmers' ability to repay loans when they are trapped in a debt-repayment cycle. A decrease in the value of their currency, coupled with erratic market prices for a commodity, can do more than bankrupt farmers. Farmers on the Malabar Coast of India rely on peppercorn exports for their livelihoods as Indian exports constituted

## Recipe Box

### The Big Mac Index

Every year the Economist publishes its Big Mac Index. The report began as a clever way to show how much currencies are inflated by comparing prices for a Big Mac. The Economist chose this sandwich because it is ubiquitous, offering one item with similar inputs (the amount it costs to make the burger, including not only the cost of the ingredients but also labor costs, facility costs, and so on). That way, whether the Big Mac is prepared in Switzerland (which historically has the most overinflated currency) or the Maharaja Mac is made in India (which often has the most undervalued currency), the Big Mac Index offers a unique and simple way to show consumers' purchasing power parity.

10 percent of the world supply in 2011.[19] Indian farmers growing peppercorn, however, have been stuck in a debt cycle of borrowing to grow more crops to repay earlier loans made to cover expenses to grow crops. A rash of Indian farmers committed suicide in 2005 after world prices fell drastically due to increased competition, leaving the farmers unable to repay bank loans.[20] The two main factors that drove down domestic and global prices were the effects of a free trade agreement (FTA) between India and Sri Lanka and Vietnam's increased peppercorn production.

**Price volatility** Price volatility is the result of changes in the value of a currency as well as in supply and demand for goods. Fluctuations in the market mean that farmers may end up paying more to produce goods than they will be worth at the time of sale. This issue led to the Dutch burning stockpiles of nutmeg as competition from the British and French increased. Reliance on cash crops subjects spice farmers and producing countries to greater price volatility. Farmers of cash crops are limited in their ability to finance production, as little credit is extended to them. Yet, to remain in farming, many need to borrow money for seeds, fertilizers, and other agricultural inputs. If farmers do not make enough from the next crop sale, they may need to borrow more money for the next seasons' planting. Many end up in a debt-repayment trap. GS governments are also at risk when borrowing to invest in agricultural sectors, and most lack the capital to invest on their own. Both currency speculation and price volatility are consequences of a GN-dominated monetary system and the factors that led GS countries to become reliant on cash crops.

## *Weather and Natural Disasters*

Dependence on one or a few cash crops for export increases exposure to weather- and natural-disaster-related losses. When the same rains that provide the necessary waterfall for tropical plants turn into hurricanes, entire crops can be decimated. Earthquakes alone can cause tremendous damage, but when the seismic activity causes tsunamis, entire plantations can be destroyed. Unlike in GN countries, where insurance companies help cover losses when weather phenomena and natural disasters occur, most GS farmers do not have insurance of any kind. The Food and Agriculture Organization of the United Nations, at its Rome Conference in 2005, raised concerns about the lack of insurance for farmers in developing countries, and the World Bank started pilot programs in 2010 aimed at increasing access to farm insurance. For instance, though more than 50 percent of India's population depends on farming, in 2010 only 25 million of the 85 million farmer households were covered by insurance in case of natural disaster.[21] Not only are crops wiped out, but farmers often do not have life insurance policies. The death of the male head of household can lead to the family's losing its land and security.

Due to British transport of nutmeg to its Caribbean colonies, Grenada grew to be one of the biggest global exporters of the spice. Prior to back-to-back hurricanes in the first decade of the 2000s, Grenada produced 12 million pounds a year.[22] This sort of natural disaster, however, has a lasting effect. Because of the time it takes for the trees to mature, six years later the country was only producing 1.5 million pounds. By 2009, Grenada had dropped to ninth place in global exports, losing millions of dollars in revenue because its nutmeg supply had dropped by 27 percent each year since the second hurricane.[23]

Agriculture in South Asia is dependent on the seasonal rains of the monsoons. Indian and Sri Lankan farmers credit the biannual monsoons with the superior quality of their peppercorn and cinnamon, which bring a higher price at export. Sri Lankan cinnamon farmers were devastated by the December 2004 tsunami that wiped out crops, killed more than 31,000 people, and displaced over 1 million.[24] Sri Lankan cinnamon, the authentic variety of the spice that is native to the country, accounts for more than 80 percent of the world's supply. For farmers who lost their crops, replanting trees took more than two years. The tidal wave not only affected farmers but also displaced cinnamon peelers, who process the bark into sticks. As in Grenada, reliance on a single commodity compromised the situation of farmers, workers, and even the country, given its reliance on export income from one spice.

### Competition

Both small farmers who rely on cash crops for a living and the states that export them are affected by competition in domestic and international markets. Individual farmers or small collectives that are not registered fair trade producers (discussed in Chapter 4) or state backed are at the whim of the global market and even possibly government spice boards that set domestic prices in an attempt to create stability. Countries embrace the neoliberal economic model to gain export partners and receive the benefits of cheaper, better-quality imports. Greater integration into the free market impacts farmers in two significant ways. First, as governments sign free trade agreements with other countries, they open up their own economies to more competition from foreign producers. Second, competition not only comes from existing producers but arises when others see the potential for income.

**Free trade agreements** FTAs are a neoliberal economic approach aimed at opening up trade between countries to increase the flow of goods across borders. Customers, in turn, should have better access to more competitively priced goods of a higher quality when tariffs and nontariff barriers are removed. Farmers already compete internationally to sell their goods in global commodity markets.

With FTAs, such as the 1998 bilateral pact between Sri Lanka and India, farmers also face greater competition in domestic markets. Import taxes would have made Sri Lankan spices more expensive than Indian spices. When the taxes are abolished through FTAs, consumers will likely opt for the least expensive spices. Sri Lankan peppercorn, cinnamon, and clove exports to India forced domestic farmers to lower their prices to compete. So, although producers in Sri Lanka and consumers in India benefit from the FTA, farmers in India need to become more competitive to stay in the farming business.

The neoliberal economic model assumes that farmers who cannot compete will leave the agricultural sector and move to one that is more productive for them, helping to increase their potential for a better standard of living. In India, unfortunately, indebted farmers who could not pay back their loans instead committed suicide. As developing countries join the World Trade Organization, they are under even more pressure to open their markets. From a macro-level perspective, farmers in those countries must consequently become more productive or leave farming for other work. The lack of mobility, marketable job skills, social welfare safety nets, and retraining, particularly in developing countries, mean that leaving farming is rarely an option on the micro-level scale.

**New Producers** Another issue that affects farmers who export crops for cash is that when other countries recognize the value of particular exports, they may be prompted to increase production. Peppercorn demand, for example, has steadily increased worldwide. The International Pepper Community, an intergovernmental organization, reported that even though production decreased in 2010 (due to weather-related issues), earnings increased by $250 million, for peppercorn sales of over $1 billion.[25] Within one year's time, peppercorn exports increased another $500 million, even though the total quantity of production dropped 6 percent.[26]

When Vietnam realized that peppercorn sales were more likely to offer better returns on investment than its coffee exports, it shifted production. Unlike for its other cash crops, there is far less global competition for peppercorn. The crop, moreover, is less expensive to produce because it requires less land and investment, making it a much more profitable venture. Because Vietnam is a communist, state-run economy, the government financed this decision, which also means that it was in a better position for long-term planning than small farmers with a more immediate need for income. In just ten years' time, Vietnam moved from only producing about 10 percent of the world's peppercorn supply to accounting for almost 35 percent, outpacing India to become the world's largest supplier.[27] No doubt this success, coupled with increasing peppercorn prices, influenced the Vietnamese government's decision to invest an additional $1.9 billion to expand its peppercorn production.[28] Despite Vietnam's dominance in production, India remains an important peppercorn exporter due to its superior product.

Farmers in Vietnam are fortunate that their government had the means to shift production; other farmers are less fortunate. Better technologies, particularly mobile phones with Internet access, afford spice farmers direct access to commodity prices, giving them a better idea of the value of their goods so that they have greater leverage when selling to export companies. The bottom line is that a country with a gross domestic product heavily reliant on cash crops tends to be poorer with fewer prospects for improving its economic situation. Until countries can shift away from the majority of their population relying on agriculture to earn a living, they will continue to encounter these issues.

## CONCLUSION

Perhaps the mystical allure of the fantastic stories spun by the Muslim merchants actually undermined their objective of keeping the source of the peppercorn, cinnamon, nutmeg, and cloves secret by piquing the interest of Europeans, sending them in search of these exotic places. Exploration—and consequently colonization—reshaped the world order. In the process of commandeering the spice trade, the Europeans laid the foundation for the modern global monetary and trade systems. As the Spaniards increased trade ties between their American colonies and the Asians, the piece of eight grew in worldwide circulation as an accepted payment for goods. As more European countries expanded their reach, currency became more commonly accepted. Traders realized that even if one merchant did not have goods worth bartering for, currency would allow them to make purchases elsewhere, giving them a wider market for their goods.

Despite spices becoming a common product in many European households by the nineteenth century, the drive to locate the source to control the supply of peppercorn, cinnamon, nutmeg, and cloves forever changed the complexion of the international system. European dominance was achieved by the need to improve the technology necessary for exploration, which was driven by the desire to control the spice trade. Not settling for just being merchants and middlemen in the supply chain, they claimed and colonized territories throughout the world. In their attempt to better compete with the Dutch for control of the market, the British and French transplanted spices from Asia to their African and Caribbean colonies, necessitating an increased presence abroad. The treatment of humans in the colonies was nothing short of brutal.

The system of credit that evolved out of the spice trade extended to countries, creating a global network of business built around lending. Demand for spices even spawned corporations in the form of the East India Companies. The monetary and trade networks that evolved from the spice trade have left an indelible mark on the world, creating a relationship between the spice merchants and the spice growers that reinforces the GN-GS economic divide.

## CHAPTER QUESTIONS

1. What factors drove the Europeans to find the Spice Islands?
2. How did the spice trade shape the international monetary system?
3. What role did emerging corporations play in the spice trade?
4. How did colonization set the stage for modern-day spice production? What are the risks of relying on these cash crops?

# CHAPTER 4

---

## COCOA BEANS

### Global Trade and Labor

Chocolate stirs up happy thoughts, evoking images from *Willy Wonka and the Chocolate Factory*, with its decadent river, and *Chocolat*, with its handcrafted delights. Holidays mean receiving heart-shaped Valentine chocolate boxes, chocolate Easter bunnies, a Halloween bag full of candy bars, and stockings stuffed with chocolate foil-wrapped snowmen and Christmas balls. Advent calendars offer the promise of a chocolate candy behind each window, while Hanukkah brings chocolate gold coins. As a mood-enhancing energy booster, chocolate actually induces happiness by activating endorphins. Dark chocolate even helps to ward off disease with flavonoids that produce antioxidants. The thought of tarnishing these images and foregoing a treat that actually has health benefits discourages consumers from considering the source of chocolate.

Most cocoa farmers have never tasted chocolate, the final product of their cultivation.[1] Because cocoa is not used in local cuisine and chocolate is rarely manufactured in producing countries, imported chocolate is an unaffordable luxury for most farmers, made even more expensive by the need to control transportation and storage temperatures to prevent it from melting in the hot climes where cocoa trees thrive. Unlike with spices, coffee, and tea, chocolate's inaccessibility to its producers makes cocoa a unique cash crop in that its end product is a delicacy largely limited to those in the global north.

Chocolate is big business, and it's only getting bigger as demand in developing countries increases. In 2011, retail sales in the United States reached $19.5 billion,[2] with industry processors and manufacturers netting $83 billion in global sales from their chocolate products.[3] Confectioners are pushing to enter emerging economies to get the Chinese, Brazilians, Russians, and Indians as hooked on chocolate as the Swiss, Brits, Danes, and Americans. The increasing popularity of chocolate in China has resulted in double-digit growth in sales, compared to just 2 percent in European countries, the largest market.[4] And since the average person in China eats less than two ounces a year, as compared to the Swiss, who consume the most chocolate, averaging twenty-one pounds each, demand will likely increase as development reaches rural areas.[5] In another emerging economy, Nestlé cashes in on the Indians' love of milk by producing milk chocolate bars, while Kraft is hoping to appeal to Brazilians' sweet tooth by investing domestically in confectionery and chocolate manufacturing. And the purchase of Petra Foods for $950 million by Barry Callebaut, the biggest chocolate manufacturer in the world, is expected to increase the company's sales in Asian and Latin American markets by 65 percent.[6]

As with bananas and coffee, cocoa production has a long history of exploiting labor and land. The Aztec Empire dominated production in pre-Columbian Central America. The Spanish then took over, monopolizing cocoa exports to Europe and relying on plantation farming and slave labor. The Spaniards exhausted the land, forcing them to move cocoa production to their holdings in the Caribbean and South America. Once the other colonial empires broke the Spanish monopoly, production expanded to include West Africa, which is now the biggest supplier of cocoa beans.

To better explain the impact of participation in the global political economy on cocoa production, this chapter begins with a look at cocoa, followed by a brief history of how the main ingredient in the Aztec drink *chocolatl* is now predominately produced in West Africa. An interdependent global food supply means that importers will seek the least expensive supplies while exporters will attempt to offer the most competitive prices. Farmers need to sell their beans to keep their farms and support their families, which pushes them to find the cheapest sources of labor to prevent those costs from eating into the meager profits they earn from the middlemen who buy their beans to sell to exporters. Cocoa production therefore offers a way to examine the effects of global trade on human security by considering trade tariffs, environmental issues, and child labor abuses.

## INTRODUCING *THEOBROMA CACAO*

The cocoa plant is native to the Amazon Basin, spreading into Central America through Mexico. Because *Theobroma cacao*—more commonly referred to as the cocoa tree—thrives in rain forest areas within a twenty degree belt around the Equator, cocoa production has also been successful in areas of Africa, the Caribbean, South America, and Asia. In West Africa, where the majority of the world's beans are grown, farms are small, usually under ten acres. Eight family members, on average, live on and work the farms.[7] Between Ivory Coast, Ghana, Nigeria, and Cameroon, over 1.5 million farms grow cocoa.

The Forastero bean variety that grows in Africa and Brazil accounts for 90 percent of the world's cocoa supply. Although this variety is more disease resistant, disease and weather conditions still result in an estimated 30 percent loss each year.[8] The Criollo, Trinitario, and Nacional varieties produce a higher-quality bean but smaller yields. The unique flavor of these beans and the impact of growing conditions on that flavor command a high price. These varieties, limited to places like Venezuela, Madagascar, Ecuador, Trinidad, and a few Central American countries, are often sold as gourmet single-source chocolate bars, while the Forastero bean ends up in mass-produced bars.

Cocoa trees take approximately two years to mature and another five to bear fruit, which means that investment in cocoa farming will not pay off for nearly a decade. Once trees do bear fruit, however, they can produce for decades. Each tree produces around seventy pods a year, each averaging thirty to forty beans, producing enough cocoa for one thousand bars of chocolate. Pods are harvested twice a year, with one main crop and a second smaller crop. Pods must be cut from the trees and cracked open by hand, typically with a machete, making cocoa farming a labor-intensive and dangerous process. Once harvested, the beans must be fermented by sun drying before being bagged for sale.

Cocoa is a fairly versatile commodity. In addition to cocoa power and chocolate, cocoa butter is another by-product of the beans. Not only is cocoa

## Recipe Box

### The Other Black Gold

When most people think of Venezuela, Hugo Chávez and oil immediately spring to mind. The country also has another very highly sought product that only connoisseurs of chocolate are likely to know about. Venezuela is one of the few countries that grow the prized Criollo cocoa, the most expensive variety in the world. The high price is in part the result of exports accounting for less than 1 percent of the world's supply. The rare Criollo variety offers a very distinctive flavor enhanced by local growing conditions in Venezuela.

Prior to the rule of Hugo Chávez, Venezuela regularly exported cocoa. Following his ascendancy, the government required fifty-two different permits to export the beans, compared to only four prior to his election.[1] Another reason for decreased exports is that Chávez seized numerous plantations to create a state monopoly, which considerably reduced crop yields. With increasing demand for single-origin cocoa, Venezuela is in a good position to make a considerable profit if the state monopoly is abandoned and farmers have an incentive to produce.

1. Simon Romero, "In Venezuela, Plantations of Cacao Stir Bitterness," *New York Times*, July 9, 2009, http://www.nytimes.com/2009/07/29/world/americas/29cacao.html.

butter edible, but the oil is also commonly found in cosmetics, soap, and even tobacco products. Roasted cocoa shells are steeped and made into tea, pods are used for animal feed, and pod gum is used as a binding agent in foods.

Cocoa beans are sold by grade. The higher the level of theobromine, an alkaloid of cocoa, the better the quality of the bean. The standard is set by beans from Ghana, which contain the highest amount of theobromine. Graded cocoa is then roasted either in the shell or with the shell removed, depending on the desired flavor. The cocoa bean, referred to as the nib, is then ground into a paste referred to as cocoa liquor. At this stage, the liquor can be used for coating, molding, or filling candy and pastries. When cocoa liquor is pressed, the cocoa butter is separated from the solids, called "cake."[9] The cake is refined into cocoa powder, while the cocoa butter is mixed with some cocoa liquor and sugar, then heated to make chocolate.[10]

Chocolate lovers have Dutchman Coeraad Johannes van Houten to thank for mechanizing this labor-intensive process in the early nineteenth century. Englishman Joseph Fry further developed van Houten's technology by combining the press technology with that of the steam engine to develop a steam-powered hydraulic press. These contributions revolutionized the chocolate-manufacturing industry. In this same century, the Swiss mixed cocoa solids with milk to manufacture the first milk chocolate bar.

## New-to-You Food: Insects

In Europe and the United States, eating insects is usually only something kids do on a dare. In Asia, Africa, and Latin America, however, insects are considered delectable. The Western distaste for chowing down on bugs no doubt stems from the time of colonization where entomophagy—or the consumption of insects as food—was just one more barbarian practice the civilized world felt it needed to abolish.

Perhaps without realizing it, people regularly eat insects, as processed foods invariably contain portions of them. In the United States, nonharmful by-products that end up in food, such as insects, are measured by the food-defect action level. The Food and Drug Administration, in its *Defect Levels Handbook*, states that up to 6 percent of cocoa in a chocolate product can contain insect parts.[1]

Often described as having a nutty taste, insects of various types, not limited to crickets, ants, spiders, grasshoppers, and caterpillars, are eaten throughout the world. Although crustaceans are really just water insects, lobster, crab, shrimp, and crawfish (aka mudbugs) are considered delicacies in the same countries that shun land insects. Westerners fail to consider that, like crustaceans, insects are packed with nutrients. Switching to diets that rely on insects for protein over animals would help to save the planet by reducing the greenhouse gas levels produced by livestock methane emissions.

Recognizing insects' potential to provide a comparatively inexpensive way to feed the world, the FAO has begun research into the feasibility of farming them to promote global food security and is even planning a world congress on the issue for 2013.[2] As global south countries develop, buying power results in an increased demand for meat in people's diets. Couple this with population growth, and the planet will be hard-pressed in the coming decades to find sustainable ways to meet demand. Eating insects in place of meat would also improve world health, as insects provide nutrients and calories without the artery-clogging saturated fats of red meat, eggs, and dairy products.

The key to convincing Westerners to consider entomophagy, however, is to find appealing ways to prepare insects. Because most people in the global north cringe at the thought of a plate of fried cricket tacos or barbequed caterpillar kebabs, some culinary artists are paving the way to make insects more palatable. Some university students in London who were concerned about alleviating hunger and promoting sustainable development teamed up with a culinary student at Le Cordon Bleu to create insect dishes that would entice rather than revolt diners.[3] The final product was an Ento Box, a takeoff on the Japanese Bento Box, which included caterpillar mousse cubes, cricket crackers, cricket croquettes, and bug paté. If the Ento Box becomes a trend, maybe more people will get hooked on bugs.

---

1. "Defect Levels Handbook," US Food and Drug Administration, http://www.fda.gov/food /guidanceregulation/guidancedocumentsregulatoryinformation/sanitationtransportation /ucm056174.htm (accessed July 13, 2013).

2. "Insects Could Be the Key to Meeting Food Needs of Growing Global Population," *Guardian*, July 31, 2010, http://www.guardian.co.uk/environment/2010/aug/01/insects-food-emissions.

3. "Pan-Fried Crickets: The Food of the Future?" *Today Food*, February 15, 2012, http://bites .today.com/_news/2012/02/15/10414868-pan-fried-crickets-the-food-of-the-future?lite.

## A BRIEF HISTORY OF COCOA

Cocoa was an important part of Mesoamericans' diet as far back as the Olmecs, who lived from 1500 to 400 BCE. As a drink, cocoa supplies calories from fat in the butter and also an energy boost that mimics the effects of caffeine. The Mayans called the drink *xocolatl*, the source of the word "chocolate," but, as would happen when cocoa reached Europe, chocolate drinks were reserved for the Mesoamerican elite.

Cocoa was so important to the Aztecs that in addition to, or perhaps because of, its nutritional value, its beans served as the official currency of their empire. Cocoa beans, like spices, are a durable food item that can be easily traded. They were a useful form of currency because they held an immediate, usable value in a way that metals did not. In addition, gold and silver were abundant in Mesoamerica, unlike in other parts of the world, where they were rare and thus highly valued. When the Spaniards colonized the Americas and the Caribbean, they continued to use cocoa beans as a form of currency, buying anything from a male turkey (at two hundred cocoa beans) to a tomato, tamale, or avocado for one bean each.[11] They even used beans to purchase land, slaves, and prostitutes.

On his visit to Honduras, Christopher Columbus became the first known European to come into contact with cocoa beans, though their economic and nutritional value was not realized until Hernando Cortez encountered the Aztecs in the fifteenth century. When conquering the Aztecs, Cortez saw that the cocoa drink could sustain soldiers on long journeys. Once cocoa was sent to King Charles V of Spain, some time passed before it became popular in Europe. Only after adapting it to their taste by adding sugar did Europeans come to appreciate the drink toward the end of the sixteenth century. Rumors spread that chocolate was an aphrodisiac, which certainly helped to attract interest.

## PRODUCTION

To meet growing demand in Europe, the Spaniards set up *encomiendas*, plantations run by expatriates using forced labor. When demand outstripped production, forced labor became slave labor. Not only were Indians pushed past the point of exhaustion, but they were dying from diseases the Spanish brought from Europe. The Spaniards turned to Africa to import slaves not only to remedy the labor shortage and meet increased cocoa demand but also to man the sugar plantations in the Caribbean that supplied the sweetener that made the drink more palatable.

Supplying slaves for cocoa and other plantations, as well as mines, encouraged the Spaniards to create a trade triangle. In order to buy slaves, they needed goods for trade. Spain used its European cocoa profits to buy stuff to trade in Africa for slaves, whom they shipped to Central America to produce more goods for the European market. These exports were then shipped to Europe to fund Spain's wars, satisfy elite tastes, and pay the wages of those making goods to ship to Africa, where the cycle started over again.[12]

Slaves solved the labor shortage, but land exhaustion presented a different problem. Cocoa plants naturally thrive in a diverse ecosystem in which other plants, grown with the trees, provide shade and fertilizing debris. Growing different complementary crops, or polycropping, served the Mesoamericans well as they could grow sustenance foods, such as peppers, melons, and bananas, along with cocoa beans. For greater efficiency, the Spaniards reorganized the plantations to focus only on cocoa as a cash crop for export. This shift to monocropping eventually ruined the supply, because the lack of shade and fertilizers promoted the spread of disease, killing off whole groves and forcing the Spaniards to relocate production to South America and the Caribbean.[13]

The Spaniards were able to maintain a monopoly on the cocoa trade until Maria Theresa married Louis XIV in 1660, uniting the Spanish and French royal houses and opening up the cocoa trade to the French Empire. The French, British, and Dutch eventually chipped away at the stranglehold the Spanish had held over the European cocoa supply for over two centuries. Trade between Brazil and another Portuguese colony, São Tomé, introduced the cocoa tree to Africa, though cocoa production did not take root until the late nineteenth century in the West African countries that now supply almost 70 percent of the world's cocoa.[14]

The Industrial Revolution gave more people buying power, but only with a shift of labor from the agricultural, rural sector to the urban factories. The result was an increase in demand for imported foods—particularly those that supplied energy at a small price. That increased demand for sugar in Europe paralleled the rise of industrialization was no coincidence; factory workers needed quick energy, which they got by adding more sugar to their tea. At the same time, laborers with more buying power frequented the chocolate houses that popped up all around Europe and drank sweetened cocoa. Demand for cocoa, tea, and sugar in industrializing countries only increased incentives for the imperial powers to expand and exploit their colonies. Treatment of natives was often brutal, cultures were obliterated, and people were enslaved and treated as subhuman. Land was exploited to the point where, in Meso-america, native cocoa crops were completely decimated.

## The Move to West Africa

Just as the Spaniards recognized the export value of cocoa from the Americas, the British and French realized the cash crop potential of cocoa in West Africa in the late nineteenth century. Instead of claiming all of the land for their empires and doling out plots to expatriates, as the Spanish had done with their *encomiendas*, the British and French instead set up administrative systems to govern cocoa farms in their colonies. The burden of funding two world wars demanded funding from the colonies, resulting in government control of cocoa exports. State monopolies continued to exploit farmers even after their colonies gained independence, leading farmers to rely on cheap immigrant labor and eventually trafficked, forced, and child labor to keep their farms. Colonization set a trend in West Africa that continues, as 95 percent of the cocoa beans grown come from small, usually family-owned and -run farms, typically less than ten acres in size.[15]

With the global north consuming an estimated 64 percent of the world's cocoa, chocolate lovers have a direct link to West Africa, where four countries collectively supply 70 percent of the world's cocoa beans.[16] Ivory Coast alone produces more than 35 percent of the world's supply (see Figure 4.1). Indonesia, though currently trailing Ivory Coast, has one of the top crop yields in the world. Production is only expected to grow, giving farmers a good return on their investment. Domestic political issues and trade issues with the European Union have hindered Nigerian cocoa exports over the last few years.[17] Despite the potential revenues from cocoa production, the government, distracted by the much more lucrative petroleum market, is making little effort to resolve its issues with the EU.

**Figure 4.1 Cocoa Production, 2012–2013.**

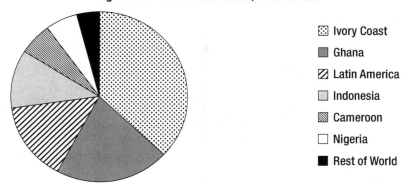

Legend:
- ⬚ Ivory Coast
- ▨ Ghana
- ▨ Latin America
- ▨ Indonesia
- ▨ Cameroon
- ☐ Nigeria
- ■ Rest of World

*Source:* *Estimates from International Cocoa Organization's Quarterly Bulletin of Cocoa Statistics- http://www.icco.org/about-us/international-cocoa-agreements/cat_view/30 -related-documents/46-statistics-production.html

---

### Recipe Box

**Conflict Cocoa**

Not only has cocoa been the source of slave labor, but the cocoa trade in Ivory Coast has provided funding for militias, just as conflict diamonds have funded insurgency groups. Since 2002, Ivory Coast has been fighting two battles. In the north, a religious battle broke out between Muslims and Christians. In the south, ethnic tensions rose when the economy turned bad, leading to a battle over land. Native Ivoirians grew hostile toward foreign landowners invited into the country during what were considered Ivory Coast's "miracle years." The nationalist-backed government declared immigrants had no legal claim to the cocoa groves they bought and farmed. The dispute was further fueled by spillover conflict from neighboring Liberia, with Charles Taylor attempting to take advantage of the power vacuum left by the death of long-time Ivoirian dictator Henri Houphouet-Boigny as a way to expand his territory and control cocoa production to fund his army.

# THE ISSUES

Although demand for cocoa is on the rise, increasing wages for farmers in West African producing countries and limited diversification and industrialization in their domestic economies make for a long road to development. As discussed in Chapter 5, Brazil is emerging as a global economy because its government was able to build on its variety of cash crops to promote foreign direct investment in agricultural and industrial sectors. Ivory Coast and Ghana, however, continue to rely on small-scale farming, which does not offer high returns or support industrialization. Economic growth is contingent on these producers moving into processing and, if possible, manufacturing to increase their development potential. Producing countries, however, rarely process the cocoa bean; even more rarely do they manufacture cocoa powder and chocolate. Cocoa farmers and exporting countries are also challenged by tariffs that discourage moving into processing, giving the multinational corporations (MNCs) yet another advantage. The sustainability of cocoa production also raises environmental and human rights issues. Short-term farming practices that increase crop yield compromise long-term output. Probably the most controversial issue for cocoa production is the use of child and slave labor. Exposés revealed forced child laborers and trafficked humans working on cocoa plantations in the biggest producing countries in the world, prompting consumer protests about these conditions. Recognizing the potential public relations disaster if associated with child slave labor and heeding threats by the US government to differentiate chocolate products by their source, corporations agreed to a protocol enacted to eliminate these abuses.

## Production versus Processing

Multinational corporations have little incentive to invest money in cocoa processing in the West African producing countries. In addition to decades of unrest in Ivory Coast, as well as rampant government corruption and a climate unfavorable to manufacturing chocolate, investing in cocoa industries on site does not offer corporations any greater earning potential than exporting the beans to their global north factories. What foreign direct investment there is in West Africa—that is, money MNCs invest to develop a business abroad—is focused on processing beans for export. MNCs are more likely to buy beans by the bag, then ship them to the Netherlands, Germany, or the United States for processing and manufacturing into cocoa and chocolate products. The real profit lies in controlling the added-value production. Consider that the export value of Ivory Coast's 2010–2011 season for its 911,497 metric tons of cocoa beans was roughly $2.8 million, whereas the top chocolate processor and manufacturer, Barry Callebaut, known in Europe for its Sarotti, Jacque, and Alprose brands, registered sales of $5 billion.[18] Similarly, the collective gross domestic product for three of the top four West African cocoa exporters in 2010 was $76.5 billion, whereas one of the biggest chocolate manufacturers, Nestlé, registered sales revenues of $99.1 billion.[19] These figures clarify the advantage processors and manufactures have over exporters that are heavily reliant on cash crops.

## Tariffs

Part of the reason for limited processing and even more limited finished goods is that until 2008, if cocoa-producing countries exported processed beans to EU countries, a tariff was assessed on any processed cocoa. The policy has since changed, with most of the producing countries having duty-free relations with the EU under its Economic Partnership Agreement with

---

### Recipe Box

#### Chocolate without Sugar?

Policies on sugar, a key ingredient in chocolate bars, directly affect chocolate manufacturers. In 2005, the World Trade Organization (WTO) found in favor of Brazil after it filed a complaint that quotas and subsidies for beet sugar production in the European Union were unfair to competing sugar producers. When the WTO set a limit on annual EU beet sugar exports, the EU paid farmers to not grow that particular crop, which is just another way of subsidizing farming. This policy came back to haunt the EU because European farmers ended up not growing enough beet sugar. Domestic shortages caused the price to rise, leading chocolate manufacturers like Nestlé to raise prices for chocolate bars to cover the increased cost of sugar. This situation raises the question of the extent to which governments should intervene in free market trade.

former colonies. The precedent the policy set, however, pushed exporters to focus almost exclusively on production. Switzerland, the biggest consumer country of chocolate, and the United States, the second largest importer of cocoa beans, continue to tax any processed cocoa imports. These policies have forestalled growth by penalizing West African producers if they attempt to develop their own industries, as processing plants would earn them a higher rate of return than just exporting cocoa beans on the world market. And a policy still in place of levying tariffs on cocoa powder mixed with sugar (i.e., chocolate) continues to discourage producing countries from pursuing manufacturing.

Despite an expanding market for chocolate in emerging economies, both raw and processed beans are heavily taxed in both producing and nonproducing countries. Duties are a form of protectionism to discourage manufacturers in these countries from relying on imported beans. In particular, Brazil, the sixth largest grower of cocoa beans, and India, with its ambitions to more than double its production, seek to limit competition in their domestic consumer markets.

Ivory Coast has an advantage over its neighboring countries, likely due to an average yearly production of 942,000 tons of cocoa beans, more than double that of its closest competitor, Ghana.[20] Each year Ivory Coast processes about two hundred thousand metric tons of beans for export, more than any other producing country. The sheer volume of cocoa beans exported from Ivory Coast offers the one incentive MNCs have for foreign direct investment. MNCs generally own the plants, giving them more of the profits, but on-site processing also provides job opportunities to Ivoirians. With a new plant that the state-owned firm ChocoIvoire opened in 2010, the country hopes to surpass the Netherlands as the top processer of cocoa, exporting more ground beans than raw ones. An increase in added-value exports affords a producing country a number of advantages. Processing beans, rather than relying on raw bean sales alone, will better cushion the country when commodity prices fluctuate. A greater reliance on processing also provides comparatively higher-wage manufacturing jobs. And since a majority of its processed cocoa is exported to the EU, Ivory Coast is not penalized by tariffs.

Although processing offers more profits to the exporting country, the real money is in manufacturing. According to the Food and Agriculture Organization (FAO), an agency of the United Nations that focuses on agricultural production in developing countries, corporations will continue to benefit from value-added production while farmers' incomes will remain low.[21] MNCs have a huge advantage because of their deep pockets and long-established brand-name products. African producers are not well positioned to break down the established pattern of the production chain and compete with the corporations

## Environmental Practices

Cocoa prices are subject to fluctuation but have been consistent over the last two decades. When cocoa prices plummeted in the 1980s, however, both Ivory Coast and Ghana turned to exporting timber. Because cocoa trees grow best in shaded areas, removing the taller trees that provided shade for the shorter cocoa trees reduced production. The process of removing the trees caused further problems as felling and dragging out the timber damaged the smaller trees.

Although traditionally cocoa thrived better in the shade, discouraging monocropping, hybrid plants have been developed to grow in full sun. Although this benefits farmers by increasing crop output, it disadvantages them by limiting production to just one crop and increasing its susceptibility to certain diseases. If that single crop should fail, farmers have no other goods to sell. Hybrids, moreover, have encouraged deforestation through the clearing of land for farming or livestock production. Cocoa production has led to deforestation through the clearing of tall rain forest trees to give cocoa trees direct sunlight. Deforestation, oddly enough, can also be caused by underuse of fertilizers in cocoa groves. Because farmers often cannot afford agricultural inputs such as fertilizers and lack access to advanced agricultural technology, cocoa farming has contributed to deforestation in West Africa.[22] As with Brazilian soybean farmers, discussed in Chapter 5, West African farmers also have an incentive to reforest areas depleted by disease and timber harvesting as land becomes scarcer. And since cassava—a staple food in cocoa-growing African countries—grows well under cocoa trees, polycropping provides not only food for farmers but also extra income from domestic sales.

Access to agricultural inputs is increasingly available through government funding, decreased prices, and funding from sustainable development programs initiated by MNCs. Sustainable development approaches increase economic growth by considering the impact that policies and practices have on humans and the environment. Companies that rely on cocoa have come to realize the importance of promoting sustainable development practices to secure the source of the product that gives their brand-name products their distinctive but consistent flavor. As a result, companies, including Nestlé, Cadbury, and Mars, have invested directly in farming communities. They recognize the benefit of offering agricultural support to improve farming techniques, encourage polycropping, and initiate community and infrastructure programs. Supporting sustainable development and reforestation ensures supplies of the uniquely flavored beans. Cadbury was one of the first companies to invest in a development project to guarantee a consistent source of the high-quality Ghanaian cocoa used in its Dairy Milk bars and Creme Eggs. Corporations also recognize that sustainable farming promotes development, thus increases the standard of living in farming communities, which helps to reduce exploitation of humans and the environment.

*Child Labor*

Relying on children to work on farms is not an uncommon practice, even in developed countries. Because most cocoa is produced on small, family-run farms, reliance on child labor has become a necessary part of the farm family's survival. What makes it problematic in developing countries is the sacrifice of schooling for work. Although child labor is illegal in most West African cocoa-producing countries, an exception is made for agricultural work, with minimum ages ranging between twelve and fifteen.[23] An estimated 1.8 million children between the ages of five and seventeen work on cocoa farms in the two countries with the largest cocoa production.[24] Although some may also go to school, attendance is affected by cultivation and harvest duties.

A number of factors influence whether children will work rather than attend school. Some children work on cocoa farms as apprentices, knowing that training will help them secure jobs as adults. Others work the family farms because they have no other choice. If they do not help to cultivate the cocoa trees and harvest the beans, their families risk losing not only their farms but their homes. Also, in rural areas, access to schools is limited, and even though education may be tuition-free, parents must pay fees for books and supplies. When cash is short, education is one of the first expenses to be cut. Having aged parents or losing a family member's work capacity due to illness or death means children are needed to supplement the family labor force. World prices are volatile, making earnings less predictable. As cocoa cultivation and harvesting are labor-intensive and seasonal, farmers often rely on their children because adults who need a steady income are less likely to work in this seasonal industry.

In many developing countries, formal education of children has not become a common social practice. One of the biggest hurdles the West African countries face is institutionalizing schooling. The coordinator for the International Cocoa Initiative (ICI) indicates that the "moral poverty of the people" necessitates the organization's holding workshops to sensitize local officials, police, and farmers about why child labor is deemed wrong and how importers will go elsewhere if such labor practices persist.[25] Another strategy implemented to address the issue is posting billboards in rural areas warning people to "say no to child labor." Educating the public is imperative if cultural norms are to change to value education. Until farmers see the worth of educating their children, using them on farms will continue to take precedence over sending them to school.

## ELIMINATING THE WORST FORMS OF CHILD LABOR

When exposés of children working on cocoa farms in West Africa started gaining attention in Europe and the United States in the late 1990s, threats of consumer boycotts forced a reaction by the US government and multinational corporations. Although two US congressmen wanted to propose a law that required manufacturers to identify the labor source of cocoa in chocolate bars, an agreement was reached that instead created the Harkin-Engel Protocol, which pursued a voluntary and collaborative effort between MNCs, intergovernmental organizations (IGOs), nongovernmental organizations (NGOs), and producing states to eliminate Worst Forms of Child Labor (WFCL) in cocoa farming. Involvement by Ivory Coast and Ghana, as the world's top two producers, was particularly necessary. Chocolate manufacturers were keen to go this route because the protocol called for self-monitoring by the companies.

Corporations exert considerable control over the demand for cocoa and hence its price. Although MNCs do not run cocoa farms, they indirectly profit from human exploitation through lower labor costs. Labor rights critics thus argue that these buyers should be responsible for setting humane standards for suppliers. Rather than deal directly with farmers, corporations rely on intermediaries who are either independent buyers, called *pisteurs*, who work for a public or private export firm, or the export firms themselves. Either farmers go to trading points, or *pisteurs* travel to cocoa farms. Because buyers are also in business for profits, the intermediaries are less likely to question the source of the labor providing the cocoa. How much a farmer earns is another issue of concern. If the farmer has to rely on the one *pisteur* who is willing to make the journey to his remote farm, then the farmer's only option is to accept the rate offered. This system, in turn, affects farmers' wages and ability to pay laborers reasonable wages, resulting in the reliance on forced labor.

Children end up in forced labor situations for many reasons, including many of the same reasons children of farmers end up working in cocoa groves. The lack of social welfare services in developing countries means orphaned children often go to live with relatives who put them to work to pay for their keep. Other children might be sold by parents who are too poor to raise them and need the money to survive. Some trafficked children are kidnapping victims. The difficulty of monitoring farms complicates accurately estimating the number of children working under forced labor conditions and distinguishing which cocoa beans come from farms exploiting children. Developing countries often lack the financial means to hire and train personnel to go from farm to farm in rural areas for surveillance.

Exploitative labor practices in the cocoa industry are not new. During Spanish control in the Americas, a Dominican priest raised concerns to soon-to-be-king Philip about the treatment of cocoa farmers, going so far as to escort a group of Mayan Indians to Spain to plead for compassion. In the late 1800s, investigative journalists exposed slavery and abusive labor conditions on colonial cocoa farms, which led the Cadbury chocolate company to file a libel suit against a London newspaper in 1901. It would take another century for the issue to come to the forefront again.

A flurry of exposés and NGO press releases at the turn of the twenty-first century revealed child slave labor on West African cocoa farms. Despite the MNCs not owning the farms or being directly responsible for labor conditions, the reports drew enough attention in the United Kingdom and the United States to lead consumers to threaten boycotts, particularly targeting Ivory Coast. As a major importer of cocoa, the US government was pushed to address the issue of child labor in West African farming. A rider to an agricultural bill that had passed the House and was on its way to the Senate set forth a policy that would classify cocoa as "slave-free" only if the manufacturer could demonstrate its source. Hoping to assuage the public's concerns while avoiding formal legislation, the major chocolate manufacturers persuaded the sponsors of the rider, Senator Tom Harkin and Representative Eliot Engel, to establish a system of self-regulation that set minimum standards for cocoa production.

**Implementing the protocol** The congressmen led negotiations with MNCs to iron out the details of the Harkin-Engel Protocol, finalized in 2001. Recognizing the difficulty of eliminating all forms of child labor, the protocol called for abolishing Worst Forms of Child Labor (WFCL) as laid out in Convention 182 of the International Labor Organization (ILO). WFCL focuses on child labor that involves trafficking, forced labor, hazardous work, or abuse. This definition distinguishes WFCL from child labor, defined as work that endangers children and/or prevents them from attending school, which is much more difficult to enforce. Recognizing the difficulty in trying to eliminate all child labor, the protocol targets the most egregious child exploitation. Although all West African cocoa-producing countries have been criticized for using forced, slave, and child labor, the main focus is on Ivory Coast and Ghana, as they produce more than 60 percent of the world's cocoa beans.

The plan of action included six goals. In addition to a public statement by MNCs acknowledging the issue of WFCL in cocoa farming, an advisory group was created to monitor progress, and the ILO was made a party to the protocol. Commitment to a joint action program of research, information exchange, establishing standards, independent monitoring, and public reporting on compliance was another goal. In addition, a nonprofit foundation was to be set up within a year. The primary purpose of the organization was to implement a field project to educate producers as well as the public and monitor progress. MNCs were also expected to take stock of their practices and build credible standards for certifying WFCL-free cocoa beans.

Within a few years, the more easily achieved goals were met. Public statements were made, an advisory board was formed, and the International Cocoa Initiative was founded in 2003 to be funded annually with $2 million in industry donations. The ICI is a partnership between MNCs, NGOs, West African producing countries, and other cocoa IGOs, including the International Cocoa Organization under the auspices of the United Nations, the World Cocoa Foundation, and the Alliance of Cocoa Producing Countries. These IGOs also work independently to promote sustainable cocoa practices. In addition, the ICI works with Interpol, which in 2009 arrested eight child trafficking recruiters and rescued fifty-four children.[26] Although these numbers are relatively small, the arrests do indicate that the issue of cocoa child labor trafficking is gaining attention.

Most of the major MNCs involved in the processing and manufacturing of cocoa and chocolate were party to the initial negotiations, including Barry Callebaut, Guittard, Blommer, World's Finest Chocolate, M&M/Mars, Archer Daniels Midland, Nestlé, and Hershey's (hereafter collectively referred to as the industry). Other corporations that did not sign the protocol, including Cargill and Kraft, later became party through the ICI. As the world leaders in cocoa exports as well as countries with reported use of child labor, Ivory Coast and Ghana were made responsible for reporting progress toward meeting the protocol. Each established agencies to implement programs and monitor progress.

In addition to steps by the organizations, MNCs, and countries to establish and monitor community programs, a third party was necessary to certify that cocoa beans were produced without relying on WFCL. The most basic form of certification involves verifying that forced child labor has not been used in the production of cocoa beans. NGOs had formed prior to the protocol to address consumer concerns regarding agricultural production standards in the coffee, banana, and tea industries. UTZ, the Rainforest Alliance (RA), and Fairtrade International are the three main organizations that certify cocoa production. Although each NGO sets a minimum standard that growers cannot use WFCL, additional standards governing agricultural, environmental, and labor issues vary.

UTZ guarantees and protects farmers' rights to organize and collectively bargain but does not guarantee a legal minimum wage after the first year of certification. The Rainforest Alliance does not protect the right to organize or guarantee a minimum price paid to farmers and only requires that 30 percent of beans be certified, which means a product can contain 70 percent noncertified cocoa and still receive an RA label. Fairtrade is the most rigorous system, mandating that labeled products contain 100 percent certified cocoa beans and guaranteeing farmers a fair minimum price and collective bargaining rights. Producers are also required to form democratic cooperatives. Furthermore, Fairtrade invests in communities to address the lack of social welfare support in rural areas of poorer countries by offering education and health services, as well as technical, agricultural, and business support. Qualifying as a farm that produces WFCL-free or higher-standard cocoa differs

┌─────────────────────────────────────────────────────────────┐
│ **Recipe Box**

**Know Your Label**

*How well do you know your candy bar label? Is the chocolate Fairtrade, UTZ, or Rainforest Alliance certified? Does the label list the cocoa percentage, letting you know the ratio of cocoa to other ingredients? What about the conche time? Are the other ingredients — sugar, milk, peanuts, or coconut — also certified products? Chances are that unless you stick to ethically traded candy bars, you won't find this information on your package. Next time you're at a checkout counter, take a look at a candy bar to see what its label does or doesn't tell consumers.*
└─────────────────────────────────────────────────────────────┘

according to the NGO involved, with any number of possible prerequisites necessary for earning certification. Some programs require farmers to undergo training programs; others include regular monitoring of worker conditions.

**Evaluating progress** MNCs agreed to implement a certification process that would eliminate WFCL on cocoa farms by July 2005. An effective system had not been put into place by the deadline, so further negotiations reevaluated foundation goals and how to remedy the lack of progress.[27] Three objectives were decided on during the talks: (1) implementing a certification system that included at least 50 percent of farms in Ivory Coast and Ghana by 2008, (2) increasing the standard of living for cocoa growers to decrease WFCL, and (3) increasing foundation funds to $5 million a year. By 2010, these objectives had not yet been met, so, back at the negotiating table, ICI members signed the Declaration of Joint Action to Support Implementation of the Harkin-Engel Protocol to establish the goal of reducing WFCL by 70 percent by 2020. The declaration is funded by $10 million from the US Department of Labor to implement programs through the ILO's International Program for the Elimination of Child Labor.[28] Critics argue, however, that the MNCs' financial pledge of a mere $2 million is peanuts when compared to their combined $8.5 billion marketing budget.[29] Even though MNCs have spent more than $75 million to implement a cocoa certification system, only $5.5 million of the reported amount went toward program implementation.[30] Clearly the amount sponsored by the corporations was unrealistic for reaching the protocol's goals.

When criticized for their lack of monetary support to the initiative, MNCs are quick to note their own direct initiatives, such as Nestlé's Cocoa Plan, Cadbury's Cocoa Partnership, and Mars's Partnership for African Cocoa Communities of Tomorrow. Companies assert community relations offer more effective results by supporting communities and farmers with funding and technical expertise. Detailed on company websites are Hershey's CocoaLink program, which relies on mobile phone technology to help farmers, Nestlé's Cocoa Plan agricultural network, and Cargill's Farmer Field Schools, which focus on social, environmental, and agriculture best practices. Other than corporations' reports on their efforts, little data exists to evaluate the effectiveness of direct initiatives.

**Tulane University: Independent monitor evaluates effectiveness of the protocol** When initial monitoring and reporting deadlines were missed in

## Recipe Box

### Check It Out

As companies move to guarantee that the source of their cocoa is child-labor-free, MNCs want to advertise the humane conditions under which it was produced— not only on their bars but on their websites. Check out the corporate websites for Nestlé, Hershey's, Mars, or Barry Callebaut to find out how they advertise their dedication to sustainable development in cocoa communities. How reliable is their information? To what extent can their individual programs make an impact on eliminating WFCL?

2005, the US Department of Labor contracted with Tulane University to act as an independent monitor. The university reported in 2011 that while some progress had been made, considerably greater efforts and resources were necessary to fully realize the protocol's objective of eliminating WFCL. Tulane monitors found that the main cocoa trading groups in West Africa were not aware of the protocol, and although government officials knew of the agreement and compliance officers had been appointed, little progress was being made. Efforts to reduce child labor and increase school attendance have been only slightly more effective in Ghana than in Ivory Coast. When surveyed by the Tulane team, between 25 and 50 percent of children in Ivory Coast and Ghana reported working on cocoa farms.[31] The monitors also found that only a minority of cocoa communities had instituted the mandated programs of the agreement.[32] Although Ghana was more successful in reaching communities to implement its community action plan, Ivory Coast was plagued by political unrest, making it difficult for agencies to function and reach communities.

Prior to the Harkin-Engel Protocol, the big chocolate producers who controlled the market had no incentive to include the source, even when they had invested community projects that they advertised in their company profiles. Seeing the origin of the cocoa beans on a chocolate bar was much more common with small manufacturers who targeted socially and environmentally conscious consumers. Companies such as Alter Eco and Endangered Species rely on the weight that the Fairtrade label gives their products in order to compete in a market dominated by mass-produced, brand-name chocolate bars.

The protocol requires that MNCs shift to using only certified cocoa in their products, reducing WFCL bean production by 70 percent by 2020.[33] Inconsistent implementation among the MNCs has contributed to the slow progress. One of the biggest factors has been the extent to which companies commit to exclusively using certified cocoa for all of their products rather than just a few brand names. Barry Callebaut has been a leading supporter of the protocol. Because concern about child labor and sustainable development has been so strong in Europe, Barry Callebaut, the largest confectioner in the world, committed to using fair trade–certified ingredients exclusively. Given its reliance on the European market, Barry Callebaut's choice makes good business sense, though the company uses the least rigorously certified UTZ cocoa beans because of their lower cost. Their greater availability is also a factor, since Barry Callebaut buys 40 percent of all cocoa beans produced every year. Guaranteeing that all its products are certified means the company needs to know it can meet demand, which is more possible using UTZ-certified beans.

M&M/Mars had been lagging behind on implementing the protocol, but the company has since made a commitment to only use UTZ-certified cocoa in all of its products by 2020. Manufacturers of mass-produced bars are also following suit, though thus far they are only committing to fair trade cocoa beans for their European products. Nestlé was the first to rebrand its Kit Kat bar as fair trade sourced in 2011, followed by Cadbury's Dairy Milk bars and Mars's Maltesers. For candy destined for foreign markets, such as Kit Kats sold in the United States, the source of the cocoa remains questionable. Outside the few European countries demanding ethically sourced chocolate, some corporations have shifted to using certified cocoa only for brands that capitalize on the niche market of socially and environmentally conscious consumers that small, fair trade companies and organizations have tapped. So while the conglomerates that control Green & Black's and Ben & Jerry's use 100 percent fair trade–certified cocoa in those brands, other brands they produce often contain noncertified cocoa. Compliance with the protocol, however, now gives corporations an incentive to verify the source of the cocoa they use for all their manufactured foods, particularly their brand-name products.

One signatory to the protocol, however, has been under fire for failing to make even the most basic steps toward implementing certification standards. The Tulane review reported that Hershey's was the only major producer that, as of 2010, still had not made a commitment to using certified cocoa or developed a plan for implementation. In response to the report and to "Boycott Hershey's on Halloween" campaigns targeting US consumers in 2011, the company stated it has implemented its own development programs, which it feels are more effective than relying on third-party-certified cocoa.[34] Cargill is another manufacturer under fire for lax enforcement of its policy requiring suppliers in producing countries to sign a statement that their contracts will be terminated if they are found to be buying beans from farmers who rely on WFCL workers.[35] The lack of progress toward carrying out the goals of the protocol is also due, in part, to the lack of funds to further implement and monitor labor activity. The ILO has struggled to implement monitoring programs for this very reason. Companies have made more progress where the market demand has given them an incentive to use only fair trade–certified ingredients.

Ethically traded chocolate offers an alternative to some farmers and their families, as well as their communities, through development projects sponsored by the cooperatives, but cocoa from certified farms accounts for only about 5 percent of world bean sales.[36] At this point, however, lack of supply is not an issue. I visited the Kuapa Kokoo, the largest fair trade cocoa cooperative in Ghana, in November 2013. Even though all of the beans they produce are ethically sourced, they are only able to sell about 20 percent of their total output at the higher fair trade price due to lack of demand. They sell the remaining 80 percent (essentially at a loss) as conventionally produced beans.[37] Producers cannot claim that they are not using ethically sourced beans because ample supply is unavailable.

The MNCs' renewed commitment to the Harkin-Engel Protocol is less likely to push companies away from WFCL cocoa than the consumer demand for brand-name, mass-produced certified chocolate bars like Kit Kat and Dairy Milk. As demand increases, one of the biggest problems MNCs will face as they shift to using WFCL-free beans is a shortage of certified cocoa. Even though producing certified beans brings a higher return for farmers in developing countries, keeping pace with demand will be a challenge as it is likely to outstrip supply due to the cost involved in training and certifying farmers.[38]

As more corporations move toward implementing the protocol, the incentive increases for buyers to guarantee the labor source of the cocoa as WFCL-free. Armajaro Ghana Ltd., the third largest cocoa buyer in Ghana, has instituted a policy to determine the "traceability and sustainability" of its commodity as a way to verify that no forced, child, or slave labor was used to cultivate or harvest the beans.[39] If the protocol is to achieve its goal of eradicating WFCL, raising awareness in consumer markets is imperative. Only by promoting sustainable development will farmers be in a position to shift their reliance for labor from children to adults.

Achieving the goals set by the protocol means promoting sustainable development. Partnerships between NGOs and MNCs, such as the protocol's International Cocoa Initiative, World Cocoa Foundation, Responsible Cocoa, and the Africa Cocoa Coalition, work with cocoa-producing communities to address environmental concerns by giving assistance to improve agricultural techniques with more sophisticated machinery and chemicals. Increased crop yields brought by these improvements can also reduce strain on the land with better fertilizers to replace depleted soil minerals, as well as decrease the need to clear rain forest to plant more cocoa trees. Development programs also focus on tree replacement in mature groves, where, over time, less productive trees are replaced with saplings. Farmers are also encouraged to continue growing shade varieties of cocoa trees since they promote sustainable land use through polycropping that enhances the soil and supports biodiversity.

After it has had ten years to achieve the goals set out in the protocol, critics question whether the industry should be left to self-regulate on the matter of eliminating WFCL or governments should instead pass laws that penalize MNCs for buying cocoa from nonverified sources. If the industry continues to self-regulate, it arguably has a greater incentive to commit to achieving the protocol, even if implementation takes longer than planned or is not deemed acceptable by critics. Corporations' reputations are at stake if they are party to the agreement but are lax in commitment. Furthermore, the same problems encountered in implementing the protocol would arise if legal repercussions were threatened. Because funds are already lacking for the ILO to monitor the situation and for West African countries to implement development programs, ensuring cocoa is WFCL-free would be just as difficult, perhaps even more so, as MNCs would be on the defensive rather than working toward a solution. Lots of money would be spent on lawsuits and trials instead of resources—limited as they are—going toward development that can eliminate WFCL.

## CONCLUSION

The cocoa situation uncovers the complexities of global commodity trade. The neoliberal free market pushes manufacturers to look for the most cost-effective way to produce goods. The free market drives employment of the cheapest labor force to harvest cash crops. Producing countries depend on cash crop sales, yet struggle to eliminate slave labor used to provide much needed income. Control of chocolate manufacturing by MNCs perpetuates the disparity between corporations, which can add value to products, and farmers, who rely on cash crop sales, because the majority of the profit is derived from the finished product. Producing countries need to bring in foreign direct investment to increase development prospects but, with a comparative advantage of cheap labor, necessarily trade off by compromising labor standards. Without cash to promote sustainable development practices in farming, governments are in a catch-22 situation in combating the corruption and poverty that undermine eliminating reliance on forced, child, and slave labor. Although Ghana fairs better than Ivory Coast, which Transparency International ranks as one of the most corrupt countries in the world, these countries are less likely to draw in much-needed foreign direct investment.

MNCs are challenged to maintain company and brand-name images while getting the best returns for their stockholders. Companies adopt cost-effective strategies at the risk of encountering criticism of their business practices. They turn to philanthropic projects in producing communities in which they have vested interests, but these efforts account for only a small portion of the necessary development funds. These projects alone, however, have not provided enough sustainable farming to eliminate WFCL. As a result, criticism drove MNCs to enter into the Harkin-Engel agreement to protect their images. Their commitment contradicts neoliberal free market trade, but the threat of consumer boycotting and a tarnished image makes intervention necessary.

Without a greater commitment by corporations to eliminating WFCL, progress will not be made. Neither Ivory Coast nor Ghana has pockets nearly as deep as the corporations to institute the necessary training and monitoring of farms. The voluntary adherence under the protocol, thus far, has proven largely ineffective as companies fail to meet deadlines. The increased demand for ethically traded chocolate serves as an incentive for MNCs to act; yet their lack of commitment to help guarantee WFCL-free cocoa beans is only likely to result in a shortage.

Although the Harkin-Engel Protocol was established in 2001 to address WFCL in the West African cocoa-producing countries, by 2011 little progress had been made, and child labor abuses continue. Some progress has been made toward increasing awareness about the issue among consumers and instituting changes in the cocoa industry, though WFCL persists. Problems ranging from enforcement to meeting demand for ethically produced beans plague efforts. Eliminating WFCL requires parties to the protocol, particularly the corporations, to step up their commitment to fund ethical farming.

Because the protocol is voluntary and not legally binding, companies like Hershey's can ignore it with impunity. MNCs have little incentive beyond consumer demand to pay more for ethically produced beans or to invest more in sustainable development. Until public relations affects a company's profits or laws are passed, real change is unlikely. The same factors that interfere with training and policy implementation in developing country producers make gauging progress difficult. The fact that monitoring remains difficult indicates that voluntary compliance has proven less than effective.

## CHAPTER QUESTIONS

1. How is the current situation on cocoa farms in West Africa tied to Spanish Mesoamerican colonization?
2. How do implementation, monitoring, and enforcement of the Harkin-Engel Protocol demonstrate the difficulties of addressing human rights issues in a global political economy?
3. Why would corporations—particularly those based outside the United States—care about US government findings regarding the extent to which they have complied with the protocol, especially when there is no enforcement mechanism?
4. What incentives do Ivory Coast and Ghana have, as sovereign states, to comply with the protocol?

# CHAPTER 5

SOY

## Multinational Corporations and
## Global Food Production

When people think of soy, tofu often springs to mind. With alternative milks gaining more attention, people are increasingly aware of soymilk. Most people do not realize, however, how versatile soy is. Not only is soy a ubiquitous ingredient in many processed foods, but it appears in many nonedible products. Its usefulness has made soy one of the most sought-after agricultural products. The humble soybean provides a unique way to understand the role that multinational corporations (MNCs) play in the global food system. More people in the world means more people to feed. Because of its versatility, soy is in steady demand in many industries, particularly the emerging biofuel sector. The single biggest contributing factor to increased demand, however, is that soy products are used for animal feed. As discussed in Chapter 1, as people's standard of living increases, so does the demand for animal protein. The growing demand for meat and fish, as evident from Figure 5.1, continues as incomes around the world rise. These factors have led to a corresponding global increase in soy production, with output more than doubling between 1950 and 2010.[1] Although the United States has dominated soybean production, Brazil and Argentina have gained ground over the last few decades, with Brazil positioned to become the world leader by the end of 2013–2014 crop season.[2]

The mushrooming global demand for meat products has piqued corporate interest. Trade in food is the trade of big businesses. MNCs tend to focus on buying raw foods on the commodities market or from a contracted grower and processing them into a manufactured good, in the way that Nestlé and General Foods buy coffee beans, which they in turn roast, package, and sell for a much greater profit. A few exceptions come to mind, such as the tropical fruit companies run by Dole, Chiquita, and Fyffes. MNCs are increasingly investing in the agriculture industry as a way to control production from the start. For centuries, family-run farms supplied urban centers with food. Globalization has caused a shift to large-scale agribusiness farms operated by multinational corporations. This scale of industrial agriculture has inspired emerging economies like Brazil, Argentina, and Mexico to move to a corporate farming model to promote economic growth and development. The shift from small-scale family farming to the industrial agriculture complex resembles the colonial shift from small farms to mass-scale plantations to meet rising demand for coffee, tea, sugar, and cocoa beans in the nineteenth century.

Brazil has been able to capitalize on global demand for soybeans, thus offering an interesting way to examine development strategies. The country currently supplies about one-quarter of the world's soybeans. As MNCs look

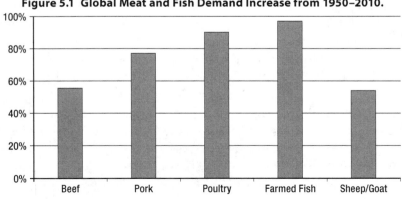

**Figure 5.1 Global Meat and Fish Demand Increase from 1950–2010.**

Author calculations based on ERS USDA data
http://usda.mannlib.cornell.edu/MannUsda/viewTaxonomy.do;jsessionid
=F208A421F41CD5072F1E8E0871C68975?taxonomyID=2

for places to invest from the ground up in the growing soybean sector, Brazil appeals for a number of reasons. First, it is the largest emerging economy in Latin America. Second, the country has a stable political system with business-friendly laws and practices. Third, it has the most available arable land as well as abundant water resources.

Brazil's recent economic development is due to its success in drawing in foreign direct investment (FDI), or investment in the country's businesses by foreign sources. Multinational giants such as Cargill, Archer Daniels Midland (ADM), Nestlé, Bunge, Monsanto, and Tyson have invested heavily in agribusiness and meat-producing sectors, helping to make Brazil the recipient of over $65 billion in FDI in 2012, the most in Latin America.[3] Moreover, due to the abundance of available land, water, and labor in their home country, three Brazilian food-processing companies have expanded into multi-billion-dollar MNCs. These enterprises have taken advantage of the country's resources and foreign corporations' interest in investing in Brazil's economy to increase their production.

To give readers a sense of how the relationship between Brazil and its foreign investors affects the global food system, the chapter begins with an introduction to soybeans, paying special attention to soy's versatility. Although already mentioned, the shift in demand is another issue worth examining in more depth. The second section focuses on production, considering the impact FDI has had on the soy industry in Brazil, on other producers, and on related sectors. The last part of the chapter examines the issues emerging from soy production in the global food system. Relying on FDI to support its export-based economy, Brazil has encountered disputes over trade barriers, including government subsidies, as well as challenges to sustainable development and problems concerning land rights and ownership.

## INTRODUCING *GLYCINE MAX*

Soybeans are native to China, where they have long been considered one of the five sacred plants, along with barley, millet, rice, and wheat. Used for over four thousand years before they were domesticated between the seventeenth and eleventh centuries BCE, soybeans have been grown on a commercial scale in China for over one thousand years. Over time, the soybean spread to other Asian countries, among them Japan, Indonesia, and India, where it became a prominent food source. Its commercial success is due in part to its high yield, as each plant produces between sixty and eighty pods with three beans each. One benefit of the soybean plant is that it enriches soil with nitrogen, a nutrient often depleted by crops (particularly corn and sugarcane), making soybeans a good rotation crop. In Brazil, soybeans were introduced as a crop rotated with sugarcane to reduce the demand for fertilizers that would otherwise be needed to nourish the soil with nitrogen.

Soybeans are one of the four main staple crops in the world along with rice, maize (corn), and wheat. Although rice is by far the single biggest crop in the world, exports are limited because of domestic demand in producing countries. Maize, in the dry form that differs from the fresh sweet corn variety, is the most traded crop, followed by wheat and soybeans. The latter, however, outranks wheat in trade value. For soy and maize, the total trade in value or volume is difficult to assess, because both are traded not only in whole form but also as oil and meal (technically referred to as "cake of soybeans"), which is the result of vegetable oil or biodiesel production. The meal remains after the oil is extracted and can then be used for livestock feed, reducing the cost of processed foods or biofuel production because nothing is wasted. So, for example, the United States is the largest exporter of whole soybeans, but Argentina is the primary exporter of soy oil and cake of soybeans.

Soybeans are classified as an oilseed crop because of their high oil content: one sixty-pound sack of soybeans yields eleven pounds of oil. As a high-yield crop that offers a good source of protein and oil and thrives in hot, humid weather, soybeans made a good forage crop for nineteenth-century farmers in the United States. As meat demand in the United States increased, soy meal's low cost and high protein value made it a popular choice as livestock and poultry feed. As a result of US policies after World War II, when soybeans became a source of not only a protein substitute and an edible oil but, more importantly, animal feed, Brazil saw an opportunity to focus on soybean production. Although it took a few decades to perfect a seed that would grow in Brazil's more acidic soil and different climate, the investment has paid off.

## A BRIEF HISTORY OF SOY

Initially in East Asia soybeans were grown for human consumption. Their composition makes soybeans a good source of both protein and healthy fats,

## New-to-You Food: Chia Seed

The Chia Pet craze took off in the United States when, in 1982, the company marketed a terracotta ram that sprouted chia seed "wool" with the catchy jingle "Ch-ch-ch-Chia Pet." At the time, few Americans likely considered eating the seeds. Fast-forward thirty years to a new craze to hit America. This time, however, the demand was for the seeds instead of the pet. Chia seeds are just starting to catch on in Europe, but first they had to overcome legal barriers. In the United Kingdom, for example, until 2012, the superfood could only be used as an ingredient in bread. Demand for the seeds, however, encouraged the Advisory Committee on Novel Foods and Processes to revise policies to expand availability.[1]

A member of the mint family, chia is a flowering plant native to Central America that bears black or white oilseeds. Perhaps as important a food source as maize to the Aztecs and Mayans, chia has emerged as a superfood. As with quinoa (discussed in Chapter 8), the Spaniards did not appreciate its value, so chia died out as an important food source.[2] Packing an incredible combination of nutrients, the seed provides omega-3 fatty acids, protein, fibrous carbohydrates, calcium, iron, and B vitamins. The seeds are fairly tasteless on their own, so they are often added to other foods, in the same way that another superfood, flax-seed, is mixed in with cereals, trail mixes, energy bars, grain dishes, salads, and baked goods. When mixed with water, seeds act as a binder that can substitute for eggs in baking or as a thickener for smoothie drinks.

When researching alternative crops for northwestern Argentina in the late 1990s, an agricultural engineer tested the plant and found that it thrived. Dr. Wayne Coates led the project that researched not only the viability of production but how to market the seed and educate consumers about its health benefits.[3] Although Australia is the world's leading producer of chia seeds, Argentina is among a number of Latin American countries that account for the other 50 percent of global production.[4] When flooding and drought led to crop failures in 2012, production was so significantly affected that stores in the United States were unable to stock enough chia seeds to keep up with the skyrocketing demand.

1. "The Chia Craze," *BBC World News*, March 22, 2012, http://www.bbc.co.uk/news /magazine-17476690.

2. "Chia Questions and Answers," Azchia, http://www.azchia.com/chia_seed_questions _answers.htm (accessed November 6, 2012).

3. "Chia Questions and Answers."

4. "Chia Seeds Move beyond Faddish Past in Bid for Mainstream Acceptance," *Huffington Post*, April 16, 2012, http://www.huffingtonpost.com/2012/04/16/chia-seeds_n_1419525.html.

and they compliment rice, which provides fiber. Although the often pooh-poohed tofu might be the only product that springs to mind when people hear about soybeans, an abundance of food products are made from whole beans or contain soy derivatives. Fermented soy makes a good sauce, miso (a paste), and tempeh (a staple in Indonesia). Curd makes tofu, which is popular in China and Japan. Immature beans steamed and eaten green, called edamame, are common in Japan, while the sprouts are used in Korean dishes. Soy products range from soy oil used in processed foods to infant formula, soy-based drinks, imitation meats, and dairy substitutes. Soy protein is dried into a product marketed as "textured vegetable protein," or TVP (a registered trademark of ADM, the company that first developed the process), and found in imitation meat products such as "beefless" burgers and "chickenless" nuggets. People in developed countries who opt for meatless diets or who want or need to limit their intake of bad cholesterol have increasingly turned to soy products.

Soybeans are a very versatile product. The biggest demand for soy is not for human foods, like tofu, tempeh, or analog meat products. Rather, the biggest demand for soy is for animal feed. The global north's insatiable appetite for meat has most affected production because soybeans make excellent live-stock, bird, and fish feed. Increased incomes in emerging economies create

## Recipe Box

### Spot the Soy

Take a look at the ingredient list for everything you eat today. How often does soy or some soy derivative (like lecithin or hydrolyzed vegetable protein) appear? Many people are not aware of the how much soy they ingest when consuming processed foods. If you really want to be diligent, take a look at the health and beauty aids you use, as you may find hydrolyzed soy protein or soy disguised as glycerides.

even greater demand. As the standard of living improves, increased buying power affords consumers more food choices. More people are choosing to add variety to their diets, including more meat, even if this means exceeding the recommended twenty-one hundred calories per day.[4] For soy production, this means that even though people could still afford to increase their calorie intake with grains, they opt for meat. People in developing countries literally pay the price for the increased global demand for meat. A meat-centered diet relies on soybeans and grains for feed. Because eating food "higher on the food chain" requires more resources to grow livestock, prices for these staple foods are consequently affected, making tofu, tortillas, and bread more expensive for poorer people.

Soybeans are not just a food source for humans and animals. Soy's amazing versatility has led to its use as a biofuel. With oil prices intricately tied to world politics, refining and usage linked to greenhouse gases, and limited supplies, the demand for alternative sources of energy has increased. Ethanol, derived from corn, has been pursued in the United States far more extensively than soybean biodiesel for any number of political reasons, ranging from government subsidies to presidential elections. In other parts of the world, however, other, more efficient crops are being turned into fuel sources. Brazil primarily

## Recipe Box

### The Amazing Soy Bean

Henry Ford developed soy-based plastics for auto-body panels. Plastics are only one of an astonishing number of industrial uses for soybeans. The nontoxic, nonpolluting, and biodegradable qualities of soybeans make them very appealing and increasingly popular in a "greening" world. Among the seemingly endless list of soy products are ink, memory foam, plywood, particleboard, soap, candles, cosmetics, plastics, antibiotics, wire, foam roofing and insulation, agricultural chemicals, and paint. Soybeans also are the source of both industrial and food-grade lecithin, another first developed by Archer Daniels Midland.

produces biodiesel made from sugarcane, but it also relies on soybeans. Not only does biodiesel reduce greenhouse gases more than corn-based ethanol, but soybean biodiesel generates 93 percent more energy than corn-based ethanol, which provides only 25 percent more energy per gallon than needed to produce it.[5] The Brazilian government is set to double the required amount of biofuel blended with petroleum-based diesel since the country produces so much soy. MNCs, including ADM and Cargill—companies already well established in Brazil—are moving to invest even more funds in the country for new biofuel refineries.[6] Access to cheap raw materials gives corporations an economic incentive to invest in refineries. Agribusiness corporations are involved in many aspects of farming. Companies' scientists develop seeds as well as pesticides and fertilizers specific to those seeds. These MNCs also own soy-crushing plants to separate the meal from the oil. Further investment in refineries using the oils derived from the crushing process also allows them to access the profitable, and growing, sector in energy production.

Although biofuel can be a profitable business, its production redirects crop output toward the energy sector and away from food exports. The shift invariably causes a shortage of grain supplies, making staple foods more expensive for poor people in developing countries. When corn prices rise, more farmers shift production toward that crop, causing shortages in other crops, such as millet and wheat, which are less profitable staples exported to developing countries. Although corn prices have only been affected thus far by the demand for corn-based ethanol, the superior efficiency of soybean biodiesel will undoubtedly affect that crop's prices in the future.

## Demand for Soy

Growth in emerging economies is changing the world food supply chain in profound ways. Economic development symbiotically creates more demand as it creates more opportunities for production. To begin, emerging economies' demand for natural resources is skyrocketing, as evidenced by rising prices for goods from steel to soybeans. China is without question the world's biggest consumer of raw materials, requiring inputs to feed its voracious appetite for industrialization (and growing population). In terms of soybeans, even though China is the world's fourth largest producer and was largely self-sufficient until 1995, growth has since snowballed to the point where imports in 2010 were fourteen times greater than just fifteen years earlier, making China the number one importer of soybeans worldwide.[7] Bearing in mind that demand for soybeans for human consumption constitutes only a small portion of usage, it is not surprising that the primary factor affecting increased demand in China is meat production. Positioning itself to become a world exporter of animal protein, coinciding with growing domestic demand as Chinese consumer buying power increases, China cannot meet its soybean demand with its domestic supply. As discussed below in more detail, China is strategically maneuvering to increase its food security and access to raw materials both through foreign direct investment and by leasing land abroad.

Due to the North American Free Trade Agreement, a country that once produced soy is now one of the top soybean importers. As an emerging economy, Mexico resembles China in its growth: not only has it moved toward more meat production, but a growing consumer demand for meat and processed foods has translated into demand for soybeans, making it the second largest importer. Having the facilities to crush the beans to produce soy meal and oil gives the country the advantage of importing whole rather than processed beans.[8] Alternatively, Japan is one of the biggest importers of soybeans destined not only for animal feed but also to meet the country's demand for food products like soy sauce, tofu, and miso.

When the infamous mad cow disease (bovine spongiform encephalopathy) struck Great Britain in the late 1990s, mass panic ensued. (To this day, I still cannot donate blood in the United States because I lived in the United Kingdom around that time.) This epidemic led the European Union to institute a policy whereby protein for animal feed could no longer come from animal sources but had to be a vegetable derivative. As a result, the EU is second only to China in soybean meal imports, and it is the world's largest importer of whole beans to support livestock production as well as meet increased consumer demand for meat-free soy-based products.[9] As in the United States, political policies drive EU farming decisions, particularly the Common Agricultural Policy (CAP). Since its inception, the EU has been working to decrease the huge proportion of farming subsidies that initially made up over 60 percent of its operational budget. Although initiatives began in 2003 to eliminate protectionist policies by 2012, the EU CAP budget in 2011 was still 28 percent.[10] The purpose of the CAP is to protect European agriculture through payouts to farmers (a form of subsidy called single farm payments), along with tariffs and quotas. With the push in Europe to go green, policies increasingly favor oilseed production to make biodiesel fuel.

Because rapeseed is more commonly planted, the EU will likely have to rely on imports of soybeans. Because EU farmers get special dispensation subsidies for growing biofuel crops, CAP payouts for soy are not likely to be eliminated anytime soon.

Brazil relies heavily on its export market in soybeans and derivatives, but it also has a healthy domestic demand due to its own burgeoning agribusiness industry growth. Domestic demand for soy-based food products and biodiesel fuel has risen along with the country's standard of living. That Brazil is poised to become the world's largest meat exporter, however, is the driving domestic force. Currently the top exporter of beef and poultry, Brazilian MNCs are jockeying to take over the pork industry as well.[11] As an emerging economy, Brazil is better positioned to exploit multiple facets of soybean production, as it can more easily align farming, processing, feedlots, and energy production facilities with its growing infrastructure than can mature industrial states. As such, growing soybeans, then processing meal and oil, which respectively go to nearby feedlots and biodiesel refining plants, is a virtually seamless connection for production.

## PRODUCTION

For emerging economies, the role agribusiness has played in promoting development offers a base for industrialization and improved infrastructure. A dominant neoliberal economy rewards efficiency with competitiveness. Soybeans exemplify the strategies Brazil has used to maximize production value. Farming has moved to an industrial agribusiness complex, concentrating as many steps of production on one site as possible. That emerging economies like Brazil are in the early stages of realizing their full potential gives them a competitive advantage over mature producers in the United States and European Union. Multinational corporations use foreign direct investment to tap into as many facets of production as possible, cutting their overhead to turn a higher profit. Brazil has worked to position itself as one of the best places for FDI through a combination of stable institutions, transparency, and a vast supply of land, natural resources, and labor. Investment in Brazil's economy has even facilitated opportunities for its national companies to expand into formidable MNCs.

Rapid growth in production and in-country crushing capability, along with increased American domestic demand, have given Argentina and Brazil an edge over the United States in soy meal and oil exports.[12] Brazil's success results from a combination of publicly and privately funded enterprises. In the 1960s, the military regime realized the value of developing the *cerrados* (wooded savannahs)—in particular, the Mato Grosso area—to increase agricultural output. Over the next two decades, the government invested in its agriculture sector by sending students to American universities to become experts in crop breeding, soil science, and regional planning.[13] The government also created an agency called Empresa Brasileira de Pesquisa Agropecuria (EMBRAPA) to coordinate and promote state agriculture by designating public monies for development of soy seeds that would grow in Brazil's more acidic soil and tropical climate with shorter sunlight hours. As a result of Brazil's strategy, agribusiness is responsible for one in every three Brazilian reals earned, 42 percent of the country's exports, and 37 percent of its employment.[14]

### Foreign Direct Investment

Brazil is a viable place for FDI for an endless list of reasons. Abundant natural resources, minimally tapped arable land, a large and inexpensive labor supply, and a huge potential consumer market all await investors. Its movement

---

### Recipe Box

**How's the Weather?**

Ever consider that the weather affects how much you pay for food? Tsunamis, droughts, and flooding impact crop production, which in turn affects how much livestock and dairy farmers pay for the feed for the animals that produce T-bone steaks, chicken breasts, cheese, and butter and how much wheat costs to make bread. Because soy is one of the main sources of animal feed, this means that the weather directly determines the price of your Big Mac. Want to know how much a Big Mac would cost in Hamburg, Germany? Check out The Economist's Big Mac index (http://www.economist.com/markets/Bigmac/Index.cfm).

from an authoritarian regime to an established and stable democracy has given investors confidence that their industries will not be nationalized. The transparency of the financial sector in Brazil, ranked among the top countries for ease of doing business,[15] places the country among developed countries in areas such as corporate governance practices and registration processes for investment.[16] Other financial factors, such as aggressive fiscal policies and investor-friendly tax incentives, combine to make Brazil a low-risk destination for foreign direct investment. Another perk for American and Chinese companies owning subsidiaries in Brazil is better access to the EU market.

Brazil has investors lining up at its doorstep, looking to guarantee exports to their countries, secure assets, and make profits. FDI has been increasing steadily, and in 2011, Brazil was the biggest Latin American recipient of foreign funds, receiving 87 percent more than the previous year.[17] The country drew in $48.5 billion for the year, followed by Mexico, with a distant $17.7 billion.[18] China's interest in Brazil, as Latin America's biggest economy, is not surprising; the former offered the largest single source of FDI in 2010, exceeding $29.5 billion.[19] This increased investment only makes the market more attractive to future investors.

Agribusiness MNCs, like Cargill and ADM, were were among the first to move into Brazil, anxious to supply seeds and buy commodities as inputs for livestock feed or processed foods. Lax sewage laws reduce the overheads for animal production.[20] Brazil is a particularly excellent location for agribusiness investment because food exports constitute a mere 1.8 percent of Brazil's total gross domestic product (GDP), leaving much room for growth.[21] The country is the leading exporter of numerous agricultural and meat products, though thus far it has only tapped 13 percent of its arable land (which does not even include the Amazon region), a fraction of the 77 percent of arable land farmed in the United States.[22] Farming in a tropical climate yields the added advantage of allowing two or even three crops per year, rather than one. For MNCs, this not only means greater crop yield but also generates greater demand for their fertilizers, herbicides, and pesticides. Agribusiness is, moreover, one of the top growth sectors for the country. Access to cheap labor and a seemingly inexhaustible supply of land and natural resources combine to create a new consumer market. More disposable income translates into an increased demand for meat and other value-added products, strategically marketed by MNCs.

A particular corporation or country may make a foreign investment in one agribusiness sector with the sole purpose of guaranteeing access to exports. Such is the case for Agro, a Saudi investment group investing in Brazil to ensure better food security in its own country. Unlike on the Arabian Peninsula, the growing conditions in Brazil are much more productive, requiring fewer inputs and less capital for better products. With $500 million to spend, Agro's main interests are poultry, grain, and soy.[23] Others see investment as a means to profits by meeting local producers' need for equipment. Focusing on just one sector, manufacturing agricultural machinery, John Deere, Komatsu, and Caterpillar have opened plants in Brazil due to the rapid growth in farming production. In addition to lowering production and shipping costs, locating plants on site also offers MNCs greater access to customers.

More common, however, is corporate investment in more than one agribusiness sector. For soybean production, this means not only developing seeds but, more importantly, breeding them in such a way that they require a company's specific brand of fertilizers and pesticides for the highest yield. The world's major seed companies recognized the vast economic potential of agriculture in Brazil; by 2000, seven MNCs had acquired more than twenty-two Brazilian seed companies.[24] Perhaps surprisingly, altering seed traits is more feasible than developing new chemicals. Buying seed-supply companies in Brazil gave those MNCs the opportunity to profit from the agrichemical sales for their fertilizer- and pesticide-specific seeds. Even though soybeans fix nitrogen back into the soil, since they are grown continuously in the *cerrados*—with two to three crops a year—the soil does not get a break. Problems with disease, weeds, and insects persist, requiring better chemicals and seeds, putting farmers in Brazil on a "pesticide treadmill."

Developing better seeds is highly lucrative. But when Monsanto engineered its Roundup Ready soybeans in 1998 (the first transgenic soy on the market, discussed in more detail below), farmers benefitted because these seeds required less water and fuel to cultivate.[25] Easier planting also cut tractor emissions, reducing the amount of carbon dioxide ($CO_2$) released into the air. The corporation has since developed Roundup Ready 2 Yield, an improved strain with better insect resistance, first used in Brazil in 2010.

### Streamlined Production

Despite its newer, but less developed infrastructure, Brazil struggles to get exports to market as efficiently as its rivals. The United States, for example, has an aged but well-developed network of roads, rails, waterways, and ports. The drawback, however, is that farming in the United States cannot be streamlined as easily as the fledgling agricultural industrial production in Brazil, with its vast, undeveloped land. Instead, the Midwest produces feed that gets shipped to the South, where it is fed to livestock. In Brazil, crops, crushers, feedlots, and even biodiesel refineries are concentrated together. Arguably, Brazil has a problem it can fix, while the United States has little room for improvement to competitively reduce its overheads.

In addition to the seed, agrichemical, and fertilizer sectors, MNCs have begun investing in crushing plants. Many of the corporations also sell livestock feed, making it worth their while to process soybeans on site rather than export raw beans elsewhere. Because Brazil has the area for development, companies can streamline production. Crushing plants separate the cake from the oil, which allows them to circumvent buying these products from another company and reduces their overhead for the animal feed and processed oils used in their own feedlots and food manufacturing plants. Bunge Food, a US corporation, is one investor that owns the crushing plants that supply its soy oil exports to restaurants, bakeries, and food producers. Similarly, Swiss-based Nestlé, the world's largest food and nutrition company, with over six thousand brands under its control, owns thirty-one factories in Brazil.[26] Others, such as Cargill, take the next step to actually produce their own value-added products, like dressings, sauces, and confectionery, on site in Brazil for domestic and export sales. To more efficiently export their soybeans, meat, and processed foods, MNCs invest in roads, railroads, and ports. Regarding its Brazilian holdings, Cargill boasts, "We also have an integrated network of over 130 grain origination offices located in the country's main agricultural areas, soybean crushing plants and several port terminals."

Companies recognized the potential to cut overhead costs even further by building their own biodiesel refining equipment and facilities and supplying their own energy. ADM first entered the Brazilian market in 1997 when it bought soybean-processing plants.[27] The MNC has since become the largest soy meal supplier and exporter, the second largest crusher and oil bottler, and operator of forty-two grain elevators in the country. In 2002, ADM opened a fertilizer blending facility, then in 2010 started construction on its own biodiesel plant to fuel its oilseed operations. The company is the sixth largest exporter in Brazil, ranking among lucrative industries exporting petroleum, minerals, and heavy industrial goods.

# THE ISSUES

Reliance on FDI and an export-based economy have advantages and disadvantages. Brazil's effort to exploit its comparative advantage in agribusiness has moved it to the top as one of the world's biggest exporters in a variety of sectors, including soybean production. Promoting its own industries through financing has made it not only a prime location for FDI but a top producer and processor in its own right. Although neoliberal policies have favored Brazil's growth and development, resistance to the free market's intrusion has sparked concern regarding the effect of rapid development on the environment, society, and sovereignty. Brazil has encountered disputes over trade barriers, including government subsidies, challenges to sustainable development, and problems concerning land rights and ownership.

The neoliberal free market has facilitated growth through a reciprocal relationship whereby emerging economies benefit from greater integration into the global food system, while MNCs gain better access to their markets. Intergovernmental organizations like the World Trade Organization (WTO) work to challenge countries' policies that favor their domestic markets to the detriment of the global market. In an attempt to minimize external competition for goods and labor, countries are inclined to subsidize their own industries, put tariffs on imports, and erect nontariff barriers, for instance, by limiting the amount of goods that can be imported. Dependence on agricultural exports has also raised concerns about the environmental impact of large-scale industrial farming. Deforestation of the grasslands and jungles leads activists to question the value of economic growth based on arguably unsustainable practices. Indigenous populations in these same regions challenge land-ownership policies and how they can use their land.

## Roadblocks to Global Business

Governments seek to protect domestic businesses and keep unemployment rates low, enacting economic policies that promote these national self-interests. Neoliberals argue that policies, like subsidies, that shelter domestic economic activities, legislation, such as quotas, that limit imports, and standards that set particular environmental conditions on products only serve to minimize foreign competition and interfere with consumers getting the best value for their money. Neoliberals draw from Adam Smith, who asserted that an invisible hand regulated the free market built on the industry of business people who were in a better position to judge market trends than politicians. Policies that interfere with free market incentives consequently disrupt efficient and effective business practices, thereby reducing the options and quality products available to consumers.

The global north has traditionally held sway over the global south, with the United States, EU countries, and Japan having more leverage in the global economy. Tariffs have been reduced considerably since the inception of the General Agreement on Tariffs and Trade in 1947, dropping between member countries by over 70 percent in the first five rounds of talks.[28] Nontariff barriers are a bit more difficult to address, since that they are ostensibly loopholes that result from governments attempting to protect workers and even the environment. Using more creative strategies to give domestic products an advantage over imports, US poultry producers have worked to secure the American market from Brazilian chicken, efforts directly related to soybeans as much of the feed for the birds is soy meal. Under the guise of health concerns, MNCs work to block white chicken meat exports from Brazil to eliminate US market competition. Tyson and other US poultry companies can thus charge more for chicken breasts in the domestic market. This strategy offsets relying on lower prices for dark meat in foreign markets as MNCs attempt to undersell domestic poultry farmers.[29] This use of a nontariff barrier benefits the MNC by allowing it to manipulate the market in order to drive out the competition while maintaining its bottom line.

Decreasing government subsidies to farmers involves very messy domestic (or in the case of the EU, regional) policy. The US Farm Bill, the European Common Agriculture Policy, and Japan's rice paddy policy, adopted after World War II to guarantee allied countries' food security, are entrenched policies that encourage farmers to grow certain crops or sometimes not to grow crops and retire land in exchange for subsidies. The Farm Bill and CAP are frequently in the news, so perhaps it comes as a surprise that Japan pays out more in agricultural subsidies either the United States or the European Union.[30]

Subsidies also come in the form of crop-insurance payments, so that if crops are damaged due to drought or floods, the government will make payouts. This policy was adopted after the farming crises of the Great Depression. At the same time that direct subsidies to farmers are being reduced to comply with international trade law, crop-insurance subsidization has increased. In less than a decade, crop-insurance payouts have more than tripled in the United States.[31]

MNCs, in particular, are the biggest benefactors of government subsidies since they control the overwhelming majority of production.[32] Domestically, they get money from what they produce as well as the supplemental subsidies from the government; internationally, MNCs are able to invest profits to earn even more money. Owners of smaller farms, whom the subsidies were originally designed to protect, struggle to keep pace with the corporations. The influence that MNCs wield in policy making increases the difficulty of eliminating farm subsidies.

Subsidies have also put American farming into overdrive by creating a permanent overproduction cycle because making money requires higher crop yields, which puts more of the commodity on the market, which drives down prices and requires an ever-increasing demand.[33] This cycle, in turn, has affected the kinds of food made (processed, value-added), where food is made (grain shipped to feedlots versus livestock and crops raised on one farm), and the way food is marketed (supersized). Government subsidies can also have an impact on food availability for poorer people. Because the US government heavily subsidies soybeans and other crops that earn higher profits,

---

## Recipe Box

### Understanding Subsidies

You are a cotton farmer in Mali, where more than 50 percent of the country's GDP comes from cotton exports. It costs you the equivalent of twenty-five US cents to produce one pound of cotton. You are lucky because, like an increasing number of farmers in the developing world, you have a cell phone with Internet access, so you can check the daily price for a pound of cotton at http://www.indexmundi.com/commodities/?commodity = cotton. Even though the price for a pound of cotton is more than what you paid to grow it, you find out that farmers in the United States and European Union are getting extra because their governments supplement whatever they earn with a subsidy. US cotton farmers received $561 billion in direct payments and crop insurance in 2012![1] Even though it costs more for farmers in developed countries to produce cotton, they will always make more than you do growing cotton. Because the overwhelming majority of world production is of the same variety, cotton quality does not vary much. The only comparative advantage that farmers in the developed countries have over farmers like you is their receipt of government subsidies, which is why neoliberals hate subsidies.

1. "Cotton Subsidies in the United States Totaled $32.9 Billion from 1995–2012," EWG Farm Subsidies, http://farm.ewg .org/progdetail.php?fips = 00000&progcode = cotton (accessed July 13, 2013).

these are increasingly favored by farmers over other crops, such as millet and sorghum, that sell for less but are staples in developing countries. So, while most people in the global north struggle with an excess of calories contributed by the value-added, supersized processed foods funded by government subsidies, poorer people in the global south struggle to get enough calories.

That these policies are outdated is evidenced by recent WTO rulings on the violation of international law by the United States regarding its subsidizing American cotton and sugar farmers.[34] Even though the WTO found the subsidies to be in violation of free trade, the terms of the US Farm Bill, which is revisited every five years, were such that the government not only has to continue to pay subsidies to American farmers but must foot the annual bill to the tune of $147.3 million to Brazil for "technical assistance and capacity building" as compensation for American violation of WTO policies.[35] Even by 2013 Congress could not agree to proposed reforms in the bill, with Democrats favoring increases for food stamps and Republicans tied to subsidizing farmers, so the United States continues to cut checks to Brazil for its violations.[36] These cases set a precedent for Brazil's complaints about US soybean subsidies since the American government subsidizes soybean farmers at about twice the rate they do cotton farmers.[37]

MNCs take an investment risk regarding protection of their intellectual property when marketing their seeds, particularly if their patent applications

### Recipe Box

#### The Seeds of International Disputes

Intellectual property rights are established to protect ideas, formulas, and creative work that would otherwise be easily copied or reproduced, leaving creators without compensation for their efforts. This very issue was at the heart of a dispute pitting Monsanto against Argentina. Because the government of Argentina denied Monsanto's patent application for Roundup Ready soybeans, when Argentinian farmers sold soy meal derived from the Roundup Ready seeds, the MNC wanted proceeds from the sales, as the intellectual property of its seeds was not protected. The soybeans were processed then sold to a Dutch company. When Monsanto filed a suit against the Dutch importers who bought the soy meal, the European Court of Justice ruled that since the soy meal is a by-product of the seeds, the farmers were not in violation of the MNC's patent claim. Monsanto therefore had no ground for its claim of intellectual property violation by the farmers. Do you think the outcome is fair to the corporation that depends on the proceeds of its sales to support further research and development of better agricultural products? Do you think farmers in developing countries should have to pay more for seeds and the special chemical fertilizers and pesticides unique to growing them?

are rejected or the approval process is drawn out. Monsanto has spent more than a decade attempting to collect royalties from Argentinean farmers for reproducing and selling the company's Roundup Ready seeds. This practice, Monsanto argues, violates the company's right to be reimbursed for its intellectual property. The dispute between the Argentinean government and Monsanto is just one example of the difficulty MNCs have protecting the time and expense that goes into developing new products.[38] Although in many developing countries protecting corporations' intellectual property rights can be difficult—due to factors ranging from insufficient funds to a lack of incentive to enforce protection laws—Brazil seems to be an outlier. The country is viewed as a safe place for protecting MNCs' investments in research and development. Although Brazilian courts are criticized for taking an excessive time to process cases, the government has worked to update its laws. This move encourages companies to reapply for patent extensions as a way to protect their developments in the country, giving Brazil an edge over Argentina. Although the neighboring country has many of the same assets to offer as Brazil, Argentina's political and financial institutions discourage FDI.

Maintaining state sovereignty and food security are also issues that arise in response to the neoliberal push to open markets; both become increasingly more difficult with greater global integration of production and trade. Accepting FDI compromises Brazil's authority as it becomes more dependent on foreign funds to spur its growth and development. Of even bigger concern is the feeling among some Brazilians that their relationship with China, in particular, is neocolonial, as the Chinese are essentially exploiting the resource-rich country. To facilitate the movement of raw materials, Brazil has constructed what has been called the "Highway to China," building Porto do Açu, a city designed as a shipping port for goods destined for China.[39] Only 16 percent of Brazil's total exports to China in 2010 were not raw materials, while 98 percent of exports to Brazil from China were manufactured products.[40] Exploitation through the imbalance in type of trade raises concerns about neocolonialism and hence threatens Brazilian sovereignty and security.

### Environmental Concerns

Resistance to neoliberal government and international policies comes in a variety of forms. One of the biggest attention getters is environmental concern about deforestation in Brazil. The Amazon rain forest tends to come to mind first, with the threat of land development in Brazil. The *cerrados*, however, have been most affected thus far by agribusiness. The biodiversity in the dry savannah forests rivals that in the wet rain forests. Development in the 1990s in the *cerrados* that predominately make up the Mato Grosso area grew out of research and development by Brazil's state agency EMBRAPA. Agriculture scientists determined the area was good for soy production because the amount of rainfall and average temperature made it suitable for soy cultivation. EMBRAPA scientists were able to develop strains of soybeans that would thrive in the acidic soil and shorter daylight hours of the tropics.

Due to heavy criticism of the government's development strategies in the 1980s and early 1990s, Brazil moved toward implementing policies to better protect its Amazon territory. The government also began to recognize, however, that if the country was to continue to rely on food production for growth and development, then it would have to pay more attention to sustainable agribusiness practices. One strategy has been to require farmers to designate a portion of their land to lay fallow or to plant trees to reforest cleared areas. As farmers have realized the long-term threat to their livelihoods, resistance to promoting sustainable practices has waned.[41] Corporations have been encouraged with carrots, but sticks have also been employed in the form of enforcement of laws that protect the Amazon region and mandate reforestation. Both farmers and MNCs are under more pressure from consumers as well, particularly Europeans looking to buy products certified as produced using environmentally friendly practices.

Another aspect of environmental resistance to neoliberal free market policies has been the use of transgenic seeds, also referred to as genetically modified organism (GMO) seeds. Those in the agribusiness industry advocate the use of transgenic seeds because they offer higher yields while putting less pressure on resources. Along with corn, cottonseed, and canola, soybeans are a main crop grown using GMO seeds. Mapping the soy genome sequence in 2009 allowed for even more manipulation to improve production and adaptation to ecological conditions.[42] Antitransgenic activists argue that we have not even begun to fully realize the health and environmental costs of using altered seeds. The Green Party and its adherents are able to influence politics in Europe more effectively than in the United States. Brazil could thus have a comparative advantage if it opted for transgenic-free soybeans, as the EU is the world's second largest importer. Because Brazil was one of the first countries to use transgenic soy, however, production of non-GMO seeds is not likely because, unless entire areas can be guaranteed as transgenic-free growing zones, farmers will not be able to have their soybean crops certified as non-GMO.

To appease activists, shareholders, and consumers, most major corporations advertise on their company websites their efforts in terms of sustainable agribusiness in their livestock production as well as their environmental and social responsibility programs. Some, like Unilever, have even gone so far as to purchase sustainable soy oil certificates that guarantee the oil has been ethically produced. Whether these actions are just a way to pay lip service to activists or will result in real changes remains to be seen. Monsanto may be sanctioned by the United Nations Framework Convention on Climate Change to receive carbon credits because its Roundup Ready seeds help to reduce the amount of $CO_2$ in the atmosphere. That Monsanto should earn carbon credits for offsetting $CO_2$ emissions seems a dubious form of environmentalism to the activists who are critical of the company's overall environmental practices.

### Land Ownership

Leasing land in a fertile developing country to control production from seed to export has become increasingly common. Having lost the bulk of its arable land to the north when the country split, South Korea is looking to lease land in Brazil. In addition to supplementing their grain and soybean supplies, the Koreans are particularly interested in security feed for their formidable aquaculture industry.[43] Limited arable land led the Japanese company Sojitz to begin soybean production in Argentina, with plans to expand into Brazil.[44] The MNC exports soy not only to Japan but also to other Asian countries.

Although the leasing of land has raised concerns (as discussed below), the proposed outright sale of land to China was even more controversial. With 20 percent of Brazil's land already in foreign hands, the government is reluctant to part with more. The result is a push for investment in production over leasing.[45] Like the Saudi investment company hoping to ensure food security, the Chinese government is taking aggressive steps. Hoping to buy land to secure soybean supplies, in 2010 the Chinese looked to Brazil's arable land. Because the Brazilian government was unwilling to actually sell the land, the Chinese instead offered $7 billion in credit to farmers to guarantee that

6 million tons of soybeans would be exported to China every year.[46] Arguably the drive behind China's purchase of Brazilian soybeans is not only the need to feed its growing population with both soy products and soy-fed animals but also the fact that the country is, in essence, buying water access. Because countries in short supply of land and water will increasingly need to rely on food imports, maintaining ownership is key to retaining autonomy. In an effort to secure its landholdings, the Brazilian government eventually banned MNCs from being the sole owners of farming businesses, forcing companies that want to operate in the country to partner with domestic firms.[47]

Neoliberal resistance has also come from groups pushing for land reform. The move toward domestic development in the 1960s, then toward global food production in the 1990s, caused social backlash in Brazil, encouraging the formation of land reform organizations to reclaim property taken outright from indigenous people or to force the government to address the issue. The influx of agribusiness MNCs has affected small landowners in a number of ways. Those who cannot compete sell or lose their land. Some end up working for the companies; others migrate to urban areas. Speculators expand into the development of uncleared land, further threatening deforestation of the *cerrados* and quite possibly the Amazon rain forest.[48] Landgrabbing by MNCs that come into the country to lease huge plots of land to farm for both the export of crops and the processing of foods for export is a point of contention as well, as activists view this as a threat to the domestic food supply.

Brazil continues to face obstacles to its development from both international and domestic forces. The government counters criticism regarding sustainability by citing a rise in the standard of living of Brazilians. In the last decade, the country's GDP has increased by over 75 percent, purchasing power of consumers has risen by almost 40 percent, and development indicators such as school enrollment, poverty levels, and life expectancy have all improved.[49] This increase in the economic situation of Brazil arguably better positions the government to adopt more sustainable practices, if irrevocable damage is not done in the pursuit of development.

## CONCLUSION

Our food supply is steadily becoming more globalized, with numerous repercussions for an MNC-driven market. Without question, Brazil has benefited from this move to a global food supply chain, exploiting the rising demand for soy to its developmental advantage. A shift in production to emerging economies attracts investment and provides employment in those countries. Mature American and European agricultural sectors, burdened by international pressure to reduce domestic subsidies, find it increasingly difficult to compete, rendering farmers in those countries more vulnerable. Consumers in emerging economies gain more purchasing power, giving them more food options, but at the cost of reducing availability of staple foods to poorer people in developing countries.

When Brazil and other emerging economies export crops or meat, they export not only the products but also cheap labor and a share of their natural resources, which are under pressure.[50] Resistance to this encroachment on Brazil's natural resources has prompted environmentalists and social land reform activists to push for reforms and protections, despite efforts by corporations and the government to redress their concerns. The search for profits and food security has not been limited to the world's biggest economies; investors from developing countries, including Saudi Arabia and the United Arab Emirates, are also turning to Latin America's biggest economy for opportunities. Brazil, in its own move to guarantee growth and development, remains challenged to meet demands for its supplies in global food production without compromising its own long-term food security.

Relying on FDI means more profits are repatriated to the parent company's home state than are invested in Brazil. As Brazil's economy has grown, its own businesses have become better positioned to invest domestically as well as abroad. Several companies have expanded by taking advantage of the country's resources, enabling them to acquire and merge with struggling producers in the United States and Europe. Others have been assisted by Brazil's establishment of the Astra Agro Fund as a way to better its own development prospects by directing more investment toward Brazilian corporations that will, in turn, retain domestic profits and even repatriate profits from their international sites back to Brazil.

Three Brazilian-based companies have expanded to become some of the world's top producers in meat exports, food processing, and biofuel. Brasil Foods resulted from a merger between two sizeable Brazilian corporations, making it the largest in the country, with multi-billion-dollar exports, and Latin America's tenth biggest MNC. Employing over 120,000 workers, Brasil Foods is by far the biggest domestic employer. Its main production is meat and processed frozen foods. In addition to its domestic operations, it operates in numerous countries and derives more than half its revenue from exports to markets in the Middle East, eastern Europe, Central America, Japan, and Africa.

Although not the top Brazilian agribusiness corporation, JBS SA is the world's top processor of meat and by-products from livestock, such as leather and collagen.[51] The corporation positioned itself as the top meat producer and processor through strategic mergers, such as by becoming the majority holder of the American company Pilgrim's Pride, and through acquisitions, such as by buying Smithfield's beef production or the pork portion of Swift & Company. Producing these lines has the added advantage of giving JSB access to the American market, as these brand names are supermarket staples.[52]

Marfrig Alimentos SA is the third leading food producer and processor in Brazil, with a variety of products ranging from meats to frozen foods. Acquiring Cargill's Seara division allowed Marfrig to add chicken and pork to its beef business, which is the fourth largest in the world. Perhaps most notable was its 2010 acquisition of Keystone Foods, a leading supplier of meat products to Subway, Yum! Brands, and Campbell Soup Company and the supplier of McDonald's chicken nuggets, hamburgers, and other meat products sold worldwide.[53]

Astra Agro Fund works in coordination with Rabobank Brasil, offering investment opportunities for agribusiness companies. It aims to take advantage of Brazil's global food production by encouraging domestic companies to invest. Given its high ranking in a number of agribusiness exports and its prospects for future expansion, this sector is deemed worthy of investment.

The overwhelming benefits of doing business in Brazil have overshadowed the few drawbacks of investment. The integration of international and regional intergovernmental organizations and the formation of bilateral trade pacts indicate not only that institutions like the WTO are able to adjudicate on trade issues but that countries accept the rulings regarding government subsidies and trade barriers. Although Brazil has a domestic demand for soy, it relies on its export market. Trade agreements, including membership in the WTO and the South American economic organization Mercosur, and bilateral pacts with the European Union and China have served to strengthen ties by reducing tariffs and nontariff barriers. Brazil's export-led growth and ability to attract FDI is, without question, due in part to its ability to exploit its soy industry.

## CHAPTER QUESTIONS

1. Why is the demand for soybeans increasing? How do these relate to increased production in Brazil?
2. What advantages does Brazil have over the United States as a soybean producer?
3. What role do subsidies play in the global production of soybeans?
4. What concerns have been raised regarding increased soybean production in Brazil?

# CHAPTER 6

——— ❧ ———

# TOMATOES

## *Immigration and the Global Food Supply*

Tomatoes are a ubiquitous food item, eaten raw or cooked, grown in gardens and hothouses, and integral in cuisines as diverse as Italian and Indian. In a lot of ways, tomatoes are taken for granted. Order a salad in the United States or Europe in the middle of winter, and you will find fresh tomatoes, thanks to production in Florida, imports from Mexico and North Africa, and lots of greenhouses. The "locavore" movement and concerns for "food miles," however, have increased demand for locally produced, organic tomatoes, pushing Americans and Europeans to eschew not only imports but tomatoes that are not locally grown. The "Think global, eat local" approach to food selection has become popular, often in response to social and environmental concerns. Arguably, however, it does a disservice to farmers in developing countries.

Domestic production and the perishable nature of tomatoes limit cash crop exports to only those global south (GS) countries within close proximity to global north (GN) countries. Mexico is the top exporter to the United States, whereas African and Middle Eastern countries bordering the Mediterranean are top exporters to Europe. Because fewer GS countries have opportunities to exploit tomatoes as a cash crop export, the two prominent international

111

issues that arise between the GN and GS countries regarding tomatoes are trade policies and reliance on immigrant labor.

GS countries have a difficult time competing with GN production due to trade policies. These include tariffs, in the form of taxes on imports, and subsidization through government support of domestic tomato industries. Tariffs on tomato imports entering the United States and European Union, supplemented by nontariff barrier policies such as regulations on environmental and sanitary production conditions, minimize foreign competition with domestic tomatoes. Food-security measures developed after World War II to ensure adequate food supplies at home and abroad, as well as Cold War strategies aimed at fortifying alliances, led to American and European farm support policies. Dismantling these outdated programs has proven difficult, despite World Trade Organization (WTO) rulings in favor of countries seeking recourse against the United States and European Union for unfair trade policies.

Reliance on immigrant labor has resulted in worker abuses in the American and European tomato industries. Although labor conditions in the global south tend to attract the most media coverage, GN consumers are far less aware of worker abuses and even labor trafficking in their own backyards. Years of activism by a small group of migrant workers in a Florida community finally drew enough attention to worker conditions to give the group sufficient leverage to effect change in the United States. An Italian labor union has also worked diligently to draw attention to farmhand abuses, eventually making headway in 2011 with passage of a law criminalizing exploitation of migrant labor. National attention thus far has been the most successful means of ensuring rights for immigrant farmworkers, as international efforts have been largely forestalled. And unlike with the push for fair trade in the cocoa and coffee industries, little attention has been given to the tomato industry because fair trade most often focuses on farmers in developing countries and not the farmhands working on GN farms. Abuse of GS workers, coupled with discriminatory competition, serves to exploit and undermine development.

Understanding the issues that have grown up around the tomato industry requires getting a sense of its origins. The tomato has an interesting history, having traveled around the globe to become an ingredient in almost every cuisine. The overwhelming majority of tomatoes in the world are produced for domestic consumption, but the trade in tomatoes—especially the hothouse variety—allows unexpected countries like the Netherlands to be a top exporter. Production of tomatoes for canning and processed foods offers some interesting twists, such as the relationship between Italy and China. A few key issues plague the tomato industry. Pricing demands put pressure on growers. One hot topic involving consumer concerns about how tomatoes are produced has given rise to a number of food movements. And probably the biggest dirty little secret of the tomato industry is the treatment of its laborers.

## INTRODUCING *SOLANUM LYCOPERSICUM*

More than four hundred varieties of tomatoes have developed and been bred over the centuries. Red is the most common color, though the spectrum ranges from white to deep purple. The yellow variety, however, is likely closer to the first tomatoes that existed. Tomatoes rarely cross-pollinate, but several hundred specially developed "heirloom" or "heritage" varieties exist and of late have regained popularity, most likely due to Michelle Obama's gardening interests and the locavore movement.

Growing up to ten feet in height, plants stems need to be staked for support, lest they end up sprawling on the ground. The tomato plant developed a toxin over time to help protect against insects and vermin, though some have developed resistance; chipmunks have been known to wipe out an entire garden in no time. Although toxic to bugs, the chemical is not harmful to humans, though it may cause an allergic reaction in some people. Tomatoes vary in size and shape, from the elongated, ovular, bite-size grape tomato to the round, squat softball-size beefsteak variety. Specific varieties lend themselves well to different products. Roma tomatoes make better sauces and pastes, whereas slicing varieties, such as the beefsteak, are better on sandwiches, and cherry tomatoes are best in salads.

Tomatoes are a versatile food item that can be eaten raw or cooked, except for unripe green tomatoes, which must be cooked before consumption. Although related to tomatillos, which can be eaten raw, tomatoes belong to a different genus, making them more closely related to gooseberries. Popular ways to prepare tomatoes include sun drying, stewing, juicing, and cooking them into sauces, condiments, and soups. Tomatoes pair well with any number of grains, pastas, meats, vegetables, herbs, and spices, so they appear in many dishes. Very low in calories, tomatoes are a primary source of vitamins A and C, potassium, and fiber. This nutritionally packed food

---

### New-to-You Food: Jicama

Infusion cuisine—that is, the melding of two cultures' cooking—has begun to increase the popularity of jicama (pronounced HEE-ka-ma), so that this root vegetable is more commonly appearing in restaurants, recipes, and grocery stores in the United States and Europe. As they did tomatoes, the Spaniards came across jicama when they colonized Central and South America. When Spanish traders introduced it to in Southeast Asia, it took root because the plant thrives in tropical areas. Today jicama is a staple food in Thai, Malay, and Indonesian cuisine.

The taste and texture of jicama resembles a cross between a water chestnut and a potato. The Aztecs domesticated jicama, which aptly means "edible roots," since this root vegetable can grow to weigh as much as forty pounds. The vines that grow above ground bear attractive, though toxic, blue or white flowers. Like cassava, yucca, and yams, which are staple foods in many developing countries, jicama is fairly inexpensive, available year-round, and extremely nutritious, with a long shelf life. This vegetable is also very versatile as it can be eaten raw, baked, steamed, braised, deep-fried, or boiled. The commonly used food thickener, arrowroot, is the powered form of jicama.

Demand in the United States is in large part due to migration. Latino influence in southwestern cuisine and Asian influence in the Pacific Northwest encouraged grocers serving these immigrant communities to stock jicama. Being very low in calories yet packed with nutrients, jicama quickly caught on with the health-food crowd, making it even more widely used. Due to globalization, jicama is widely available across the United States. Ironically, it is just now gaining interest in Spain, the country responsible for its spread across the globe.

---

also contains an abundance of lycopene, a phytochemical deemed to have disease-fighting properties.

The perennial question of whether tomatoes are vegetables or fruits is largely the result of a legal decision by the US Supreme Court. Tomatoes are the ripened ovaries of a flower, making them a fruit botanically, though legally they are considered vegetables. The confusion results from the 1893 ruling in *Nix v. Hedden*, in which the Court classified tomatoes as vegetables in order to tax sales through customs regulations. At that time, fruit was not subject to tariffs. The popularity of tomatoes encouraged benefitting from taxing trade, so for legal purposes, they became vegetables. Justice Horace Gray makes an interesting argument in his opinion, observing that even though botanically tomatoes are a fruit, people don't eat them as such; because they are treated as vegetables, they should be taxed as vegetables. Outside the United States, however, tomatoes are more often than not considered fruit.

> ## Recipe Box
>
> ### Superfoods
>
> Are "superfoods" for real or just another ploy devised by advertisers to sell stuff? Blueberries and dark chocolate are touted for their antioxidants. Walnut and flaxseed get press for their omega-3 fatty acids. The humble tomato is also considered a superfood for its lycopene. These ordinary foods might seem too banal to be superfoods. Maybe exotic imports like mangosteen, açaí, and goji berries are more credible candidates. What qualifies a food as a superfood, after all? In addition to being packed with vitamins and minerals, superfoods are more nutrient-dense per calorie, making them among the best foods for reducing the risk of a variety of diseases. So, are these foods miraculous cure-alls? Eating a bushel of tomatoes a day does not ward off a heart attack.
>
> When it comes down to it, naming superfoods is a strategy by health advocates to draw attention to good foods. The unfortunate effect is that people think eating superfoods cancels out their less healthful choices. No superfood, or even superpill, exists that will spare humans from disease. A healthy body is more readily maintained with healthful foods eaten in moderation, with the occasional decadent indulgence, rather than through reliance on superfoods for a quick fix.

Commercial seeds and plants used in agribusiness or sold by catalog or at gardening centers are hybrid strains. Seed companies and corporations that use a lot of tomatoes in their products have developed varieties for particular conditions and purposes. Tomatoes destined for canning, for instance, have been bred to be oblong for machine harvesting and have fewer seeds and less water content. These crops go from fields to cans within a matter of days— and sometimes even hours. This streamlined process allows the tomatoes to remain in the fields until they reach peak ripeness, making them much more flavorful than commercially grown tomatoes. Those destined for grocery store shelves not only have longer distances to travel to market but also spend time on the produce shelf and at home before being used.

Tomatoes are also bred to better withstand cold weather, resist insects and vermin, and even grow for specific durations to allow for a steadier harvest throughout a season for home gardeners and smaller commercial outdoor farmers. Although they grow year-round in warmer places, tomatoes are usually planted annually, as they cannot survive through winter freezes. Sometimes tomato plants "voluntarily" grow a second season in areas where the plants die in winter. This happens when seeds from the previous year's crop fall into the soil, then germinate the next year.

Tomatoes do not refrigerate well as the flesh turns mealy. Ripened produce is highly perishable, needing to be stored at between fifty-four and eighty degrees Fahrenheit and out of direct sunlight. When fresh tomatoes will be shipped, the destination determines how long the produce can be vine ripened. Most often, chemicals are used in commercial tomato production to extend their shelf life before they reach the point of sale. Ethylene is an organic compound used to make green tomatoes appear ripe. Mature tomatoes would rot before reaching grocery stores. In order for the highly perishable tomato to be picked, boxed, shipped, and shelved, then purchased and eaten, fresh tomatoes are green tomatoes in disguise and might ripen a bit further.

## A BRIEF HISTORY OF TOMATOES

Think of tomatoes, and, without a doubt, Italy comes to mind, with images of pizza and pasta. The plant, however, is not native to Europe. The tomato's roots have been traced back to the Andes region of South America. The plant spread to Mexico through regional interaction, where European explorers encountered it in the late 1400s. The Aztecs first cultivated the *tomatl*, which influenced the Spanish name *tomate*. By the sixteenth century, tomatoes were commonly eaten in Spain and Italy. The tomato's reputation as an aphrodisiac was also carried back to Europe, where the French popularly referred to it as *pomme d'amour* (apple of love) through the seventeenth century until *la tomate* became a common food.

Like potatoes, eggplants, and tobacco, tomatoes belong to the nightshade family, so their poisonous leaves initially discouraged people from eating them. In some areas of Europe, particularly England, tomatoes were not eaten but grown only for observers to admire the flowers and fruit. The tomato, perhaps surprisingly, took a circuitous route to America and Canada via colonists who brought the ornamental plant with them, rather than spreading north from Mexico. By the eighteenth century, people had widely come to accept that tomatoes were not poisonous. As with other plants the Europeans found in the Americas, colonization spread tomatoes across the globe, integrating them into any number of cuisines, from the Philippines to Morocco.

The high acidity level of tomatoes lends well to preservation through canning, which is perhaps the reason that ketchup was popular before tomatoes appeared in salads. Campbell's introduced another popular canned product, cream of tomato soup, in the mid-nineteenth century, followed by Heinz Baked Beans, which became very popular in Britain later that century. Eventually tomatoes became appreciated as the versatile food they are, making their way out of the can and onto salad plates and eventually becoming a common sight year-round, thanks to hothouse production.

## CONSUMPTION

The top consumers per capita of tomatoes in the world are in Egypt, Greece, Armenia, and Libya, with more than ninety kilograms eaten per person each year.[1] Not surprisingly, many Mediterranean countries top the list, with Americans eating their fair share, though US consumption is only about half that of the top countries. Year-round availability of tomatoes in the global north is due to the combination of outdoor and greenhouse production. In the United States, for example, California and Florida can produce tomatoes during most months of the year, with the remaining months filled by greenhouse suppliers and imports from Mexico. Much of Canada's supply is from greenhouse production since temperatures permit a limited outdoor growing season. Europeans are steadily supplied with outdoor tomatoes from the Mediterranean region and Africa, supplemented by hothouse production across Europe.

Fresh versus processed tomato consumption roughly correlates to a country's level of development, with GN countries tending toward processed consumption and GS countries toward fresh tomatoes. In the United States, almost 90 percent of all tomatoes produced are destined for processing,[2] versus the 98 percent eaten fresh in Central Asia.[3] Another interesting consumption pattern is that, although people in the African and most of the Middle Eastern countries bordering the Mediterranean consume very few processed tomatoes, fresh tomatoes are commonly used in cooked dishes. The European Mediterranean countries, however, consume about 20 percent more processed tomatoes, even though they are also big producers of fresh tomatoes.[4] Perhaps most notable is India, which ranks second in world production; Indians almost exclusively eat fresh tomatoes, with very few grown for processing.

When inflation hits developing countries, tomato prices can force poorer people to cut back on this staple food item. Political turmoil in 2011 caused tomato prices in Egypt to more than double.[5] Slowing economic growth and increased exports to Pakistan resulted in the doubling of tomato prices in India, where one kilogram (2.2 pounds) of tomatoes increased to twenty rupees.[6] Although this amount represents only about thirty-five US cents, it makes a huge dent in many pocketbooks in a country whose gross domestic product per capita is $1,400.[7] Because tomatoes are a staple in Indian diets, a person earning $1,400 a year who buys one kilo of tomatoes each day spends 9 percent of his yearly income just on tomatoes. Urban prices are even higher: a kilo sells for forty rupees, making an even bigger dent.[8] Translated into what this increase would mean in terms of US dollars, a kilo of tomatoes would cost $12 a day and $24 in the city.[9]

A regular concern with fresh produce consumption, particularly of lettuce, spinach, cucumbers, and tomatoes, is outbreaks of salmonella and *E. coli*; with sun-dried tomatoes, the concern is hepatitis A. Salmonella is a bacterium that infects produce. Before shipping, tomatoes are treated with chlorinated water to kill bacteria, but sometimes enough survives to cause infection. *E. coli* is a bacterium that causes infection and can lead to death, as evidenced by the thirty-one Germans who died in 2011 after eating tainted sprouts. During that scare, the government also cautioned consumers to avoid raw tomatoes, which might also have been affected. Sun-dried tomatoes contaminated with hepatitis A were sold in the Netherlands in 2010 and in the United Kingdom in 2011. Although hepatitis A is rarely life threatening, in people who are not immunized against the virus, infection may result in hospitalization. Lack of farm and packing plant inspections, intensive farming methods, and increasingly tainted water supplies account for increased food contamination. Anytime there is a scare, until the outbreak can be traced, tons and tons of produce rots in fields or gets tossed into supermarket Dumpsters. The European Union compensated farmers to the tune of US$306 million for produce that rotted in fields or went bad in warehouses due to the *E. coli* breakout.[10]

## PRODUCTION

The top tomato producer in the world, by far, is China, which grew 41.9 million tons in 2010; the next biggest producers, the United States and India, grew only 40 percent of China's total.[11] Egypt, Turkey, and Italy round out the top six. In terms of imports and exports, tomato production is separated between fresh and processed tomatoes. The United States and Turkey are the only top-ranking producers that export fresh outdoor tomatoes, whereas hothouse production allows the Netherlands to be the global leader in fresh tomato exports.[12] Of the top twenty fresh tomato exporters, eight countries border the Mediterranean, giving an indication of not only the importance of tomatoes in those diets but also of the export value of the product. The top tomato importers, not surprisingly, are developed or emerging economies, as they have greater buying power.

Processed tomato exports differ primarily in that Italy is at the top, largely due to an interesting relationship with China. Domestic production in China is the result of Communist Party policies aimed at small-farm capitalist growth, initiated in the 1980s to achieve food self-sufficiency.[13] Families with small plots are financed to build greenhouses to grow fresh produce. These tomatoes are then processed in China before being exported to Italy, where they are reprocessed and exported. An Italian label attracts more consumer interest than pastes, canned tomatoes, and sauces from China, consequently exaggerating Italy's production numbers. Italy's domestic production and processing continue to be aided by government subsidies, as farmers and industries will receive US$230 million each year through 2015.[14] In 2009, Italy outpaced second-place Spain in processed-tomato production by more than eight hundred thousand tons.[15]

**Figure 6.1  Tomato Production 2012 (Millions of Tons).**

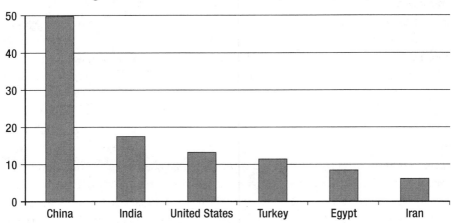

*Source:* FAOSTAT, 2012, Tomato Production.

The overwhelming percentage of tomatoes grown in developed countries are intended for processing, allowing for mechanized harvesting, which reduces the cost. As discussed below, fresh tomatoes are considerably more labor-intensive, requiring handpicking, which makes them comparatively more expensive than canned products. The H. J. Heinz Company uses more tomatoes than any other company worldwide, processing over 2 million tons that go into any number of its products, from its world-renowned ketchup to Smart Ones Angel Hair Marinara.[16] The company produces its own hybrid variety used by farmers who grow tomatoes solely for Heinz. More often than not, a corporation contracts with farmers to supply a specific variety of tomato for a particular purpose. Local conditions at times offer a bonus by producing a certain flavor. Corporations also strategize by using a tomato variety that is less demanding in terms of irrigation, fertilizers, and so on.

Developed and emerging economies increasingly rely on greenhouse farming to guarantee year-round fresh tomatoes and increased production for processing and export. In the United States, for example, shipping field-grown tomatoes south to north during the winter months means picking barely vine-ripened tomatoes, minimizing flavor and affecting texture. Greenhouse production may also require picking earlier than for those field-grown closer to market, but it allows for closer proximity to markets year-round. Canadian growers adopted this method in the 1990s, with the United States and Mexico following suit.[17] Although investment costs are considerably higher, agribusiness companies continue to invest in greenhouse tomatoes in developed and emerging economies because consumers are willing to pay for a regular supply of fresh tomatoes.[18] These tomatoes are often sold in clusters on the vine to lend a fresher appearance. Consumer demand alone is not enough to offset costs, so companies also look to sell to restaurants to make a profit.

The hothouse equivalent of industrial parks dot the Mediterranean coastline of Turkey, where greenhouses grow tomatoes to meet the huge domestic demand, as well as for export throughout Europe. The food supply corridor running from Beijing to Shanghai in China resembles that in Turkey,[19] supplying more than one-half of the country's tomatoes.[20] Greenhouse farming is increasingly used in developed and emerging economies for fresh produce production. Controlled conditions regulate temperature, guarantee regular watering, protect plants from weather damage, and significantly reduce the need for pesticides and weed killers.[21] Tomatoes grow faster under these conditions, taking at least one month less than those grown in the field, increasing the overall amount produced each year.[22] Tomatoes originated in the dry, hot, well-irrigated areas of the Andes, so they grow best in places that mimic those conditions. In regions with hot, humid seasons, such as Nigeria, which is the thirteenth biggest producer in the world, tomatoes are more susceptible to disease and pests. In some developing countries, such as Kenya, nongovernmental organizations (NGO) have funded growers to build hothouses for domestic production because during the wet season, tomatoes are more likely to get damaged, jacking up the price for people who depend on this staple food.

## THE ISSUES

Tomato production for export is concentrated in the global north and a few GS countries. Because tomatoes are a key ingredient in most cuisines around the world, countries that can produce them do so to meet domestic demand. As previously mentioned, tomatoes are also highly perishable, reducing the number of miles they can travel before rotting. For both domestic and export production, pricing raises some issues. Growers are affected by prices set by retail grocers, weather conditions, political crises, and economic policies.

Consumers in GN countries are increasingly paying attention to how tomatoes and other foods are produced, under what environmental conditions, and how far goods have traveled. One aspect of food production particularly related to fresh produce that tends to slip under the radar of many consumers is who is involved in production. The most pressing issue in the tomato industry in the United States and Europe involves the use of immigrant laborers, who often migrate as seasons change, to pick produce.

### Prices

Tomato production has provided a fairly stable income for farmers over time, though dependence on commodities (as seen in other chapters) puts farmers in a more vulnerable position in comparison to people in the manufacturing and service sectors. Leverage by retailers over price paid, as discussed in Chapter 1, has reduced farmer earnings in the United States by about 10 percent since the 1980s.[23] Global retail chains and multinational food companies have considerable bargaining power when contracting for products. The spread of big retail chains in developing countries has an effect not only on farmers, by influencing the price paid, but also on suppliers, by making more stringent demands. Walmart and Carrefour, two of the biggest retail grocers in the world, are moving into markets previously filled by small grocers, and multinational corporations (MNCs) are less tolerant of mediocre-quality produce and late deliveries.[24] To remain a chain supplier, farmers have to upgrade their service and product, or they will be replaced by another supplier willing to provide a constant, consistent flow of produce. Small farmers are often pushed out of the supply chain because they cannot compete with agribusinesses, as they are financially unable to accept below-production prices for their produce. One tomato farmer in India produces eight to ten tons of tomatoes each season, yet can barely make a living because, after investing $715 in seeds, pesticides, and fertilizer, he only earns about $1,000.[25]

Factors like weather conditions, strikes, conflict, and government policies also affect prices. In 2010, drought devastated tomato crops in northern India, and in 2012 floods damaged crops in Taiwan. Water shortages in 2012 in California resulted in extensive layoffs. Migrant farmhands in Italy protested work and living conditions by going on strike in 2011. Farmers in Syria, where tomatoes are the fourth biggest agricultural commodity, suffered losses from civil unrest.[26]

Tariffs, quotas, nontariff barriers, and subsidization policies give advantages to farmers in developed economies. Countries impose these measures to protect domestic production. The institution of the WTO allowed that organization to better address tariff and nontariff barriers than its predecessor, the General Agreement on Tariffs and Trade, which was not a formal organization but a set of multilateral trade policies. Because the WTO has the power to rule on disputes, countries are increasingly discouraged from implementing trade barriers. As discussed with sugar subsidies in Chapter 4, countries are more inclined to change their policies when a ruling by the WTO finds against them. Attempts to amend these policies, nevertheless, take time and often require a direct incentive to encourage implementation.

Under some circumstances, however, the WTO permits countries to retain tariffs. The European Union, for example, maintains tariffs to protect its wheat production, as well as pays out subsidies for produce under "special agricultural safeguard" arrangements.[27] GN producing countries are more likely to add seasonal tariffs, adopt health and safety restrictions, and set quotas to protect domestic produce sales from imports. The dumping of excess tomatoes from countries that subsidize tomatoes also affects farmers in developing countries, as they cannot compete with the cheaper prices.

Government subsidies impact market competitiveness, favoring the GN countries that can afford to earmark funds. As with soybeans and tuna, the United States and EU countries continue to support the agriculture and fishing industries, even though the threat of food shortages in the twentieth century that drove them to enact protective measures is no longer viable. Developing countries are particularly at a disadvantage because agricultural subsidies were largely eliminated as conditions for lending in the 1980s. Farmers in developing countries struggle to afford inputs such as fertilizers and seeds that were subsidized prior to restructuring. Farmers in sub-Saharan Africa have been particularly affected by these policies, where low input use has resulted in low food production.[28] Small farmers in GN countries are disadvantaged by subsidization as agribusiness averaged more than $1 million in funding under the US Farm Bill's federal crop-insurance program, whereas small farmers received about $40,000.[29] International pressures from countries filing subsidies disputes against the United States with the WTO encourages the US Congress to revise the Farm Bill, though, as explained in Chapter 4, subsidy reductions are complex and take years to accomplish.

Although the European Union has been actively working to reduce payouts in the tomato sector, developing countries find it difficult to compete. Tomato farmers in Italy, for example, earn an additional forty-one cents for every dollar of tomatoes sold, allowing them to undercut farmers in countries that do not subsidize the farming industry.[30] Due to its proximity to the EU market, Ghana is in a position to exploit its fresh tomato production as a cash crop export. Not surprisingly, Ghana has experienced difficulty breaking into the European market. EU subsidies and policies that limit competition with domestic tomatoes by claiming that production conditions do not meet EU standards have acted as a nontariff barrier on imports.[31]

Because Ghana was required to privatize state-owned processing factories under structural adjustment programs in the 1980s, farmers switched to tomato varieties bred for fresh consumption. Privatization opened the door to European canned tomatoes, which came to dominate the Ghanaian market.[32] Although the country is equipped to process tomatoes, farmers would have to shift production to canning tomatoes. They have little incentive, though, because of the stiff competition they would face from subsidized European imports.[33] With EU tomato processors receiving more than $300 million in

---

### Recipe Box

**The Road to Tomatoes**

Even though the terms of IMF and World Bank borrowing are often criticized for being overly stringent, in one instance, intervention seemed to have a positive effect as Ghana actually improved under structural adjustment program policies. Infrastructural improvements made it possible for more farmers to travel to market and to transfer goods for export. Transporting highly perishable produce like tomatoes became much more possible for Ghanaian farmers. Along with state-set cocoa prices and an abundant labor supply, almost half of Ghanaian cocoa farmers were encouraged to switch to tomato production.[1]

1. Rachel MacClean, *Informal Institutions and Citizenship in Rural Africa: Risk and Reciprocity in Ghana and Côte d'Ivoire* (Cambridge: Cambridge University Press, 2010), ch. 6.

---

subsidies annually, Ghanaian farmers have little chance to compete and lack bargaining power for getting their tomatoes processed.[34] Limited processing capacity leaves the country dependent on fresh produce instead of value-added goods.

On the heels of a rash of tomato farmer suicides in the late 2000s, the Ghanaian government set up a workshop in 2010 to strategize ways to improve tomato production and increase processing prospects. Competition from imports pushed down the price of tomatoes, burdening farmers with debt. Like the peppercorn farmers in India who were pushed to suicide when unable to repay their debts, Ghanaian farmers felt they had no other option but to end their lives.

### "Think Global, Eat Local (and Organic)"

Competition has emerged in GN countries between the capitalist system that pushes for greater economy in production and the locavore movement. Local and regional produce have grown in popularity as better food because it is grown nearby by small farmers struggling against agribusiness to make ends meet. The locavore movement urges Americans and Europeans to save farmlands from ending up as paved parking lots for the next megamart. In reality, however, agribusiness is a far more efficient producer of food, leaving a smaller carbon footprint on the earth.

Despite arguments that opting for a locavore diet is better for the environment and more socially just, this thinking is considered a "local trap" that food activists and researchers fall into because they fail to acknowledge the greater implications of local-scale reliance.[35] Promoting national food independence by eating primarily locally produced foods has unintended consequences for people in the global south, as this small-scale strategy undermines development ecologically and socially. These "First-World fetishes," as one author calls them, push for farmers' markets and supermarkets to stock local produce, which often does not include genetically modified organisms (GMOs) and is organically grown.[36] These foods, however, are more expensive and thereby privilege wealthier people at the risk of providing less food locally and globally.

A "globavore" approach to eating is actually more energy efficient—even with transportation factored into the equation. GS farmers and the planet would be better served by farming on a large scale, growing GMO crops, and exporting food from places that can more sustainably produce it. Field-grown tomatoes shipped from Africa to Europe, for instance, require far less energy to grow and transport than those produced by hothouses in the Netherlands.

## Recipe Box

### Tomatoes Sprouting Gills

The public got wind in the 1990s that scientists were attempting to improve tomatoes' resistance to cold temperatures by splicing Atlantic cod genes into their DNA. Questions abounded about whether people with fish allergies would be allergic to the tomatoes, if vegetarians would be violating their pledge to avoid seafood if they unknowingly ate these tomatoes, and what Frankenfood would be next? Despite attempts to introduce a genome that would make tomatoes more impervious to the cold, the "fish tomato" never materialized. Yet the debate over the value of GMOs continues to pop up on political agendas, particularly in Europe, where protests against companies developing transgenic plants have provoked destruction of GMO crops.

A change in diet can address concerns about the impact of "food miles," or long-distance distribution of food, and better help the planet. Producing red meat and dairy actually contributes more to carbon emissions because of the methane produced by livestock, so moving away from these products and replacing them with chicken, fish, and eggs—or better yet, a plant-based diet—does more to save the planet than exclusively eating locally sourced food.[37] Although air transport of fresh foods is detrimental to the environment, shipping produce one thousand miles by sea uses less fuel per ton than driving it one hundred miles by truck.[38]

Reliance on organic foods, whose production rejects GMO seeds along with chemical fertilizers, herbicides, and pesticides, is also unnecessarily harsher on the planet. A joint university study found that organic methods are, on average, 25 percent less productive than conventional methods, particularly for staple foods.[39] In order to sustain current levels of crop production in the United States using only organic fertilizer, 5 to 6 billion more cows would have to be raised to supply enough manure.[40] Not using the herbicides that allow farmers to forego tilling fields before sowing seeds would cause a dust bowl equivalent of topsoil to erode.[41] GMO seeds also offer hope for producing tomatoes that not only require fewer pesticides but improve upon the dull

---

### Recipe Box

**Feeling Better about Food Choices**

The adage "You are what you eat" might make us think twice before choosing a conventionally grown tomato over an organic one in the grocery store. To feel help us feel even better about ourselves, Dole began putting stickers on their organic produce so that consumers could see where their food is grown. On the Dole Organic website (http://www.doleorganic.com), consumers can input the number of the farm on their produce label for a virtual visit to that farm, where they can "meet" the farmers who grew their food. Despite the many disadvantages of organic farming for poorer people and the planet, one of its few benefits is that workers are not exposed to harmful pesticides and fertilizers used in the produce industry.

flavor of commercially grown tomatoes by developing a nonripening gene to extend the shelf-life of fresh tomatoes.[42]

The unfortunate outcome of growing produce—especially tomatoes—in locations like Florida where they do not thrive without excessive chemicals is that workers suffer. Reports of the chemicals used in field-grown tomato production and the harm spraying causes farmhands cause real concern for workers' lives. The sensationalized reports of possible health effects for consumers are unsubstantiated scare tactics used by the media to gain audiences. The need for chemicals comes from growing tomatoes in a place completely unsuitable for the plant. While California has reported health issues with pickers, the numbers are nowhere close to those in Florida, where producing unblemished tomatoes requires eight times the amount of chemicals.[43] Because the state is one of the few places in the United States where tomatoes can be grown in the winter months, entrepreneurial farmers figured out how to grow tomatoes in humid, soil-less conditions, so that Florida now supplies one-third of all fresh tomatoes in the country.[44] Because the land and climate are not suitable to growing tomatoes, an excess of chemicals are required for production, in turn exposing pickers to harmful work conditions. The spraying of fields when farmhands are harvesting has caused numerous health problems in the form of cancer, respiratory difficulties, and birth defects.

Organic farming has definite advantages. Farms benefit from raising diverse crops. Owners have greater autonomy from the big businesses that control GMO seeds and their necessary inputs, and workers are preserved from risk of exposure to chemical fertilizers and pesticides. Some plots have demonstrated yields comparable to conventionally grown crops. Consumers feel better about supporting these farms. Another concern about using GMOs is their effect on flora and fauna. Bee populations are at risk, and unwanted weeds are growing more resistance to chemicals. The unfortunate reality is that supporting the world's population—especially its future populations—through organic farming is not possible.

A number of factors make conventional farming that relies on GMO seeds more effective in terms of not only producing crops but protecting the environment. In most parts of the world, farmers lack the necessary inputs to reap yields comparable to conventionally produced foods. Insufficient development funds, coupled with the biological wall that evolution has hit for naturally grown plants, limit the possibility to match the pace of food demand with food production in most parts of the world.[45] With a steadily increasing global population, increasing reliance on locally grown organic foods is not practical. Another strike against organic farming is the amount of land necessary to support increases in the use of this method. Conventional farming was estimated to save an additional 750,000 square feet of new land from the plough in 2011[46]—the equivalent of the sea territory covered by the 1,225 Marshall Islands in the northern Pacific Ocean. Conventional farming also decreases reliance on fertilizers, pesticides, and other chemicals added to crops, since seeds are increasingly being programmed to be heartier, fight off pests, and yield greater output per plant.

Yet the locavore movement is growing traction. The unfortunate consequence of increased reliance on organic products is that, since yields are lower on organic farms, they require more land to meet increasing demand, pushing up the price on conventional foods for people who can't afford to indulge in "First-World fetishes." With an increasing number of MNCs, like Dole, jumping on the organic bandwagon to tap the wealth of those willing to pay extra for these products, more environmental damage will occur than through conventional production. The neoliberal economic model encourages these MNCs to meet the demands of GN desires at the risk of jeopardizing the food security of poorer people around the world.

## Migration for Labor

A representative from the United Farm Workers of America (UFW) appeared on *The Colbert Report* in 2010 in an effort to raise awareness about rights for undocumented farm laborers with the "Take Our Jobs" campaign. The farmworkers invited Americans literally to take their jobs, since popular opinion holds that illegal immigrants steal American's jobs. The point of the campaign was to show that Americans are not really interested in filling these positions, so the country is dependent on immigrants. To underscore its point, the UFW invited workers to replace them in the fields, offering to help those interested connect with their employers. Of the eighty-six hundred people who expressed an interest in farmwork, only seven took jobs.[47] Not only is farm labor backbreaking, disrespected work, but farmhands have to migrate as crops ripen in different parts of the country to earn whatever money they can in a year.

When the House Judiciary Committee's Subcommittee on Immigration, Citizenship, Refugees, Border Security, and International Law raised the issue of immigrant farm labor in 2010, Stephen Colbert testified on behalf of the UFW. Responding, in character, to the subcommittee, he suggested that because "Americans are far too dependent on immigrant labor to pick fruits and vegetables ... the obvious answer is for all of us to stop eating fruits and vegetables."[48] Although Colbert took a comedic approach to the subject, he was trying to draw attention to this serious matter, which is the same reason he spent a day in August working on a farm.

In most parts of the United States and Europe, crops are grown seasonally rather than year-round. Unlike hothouse tomatoes, field-grown crops rely heavily on migrant farmhands. Foreign-born laborers constitute 60 percent of agricultural workers in the United States.[49] Some of these laborers are in the country legally; many others are not. Of the illegal immigrants, some have been trafficked; they are trapped in involuntary servitude to farm owners until they pay off their debts. The issue is rooted in the desire for cheap labor. The problem is that people in the global north do not aspire to the mostly seasonal, backbreaking labor of picking tomatoes. Illegal immigrants willing to do the work do not have protection under the law; if they do, they may be unaware of their rights or unwilling to compromise the possibility of earning money to lodge a complaint. Workers endure harsh conditions and brutal treatment. Many emigrate to earn money to send to their families. Employers have leverage over laborers, threatening to report those who are illegal if they fail to comply. Field managers are likely to dock their pay if they complain. Traffickers have a business to protect and don't even hesitate to use death threats to keep workers in line. Without paperwork, illegal-entry and trafficked humans lack status, making them fear the law as much as their bosses.

Immigrant laborers in other developed countries face similar circumstances and conditions: poor living conditions, ridiculously high rent and food prices, no health care or benefits, and pay far below minimum wage. Employers are able to exploit pickers because of the questionable legality of their work status. Farm owners are able to distance themselves from culpability in using both illegal immigrants and trafficked humans, hiding behind layers of underlings who are directly responsible for the laborers. In cases where arrests have been made, prosecutors find it difficult to link owners to these activities.

Greed on the part of farm owners might seem like the obvious explanation for workers' conditions, but these owners are forced to find ways to cut costs to match the competition and face pressure from corporations to lower prices. Because agricultural inputs such as the price of land, fertilizers, seeds, and so on cannot be negotiated, wages are one of the few controls farmers have to improve their bottom lines. And for farms that sell fresh tomatoes, labor prices are a significant factor since the crop must be picked by hand. Of course, the situation does not excuse exploitation, but it explains why owners are inclined to pay as little as possible.

**Migrant workers in the United States** Reports of human trafficking, worker abuses, and poor living conditions for farmhands led workers in Florida to form a community group in 1993 to deal with their situation. Those workers were better able to organize because Florida is one of the few places where tomatoes are grown year-round, allowing the farmhands more permanent work and living conditions. Instead of earning a minimum wage, the more than thirty thousand tomato pickers in the state are paid by the number of bushels picked in a day. Because any number of factors can delay picking, and any amount of time spent on work-related activities is not compensated, farmhands earn $10,000 to $12,000 a year, though that number is distorted because field manager pay, which is slightly higher, is also included.[50] This pay does not include health-care benefits, sick leave, or retirement plans. Workers have to cover their own health- and dental-care costs, which many just cannot afford on such low wages. Below-poverty-level wages and poor work conditions led the community group to organize into the Coalition of Immokalee Workers (CIW), which has since made amazing strides in pushing national food and grocery store chains to sign onto its Campaign for Fair Food, now called the Fair Food Program, whereby they agree to pay an extra penny per pound for their tomatoes, with the extra money going directly to the pickers. If farm owners fail to pass the penny on to their workers, they lose their MNC contracts. CIW has also worked to raise awareness about human trafficking with its Modern-Day Slave Museum. Recreating a box truck used to imprison workers, the mobile museum travels up and down the East Coast of the United States to raise awareness about human trafficking and the squalid, confining conditions of the slaves.

After ferocious battles with the two biggest farms and the Florida Tomato Growers Exchange, the organization finally got the necessary support of the owners to implement the penny-per-pound system.[51] Although a penny might not seem like a lot, consider that just one bushel of tomatoes weighs between thirty-two and thirty-five pounds.[52] A worker in Florida earns forty to forty-five cents per bucket.[53] If the worker fills ten buckets an hour, each holding one bushel, and works for eight hours, at most, the farmhand makes $36 a day. An extra penny means that the farmhand can earn almost a dollar more a day. This supplement might not seem like much, but it represents a 2 percent increase in annual income.

CIW was also able to negotiate a number of additional supports to improve worker rights and conditions, which, along with the penny-per-pound agreement, promote increased transparency in the supply chain and reduce the risk of worker abuse and human trafficking. Although successful thus far in persuading the biggest restaurant chains, CIW has yet to garner support from supermarket chains. For several years, Whole Foods was the only grocery store to sign the agreement, though after fifteen years and much criticism, Trader Joe's finally agreed. These chains, however, only buy a small portion of the fresh Florida tomatoes sold throughout the United States, encouraging CIW to continue its mission. Progress made by the CIW encourages other grassroots groups to organize to push for change when the government's efforts and effectiveness are limited.

**Migrant workers in Italy** As in the United States, migrant workers are necessary to harvest fresh field tomatoes in Italy. Work and living conditions in the two countries mirror one another, as farmhands pay exorbitantly to live in slums and buy food, only to be abused by corrupt field managers to earn a pittance. Dubbed "Europe's tomato slaves," workers from North Africa and eastern Europe migrate in August to earn money to send home.[54] Reports of threats, beatings, and racial abuse by "gangmasters," who act as brokers between workers and farm owners, are not uncommon. Because the immigrants have no benefits, if injured they have to rely on mobile health clinics run by NGOs like Doctors without Borders. Farm owners rely on migrant labor primarily for two reasons. Like Americans, Italians feel the work is beneath them. To make ends meet, owners need to cut costs somewhere to compete for sales. As they cannot negotiate lower prices for agriculture inputs, paying lower wages is the only solution enabling small farmers to earn a living.

FLAI-CGIL, a food, farm, and hotel union formed to address workers' issues, has been pushing the Italian government to recognize the problem. With no response, the union promoted the *Oro Rosso*, or "Red Gold," campaign to raise awareness about migrant laborer abuses.[55] Although it was far less visible than the Campaign for Fair Food in the United States, its strategy differed in that the FLAI-CGIL went to fields and slums to distribute information to the workers, alerting them to their rights to unionize. Its next step was the national "Stop *Caporalato*," or "Stop Illegal Hiring," campaign, which gained support from political parties and trade unions to push a bill through the Italian senate in 2011 to criminalize "illicit brokering of labor based on the exploitation of the work," which affects 550,000 migrant workers every year.[56]

In addition to the illicit brokering of labor through human trafficking, exploitation includes workers' earning below minimum wage, resulting in pay between $25 and $38 a day.[57] If pickers put in an eight-hour workday, they earn between $3.25 and $4.75 an hour. The need for income and competition to keep their positions make them more amenable to working longer hours, meaning an eight-hour workday is a very conservative estimate during harvest time. Although pressure by the union demonstrates that governments can be pushed to address migrant labor issues, the extent to which implementing the law will change work and living conditions remains to be seen. Perhaps the survey conducted by the government in 2012 not only shows progress but also indicates its intention to follow up on migrant labor issues.[58]

Laborers may risk losing work if they push for higher pay and benefits. Farm owners will upgrade as soon as investing in mechanized harvesting equipment proves more cost-effective than paying pickers. Because the Coalition of Immokalee Workers targeted restaurant and grocery chains to pay the additional penny per pound, farm owners did not incur any additional wage burden. The extent to which the Italian law is enforced may push tomato farmers to invest in harvesters and forego manual laborers. Increased labor costs in Italy may also result in increased competition from neighboring exporters with lower standards.

Globally regulating labor standards has proven difficult. Although GS countries should seemingly favor setting universal standards, they argue that the low cost of labor is one of their few comparative advantages in the global economy. This position has prevented the WTO from implementing international labor regulations.[59] As an agency of the United Nations, the International Labor Organization is only as effective as member countries allow it to be, as the cocoa labor situation, discussed in Chapter 4, demonstrates. GS states are in the precarious situation of needing to use their labor to their competitive advantage, making it more difficult to institute laws if they are not uniform across all developing countries. Even when they want to set standards, developing countries are in less of a position to adopt, implement, and enforce laws, given that they have limited resources and struggle against corruption. Businesses are the key to effecting change, though they need an economic incentive to implement minimum standards.

## CONCLUSION

Concern for human rights abuses in the tomato and other industries gave rise to the fair trade movement in the 1980s.[60] One of the biggest driving factors behind its conception was ensuring that workers in developing countries were not exploited. MNCs and NGOs operate companies that set standards for fair trade. The only qualification to earn a fair trade label is a guaranteed minimum wage. Labels otherwise vary in stringency for qualifications, with Fairtrade International having the highest standards.

Fair trade goods are not synonymous with organically produced products. Fair trade focuses on the labor behind the produce, while organics focus on the product. Although fair trade–certified tomatoes are often also organic, the reverse is not necessarily the case. The biggest difference is that workers may not receive the livable minimum wage guaranteed by the fair trade process even though the tomatoes are grown organically. Because the use of chemicals can be detrimental to the health of workers, fair trade production may encourage growing organic produce. Organic farming presents a number of barriers. This type of farming offers lower crop yields, while at the same time requiring more land, water, and natural fertilizers, pesticides, and herbicides. These factors also make farming organic products more labor-intensive. The small demand for products that are both fair trade and organic is likely to dissuade struggling families in developing countries from selling certified produce.

Exposés of picking conditions in the United States and Europe have encouraged a push for fair trade tomatoes. Although the Coalition of Immokalee Workers is not a fair trade organization, ground gained by its Campaign for Fair Food has helped farmhands earn a more livable wage with the additional penny per pound MNCs were willing to pay for tomatoes. Fair trade tomatoes are late coming, as worker conditions in the tomato industry have received less attention in comparison to those in the coffee and cocoa industries. Perhaps one reason for the lack of publicity is that, unlike imported commodities, tomatoes are produced domestically, so consumers are more inclined to turn a blind eye to injustices happening at home. The low demand for fair trade tomatoes has thus far been another factor contributing to slow growth. Few farms grow fair trade–certified tomatoes in the United States and the European Union, which means that few companies sell certified processed tomatoes.

The Food Alliance, a collaborative project conceived in 1993 in the Pacific Northwest, is the only certified fair trade label for tomatoes in the United States, Canada, and Mexico, with over 320 certified farms.[61] Minimum requirements to earn certification focus on sustainable agricultural practices for humans and the environment. Farm conditions must promote safety, be nondiscriminatory, offer employee benefits, and pay the minimum wage. Farmers must use non-GMO seeds, minimize reliance on chemical pesticides and herbicides, and adopt water, soil, and wildlife habitat-conservation measures. Farms are subject to third-party inspection to ensure standards are implemented and upheld. Foods certified by the Food Alliance bear a fair trade–certified label.

The European Trade Union Institute, in reaction to treatment of migrant tomato pickers, is working toward devising a fair trade strategy to ensure minimum livable wages and humane conditions. FLAI-CGIL, the Italian union pushing for migrant labor rights, is pushing for an industry-wide fair trade certification program. Instituting a labeling scheme would increase awareness and improve conditions for pickers. Getting the country's senate to pass such a bill would be monumental, though the implementation of such regulation would be costly and undoubtedly meet with great resistance.

Examining tomatoes offers insight into other perishable food commodities. A number of vegetables (green beans, asparagus, and lettuce) and the overwhelming majority of fruit (apples, oranges, grapes for raisins, and strawberries, to name a few) grown in developed countries have to be hand-picked. Labor costs burden farm owners, who have few options for cutting costs beyond wage reduction. Reliance on migrant workers has encouraged human trafficking and mistreatment of undocumented workers. GN farm policies and trade practices disadvantage developing countries. The push to eat locally, organically produced tomatoes in order to reduce food miles and protect the environment also serves to undermine opportunities for farmers in developing countries. Organized movements in the United States and European Union have helped to address worker injustices, though widespread produce-industry improvements remain necessary.

# CHAPTER QUESTIONS

1. What difficulties are associated with providing fresh tomatoes year-round in most areas in GN countries?
2. What factors affect a reliance on tomatoes as a cash crop in the global south?
3. What factors should one consider when opting for a locavore diet over a globavore diet?
4. What labor issues prompted the formation of the Coalition of Immokalee Workers and FLAI-CGIL?

# CHAPTER 7

---

# TUNA

## *The Global Environment*

Japanese restaurants are popping up in the most unexpected places. In Krakow, Poland, sushi bars line a street in the old Jewish quarter of the city. If you're visiting Marrakesh, Morocco, and craving sushi, just head to the trendy Gueliz district. Whether in Mexico City or Bangkok, a tourist is likely to happen upon this Asian fare. Even walking into a local supermarket nowadays could bring a shopper face-to-face with a sushi chef.

Ask average Americans what they think of when they hear the word "tuna," and their answers will include "tuna salad sandwich," "tuna noodle casserole," and maybe even "Chicken of the Sea," a brand of canned tuna. These family-friendly, budget-conscious options contrast dramatically with $24-a-piece otoro sashimi, which uses the best cut of tuna.[1] High demand in Japan for bluefin, bigeye, and yellowfin tuna, coupled with a growing demand worldwide for sushi and sashimi, contributes to the depletion of tuna stocks, as does demand in Mediterranean countries. Tuna's extinction would have an irrevocable effect on the ocean's ecosystem. This change would not only upset the balance of underwater life but threaten the welfare of poor people dependent on fishing for survival.

Unlike many other endangered fish, tuna, as a migratory species, depend on international cooperation and policing for protection. The difficulty lies not just in securing funds and personnel to monitor international waters and docks where tuna might arrive. Work toward establishing international agreements to regulate fishing for tuna has been undermined by economic self-interest. To promote conservation, countries have established regional fishing management organizations (RFMOs) in the five areas of the world where tuna populations are concentrated. Their effectiveness, however, is limited by the cultural, economic, and political divides that influence policy making. With nongovernmental organizations (NGOs) creating common awareness about the threat to tuna, RFMOs are attempting to push states to adopt a rights-based management (RBM) approach to protecting this common good. Although aquaculture may take some pressure off of wild tuna by breeding fish for market, conservation efforts will still be necessary to maintain sustainable levels in the wild.

## INTRODUCING *THUNNUS*

More than fifty species of *thunnus*, or tuna, swim in the oceans and seas of the world, though only six species of true tuna are commercially fished.[2] Of these, two types of bluefin, Atlantic and southern, are considered the most endangered, whereas albacore, bigeye, and yellowfin are classified as vulnerable to extinction if demand at its current level continues. In 2011, the Pew Environmental Group reported that 140 percent more bluefin tuna was fished in the Mediterranean than was declared by fishers.[3] With Atlantic bluefin stocks estimated to have fallen by more than 80 percent since the 1960s, disagreements over protection—coupled with rise in demand for bluefin—threaten the sustainability of this and other overfished species of tuna.[4] Although the Pacific bluefin currently appears to have healthy stocks, debate over the accuracy of its numbers has led to recommendations for intervention.[5] Shortages of one species of tuna shift demand to other varieties, putting them in jeopardy of extinction.

Although tuna is a renewable resource, overfishing risks wiping out the commercially fished species. Tuna are a migratory fish that continually need to move in order to get enough oxygen, swimming up to forty miles per hour. These fish are pelagic, meaning they live in open waters, and generally concentrate in a ninety-degree band around the equator. Some species can increase their body temperature, which allows them to survive further north or south; this also gives them greater range in migration patterns.

At the high end of the aquatic food chain, tuna grow to be enormous—up to twelve feet long and weighing several hundred pounds. Yet they are amazingly fast, so much so that engineers have replicated the physiognomy of tuna to create faster aquatic robots. Because of their size, their maturation time is much longer than for other commonly eaten fish. Fewer tuna in the ocean means fishers will accept smaller, immature catches. Fishing tuna as juveniles before they mature limits the number of females who remain to reproduce.

Burning so many calories with their constant movement, tuna spend a lot of time eating other fish, mainly sardines and anchovies, but they will eat almost anything. Because tuna are close to the top of their food chain, they accumulate heavy metals from the fish they eat that have been exposed. Despite health concerns about mercury poisoning from eating tuna, demand for the fish continues to increase. With the recent media attention to the health benefits of omega-3 fatty acids, consumers have increasingly turned to tuna for this essential dietary supplement.

Conservation of tuna is necessary to protect the ecosystem. Tuna are the natural enemy of jellyfish and help to control the jellyfish population, which, if left uncontrolled, can wreak havoc on other marine life and, ironically, on the fishing industry by damaging nets and engines. Jellyfish blooms along the coast of Greece were so bad in 2013 that the British Foreign Office issued a travel advisory to tourists heading to the country's beaches.[6] Some argue that commercial whaling is necessary to protect tuna stocks, as killer whales are their natural predators. Sharks are also enemies of the fish. Schools of tuna will swim with dolphins, which scare away the sharks, since only the largest sharks are known to attack groups of dolphins.

Tuna fishers often track dolphins because they swim together. Fishers have even developed devices that attract dolphins to better concentrate the tuna. As the nets are reeled in, however, dolphins get caught as bycatch and drown.[7] In an attempt to protect dolphins, a dolphin-safe tuna campaign started in the 1980s. Recognizing dolphin-safety concerns, in 1998 the Inter-American Tropical Tuna Commission instituted the multilateral Agreement on the International Dolphin Conservation Program in an effort to limit dolphin mortality as bycatch in tuna fishing. The World Trade Organization (WTO) is much more likely to tolerate this sort of policy due to its unilateral, nondiscriminatory enforcement. Although the dolphin-safe campaign proved a success in raising consumer awareness, resulting in legislation that required the fishing industry to implement changes, Atlantic and southern bluefin tuna are steadily heading toward extinction, with a 60 percent average decline across varieties from 1954 to 2006.[8]

## A BRIEF HISTORY OF TUNA

Tuna consumption is a rather new phenomenon because these fish swim farther off of the coastline, making it less likely for local fishers to encounter this migratory fish. Industrial fishing really took off in the mid-twentieth century, at which time tuna became more readily available. Industrialization in Japan after World War II helped to modernize the country's fishing industry. Even though tuna only recently become part of the Japanese diet, the fish is now both a staple food and a delicacy in the country. Not until the 1950s, when the islands were introduced to American beef, did the Japanese develop a desire for the heartier, fattier "red" fish.[9] Until then, the islanders had traditionally eaten the more healthful, leaner "white" fish options.

---

### Recipe Box

**Is Dolphin-Safe Tuna _So_ 1980s?**

Public outcry in the early 1970s pushed the US Congress to pass the Marine Mammal Protection Act to protect dolphins from US tuna fishers. In the 1980s, Congress banned imported tuna that did not comply with US dolphin-conservation standards. The "dolphin-safe tuna" labeling program immediately generated contention with other countries, which claimed that these environmental standards were put into place only to block imports to protect the US domestic fishing industry. Mexico was especially affected by this policy and argued with the United States for a decade about the legality of the act. In 2008, a WTO dispute-review panel finally ruled that the label acted as a nontariff trade barrier. Mexico benefited from the ruling and their tuna exports now qualify as both legal and duty-free coming into the United States—a challenge to American-owned canning MNCs as well as environmentalists.

---

The ability to fish farther out at sea for longer periods with better equipment has helped fishers meet the growing demand for tuna among the growing populations in East and Southeast Asia, with their improved standards of living. Americans living in Japan after World War II returned to the United States to demand tuna, and the more recent sushi fad has considerably increased the popularity of the fish outside East Asia.

## PRODUCTION

Traditional fishing methods dominated on the seas from the time boats were first built. Countries, through custom, initially understood that their territory extended three miles into surrounding waters. Naval and military advancements eventually pushed that line to twelve miles. Greater advancements in fishing brought about an agreement through the United Nations Law of the Sea Treaty to extend countries' claims to two hundred miles, creating an exclusive economic zone (EEZ) as an extension of their territory.[10] Water outside the EEZs is considered the high sea and is not controlled by any one country.

Several innovations in the twentieth century have enabled fishers to better take advantage of these fishing zones. Improved returns on investment pushed investors to move toward industrial fleet fishing, creating considerable competition with individually owned and operated fishing vessels. Desire to increase catch size led to the development of purse seines and long-liners with fish-aggregation devices, such as buoys, to attract fish more easily. Technological advances in refrigeration, along with GPS tracking and acoustic fish finders, made fishing on the high seas a much more economically rewarding venture.

By the 1960s, purse seine and long-line fishing began to replace traditional fishing methods for catching tuna. A purse seine is a huge net weighted at the bottom that is dropped over a school of fish, encircling it. The net is then drawn shut with a rope to trap the fish inside. The vessel uses a mechanized pulley to haul in the catch. The fish are then transferred into cages for transport to processing centers. Long-liners are long fishing lines with baited hooks and buoys attached to keep them from sinking. The point of these devices is to increase catch size per voyage. The shift from traditional hook-and-line methods to purse seine nets and long-liners increasingly pressures fish stocks because fewer fish survive to reproduce. In the 1950s, for example, tuna fishers annually netted about half a ton of all types of tuna; in 2010, commercial fishers caught about 6 million tons.[11] Another effect of using these more advanced methods is that sea life other than the intended catch is caught in the nets and on the lines. Sharks, sea turtles, and other fish end up as bycatch and are left to die instead of being separated out and returned to sea. While more efficient for the commercial fishers, this practice actually undermines their business prospects by depleting the food source of the tuna that eat these fish. This practice also results in smaller and fewer fish for island and coastal peoples who depend on fish for their survival. Although bycatch is heavily regulated in the United States, other countries are less diligent in their enforcement. Protecting bycatch on the high seas proves even more difficult.

The development of satellite navigation systems has made it easier to track schools of fish to specific areas on the high seas. Whereas tuna may have once had a safe haven in the open sea, this sophisticated tracking equipment means far more vessels are willing to venture farther for the catch, giving tuna less time to spawn and mature. The enormous carrying capacity of corporate-owned commercial fishing fleets using purse seines and long-liners means far more fish are caught and hauled on each voyage. All of these advances reduce the odds of enough tuna surviving to reach adulthood, reproduce, and sufficiently repopulate the stock.

Until vessels equipped with superfreezers were designed, tuna fishing for raw consumption was constrained by distance to market. Because the overwhelming demand for bluefin tuna comes from Japanese consumers, about 80 percent of all tuna caught in the Atlantic Ocean and Mediterranean Sea ends up on plates in Japan.[12] Technological upgrades allow fishers to freeze tuna aboard the vessel, meaning voyages are constrained only by the capacity of their freezers. This process preserves the fish's flavor, texture, and color so that, when thawed and served, the fish appears freshly caught.

Technological advances in fishing have stiffened competition between vessels. Catch limits, such as quotas in a fishery, result in even greater rivalry between parties as they race to collect as much fish as possible before the maximum is reached. Increased competitiveness pushes fishers to take out loans for newer, better vessels, which means they have to earn enough to repay the loans, further fueling the competition.

# THE ISSUES

Because tuna is a migratory fish, attempts to protect this common good from overfishing have been hindered by numerous factors. Technological advances, coupled with population pressure on resources and increased demand for tuna, threaten sustainability. The important role of tuna in the food chain is worth reiterating. Removing this predator would upset the balance of the aquatic ecosystem, particularly as tuna are one of the few enemies of the jellyfish. Smaller fish would then face competition from increasing numbers of jellyfish, threatening other links in the food chain. The impact on this ecosystem would create a global collective or common goods problem.

Common goods include anything that humans share and benefit from without having to pay for. Common types of global common goods are water, flora and fauna, the ozone layer, and rain forests, to name a few.[13] For example, one person's breathing fresh air does not affect another person's ability also to breathe; nor can the person breathing exclude others from taking in air by the mere act of respiration. When too many people abuse a common good by polluting the air, depleting wildlife, or razing rain forests, everyone is at risk of losing that good's benefit. This outcome, often referred to as the "tragedy of the commons," results from too many free riders taking advantage of global resources.

Protecting common goods requires cooperation to protect resources. Because global common goods cross political borders, attempts by one or a few countries to conserve a shared resource will not be enough. At minimum, the majority of actors involved—in this case, in tuna fishing—need to be on board for a strategy to be effective. A number of issues arise in attempts to protect limited resources. Cultural differences, access to technology, and economic policies interfere with devising a global strategy involving sovereign states.

## The Need for Cooperation

When dealing with global common goods such as tuna, conservation efforts require a concerted effort. As long as bluefin tuna remains a delicacy and the global demand for Japanese cuisine grows, the market will continue to place an exorbitant value on the fish. A 511-pound bluefin tuna was auctioned at the world-renowned Tsukiji fish market in Tokyo in 2010, fetching $175,000,

## New-to-You Food: Lionfish

You may not be familiar with lionfish, a tropical fish that makes a beautiful addition to any tropical fish tank. Concerns about this exotic fish are the exact opposite of those facing tuna. Lionfish have invaded coral reefs along the Atlantic coast of the United States and Caribbean countries. The insidious proliferation of lionfish has been traced back to the smashing of an aquarium tank in Florida during a hurricane in 1992, washing just six lionfish into the Atlantic Ocean.[1] This nonnative fish has since multiplied to the point of threatening the balance of the ecosystem, since the lionfish do not have natural predators in this nonindigenous location. Tourist boards in the United States and Caribbean are concerned with the increasing population. Lionfish congregate around coral reefs and sting divers. They also eat the colorful reef fish that tourists come to see. The predators are also harming the fishing industry by feeding on native species such as snapper and shrimp.

In order to control the spread of the lionfish, the US National Oceanic and Atmospheric Administration (NOAA) launched its "Eat Lionfish Campaign" in 2010 as a way to stir up consumer demand for the fish. A number of environmental organizations got together with NOAA to encourage people to catch and eat lionfish, arguing that doing so would actually promote sustainability. The campaign was an attempt to get chefs, restaurateurs, and fishmongers to encourage fishers to catch the predator to fill what NOAA hopes will be a growing demand.

MSNBC followed with a piece titled "Do Your Civic Duty: Eat This Fish," encouraging people to eat the fish so fishers would have an incentive to save the coral reefs.[2] Deep Creek, Maryland, decided to hold a Lionfest Cook-Off to entice chefs to develop recipes that diners would request in restaurants.[3] Competitors in the Bahamas caught 1,408 lionfish during a derby aimed at saving coral reefs, with several cities in Florida scheduling similar events to help put a dent in the population.[4]

So, is lionfish any good? Many people think so. The main reason it is less likely to appear on menus or at the fish counter is that many people have never heard of it. Some say it tastes like grouper; others maintain that when prepared as seviche, it goes well with nacho chips. Next time you are craving seafood, why not help save the coral reefs and eat lionfish?

---

1. "Spreading Lionfish Invasion Threatens Bahamas," NPR, August 9, 2009, http://www.npr.org/templates/story/story.php?storyId=111695369.

2. "Do Your Civic Duty: Eat This Fish!" *NBC News*, August 10, 2010, http://www.msnbc.msn.com/id/38632799/ns/us_news-environment/t/do-your-civic-duty-eat-fish/#.T8-7FVKuW2s.

3. "Lionfish Cook-Off at Conch Festival," Tribune 242, June 4, 2012, http://www.tribune242.com/news/2012/jun/04/lionfish-cook-off-at-conch-festival.

4. "Do Your Civic Duty."

or more than $400 per pound.[14] The next year, the record was beaten with the sale of a 754-pound tuna for almost $400,000.[15] Then in 2012, the record was broken once again with the sale of a 593-pound tuna for $736,000, at $1,238 per pound![16] Note that the more recent, smaller catch sold for 46 percent more than the previous year's bigger catch, indicating the increasing value of huge fish in the market. The demand that rewards such a high price for bluefin tuna makes it easier to understand the motivation to stay in the very competitive tuna industry.

The catch of these enormous tuna belies the reality of the situation; fewer tuna are reaching full maturity because of increased demand and better technology. The days of five-hundred-plus-pound tuna are nearing an end as the bluefin is verging on extinction. Catches as large as these are quite rare in the Atlantic, where bluefin tuna has been heavily fished since the 1960s, when industrial fishing fleets replaced traditional fishing methods. The allure of catching "the big one" is not the only reason that tuna fishers, despite increasing competition, stay in the business. Although tuna accounts for only a small percentage of all fish sold, fishers are enticed into the industry by tuna's significant value per pound as compared with other fish.

Efforts to protect this common good are constrained by states' self-interest. Culture shapes countries' decisions, registering vessels under flags of convenience (FOCs) offers economic benefits, laundering and poaching undermine legitimate fishing, and government subsidies interfere with developing a coordinated policy. All of these variables interfere with fishery management and limit the potential for effective governance of this common good. In order to ensure sustainability over extinction, protecting tuna requires more effective, stronger monitoring, controlling, and surveillance (MCS) of fishery zones by international institutions.

## Cultural Differences

Tensions between East Asian countries, where tuna is a dietary staple, and other parts of the world, where consumer demand for the fish is less, challenge the coalition building necessary for successful conservation. Even if an agreement can be reached, the degree to which countries can—or will—enforce international law erects another hurdle, as the self-interest of states may hinder them from fully cooperating. Both Taiwan and Japan have either been unwilling or unable to enforce quotas established for bluefin catch limits.[17] When the European Union proposed adding a ban on trade in bluefin tuna to the Convention on International Trade in Endangered Species (CITES), a key opponent was Japan. Consider, however, that banning the tuna trade would be like banning cattle production to reduce greenhouse gas emissions, as the livestock give off more carbon dioxide than vehicle exhaust.

## Villages versus Corporations

Island and coastal people traditionally depend on seafood for calories, protein, and fat. As many as 3 billion people rely on fish as a dietary staple.[18] These same people often depend on fishing to earn money, selling the better, bigger fish and keeping the less desirable catch to feed their families. These small fishing villages are in competition with big trawlers owned by corporate fishing fleets and outfitted with high-tech gear. These enormous vessels crowd out smaller, less sophisticated, independently owned vessels. Fishing industry corporations and unions can afford to hire lobbyists who push for favorable legislation by pressuring elected government officials. Corporations also own processing plants, cutting out intermediaries between themselves and the market.

Multinational corporations (MNCs) also assume the role of importers in Japan. Mitsubishi, best known for its automobiles and electronics, is one of the biggest traders of bluefin tuna in the world. Although it admits to processing between 30 and 40 percent of all the bluefin sold in the Japanese market, others estimate the company controls as much as 60 percent of the market.[19] The company imports the fish predominately from the Atlantic and Mediterranean regions. Because the fishing season is so short, Mitsubishi freezes the fish to have a ready supply for the Japanese market throughout the year. Controlling such a large portion of the market means the company can leverage prices with its ability to increase or decrease market supply.

## Flags of Convenience

Under international law, boats must be registered with a country and are bound by the laws of that country. Flags of convenience are a means of registering a vessel with a foreign country of which the owner is not a citizen. After World War II, newly independent countries realized that offering FOCs could raise some much-needed foreign currency. This option has grown in popularity over time, with more than 60 percent of vessels sailing under an FOC, and reports show that the numbers are on the rise.[20]

Seafarers can conveniently avoid domestic and international laws to which their home countries might be a party. FOCs essentially offer anyone using the sea for trade or transport a sort of international system loophole, allowing fishers to be free riders on common goods since they can avoid regulations such as quotas or size limits on fish. Researchers estimate that, varying by regional fishery area, between 10 and 30 percent of bluefin tuna is caught by FOC vessels.[21] These rivals to vessels registered in their home countries catch tuna and drive down prices for this depletable resource by adding extra tuna to the supply caught by registered fishers.

FOC vessels can be denied entry to ports of countries that are party to fishing agreements. The European Union has adopted this strategy for some fish, but those countries only account for a portion of the ports where the endangered Atlantic bluefin swim. FOC vessels can just as easily dock in Morocco as Spain to sell their tuna. Until FOC vessels have an economic incentive to register with their home countries, these fishers will continue to cheat the system. The most compelling reason fishers would have for not registering for an FOC is denial of access to markets to sell their catch.[22] They will continue to opt for the more convenient registry until given a greater economic incentive.

## Fish Laundering and Poaching

It should come as no surprise that corruption plagues an industry with such high potential returns. Fish poaching, laundering, and cheating on existing quotas are not uncommon. Fishery experts estimate that "pirate fishing" deprives legitimate fishers of approximately $17.5 billion each year.[23] One of the biggest challenges in regulating the fishing industry is identifying the origin, or provenance, of tuna brought to port. Corruption is so prevalent in the fishing industry that "illegal, unregulated, and unreported" fishing has its own acronym and is referred to as "IUU catch." Particularly vulnerable to piracy are developing countries that lack the means to sufficiently patrol their EEZs.

Vessels flying FOCs are frequently associated with these nefarious activities. A typical tactic to avoid catch limits is to transport the fish to an intermediary country.[24] In port, a factory ship might mix legitimately and illegally obtained fish, exporting it under that country's regulations. Another way to conceal the provenance of the catch is to mislabel the fish as a different species. These corrupt practices of poaching fish in restricted areas and selling fish as something it is not contribute to the depletion of tuna stocks and make it more difficult for legitimate fishers to earn a living.

## Government Subsidies

As seen in Chapter 5 on soy, any effort to challenge policies eliminating government subsidies is a hot-button issue, riling up the constituents and corporations who benefit from these payouts. In addition to monies earmarked for fisheries management, tuna fishing industries receive government support. Between 1996 and 2004, 29 percent of all American federal and state government fishery subsidies were directed at the tuna industry, amounting to $189.2 billion.[25] The European Union spent even more, doling out $44.4 million toward modernization of bluefin tuna vessels and, unfortunately, not even requiring upgrades to more fuel-efficient models.[26]

Subsidies come in the form of purchasing surplus fish, footing the bill for fishing access payments, and providing disaster relief.[27] Surplus fish removal subsidies provide governments with a way to help maintain a steady market price for fishers. Fishing access payments essentially allow fishers to buy vessel permits to access other countries' EEZs. Disaster aid is paid out directly to fishers affected by natural or human-induced events, such as hurricanes and oil spills. In addition to these direct subsidies, commercial fishers in the United States and European Union countries enjoy exemption from federal and state/provincial fuel taxes.[28] Some US states even exempt fishers from state sales taxes on gasoline and diesel, and some EU members give fuel credits. Countries struggle to balance demands for subsidies, while also providing funds for MCS conservation support.

Government subsidies protect fishers during hard times, thereby discouraging them from leaving fishing; corporations receive funding as well. Subsidies offer rewards for remaining in an overpopulated industry, effectively guaranteeing an income. Pressures from MNCs and unions make it difficult for governments to cut these subsidies. The increased power of the WTO through its dispute-resolution mechanism, however, is likely to resolve the issue eventually. Because subsidies are nontariff barriers that interfere with free trade, precedent rulings by the WTO indicate the organization will not tolerate discriminatory policies that unfairly advantage global north (GN) fishers over those in developing countries.

Self-interest complicates cooperative efforts, putting roadblocks in the way of developing a universal plan to conserve tuna. In order to implement effective monitoring, controlling, and surveillance techniques, those involved in the tuna industry essentially need to agree on how to divide tuna stocks in a sustainable way that minimizes cheating. This objective requires addressing issues related to economic responsibilities, rights distribution, public awareness, and whether aquaculture offers a solution for saving the tuna population.

## Monitoring, Controlling, and Surveillance

Relative to most other endangered fish, tuna present a unique challenge for monitoring, controlling, and surveillance activities. Because tuna migrate into international waters, monitoring fishing activity is even more difficult. They cross not only countries' territorial borders when migrating but also open, unpoliced international waters. Atlantic bluefin, for example, move all the way across the Atlantic Ocean from North America to Europe. The migratory nature of the fish raises difficulties on both the high seas and at port. Effectiveness varies based on states' willingness to follow set quotas, monitor ports, and coordinate data with other countries. Even if a state could control its own EEZ, policing fishing vessels outside these zones would be expensive. The most efficient way to monitor catch size would be to patrol the ports of entry. If enough countries are not a part of an agreement, however, free riders can take advantage of the common good by delivering their catch via nonparty states where set quotas are not enforced.

## Cooperative Efforts

Although unilateral action is possible when dealing with nonmigratory fish, multilateral action is necessary if tuna-conservation efforts are to be effective. What began as a bilateral agreement signed in 1949 between the United States and Costa Rica evolved into the Inter-American Tropical Tuna Commission, the first intergovernmental organization (IGO) to collectively govern the tuna common goods issue. Although its earliest efforts to set quotas on yellowfin tuna in the eastern Pacific Ocean proved less than effective, the organization has since established one of the most successful resolutions to date. Concern for dolphin as bycatch in tuna fishing brought about the Agreement on the International Dolphin Conservation Program, which demonstrated that multilateral cooperation could be an effective means to limit dolphin mortality.

The first cooperative attempt aimed at protecting tuna in one specific region, the Atlantic Ocean, was initiated in 1967 with the International Commission for the Conservation of Atlantic Tunas (ICCAT) in 1967. The objective behind the founding of the IGO was to provide the resources necessary to manage fish stocks. The forty-eight island and coastal country members set catch limits through quotas and support conservation research to achieve a sustainable balance of tuna and tuna-like species (such as mackerel, skipjack, and spearfish). Due to their trade in tuna, Japan, South Korea, and China, though not bordering the Atlantic or one of its seas, specifically became signatories to the agreement as "distant-water fishing countries" because they fish in the high seas of the Atlantic.

Despite a reduction in quota limits in 2010, ICCAT has received much criticism from environmentalists maintaining that its catch limits are too generous to allow for sustainability of the fish. The primary difficulty in reducing quotas, however, is that the sovereign members deciding the policy have to consent to the number set. Because countries felt ICCAT was ineffective in protecting the Atlantic bluefin, in early 2010, the European Union petitioned CITES to include that fish on its Appendix I, a classification for species under threat of extinction, often due to trade. Despite support for this initiative, these tuna failed to gain Appendix I listing. Fearing the effect a ban on trade would have on people dependent on fishing for their livelihoods, global south (GS) coastal states sided with the developed fishing industry countries, led by Japan and Canada, in opposing the highest protection listing by CITES.[29]

Later that year, the European Commission made efforts to persuade member states to collectively propose a significant quota reduction to ICCAT for 2011 catch limits. Under pressure from Mediterranean countries that depend on the fishing industry, the EU countries rejected the proposal, arguing that the 2010 ICCAT quotas made earning a living difficult enough without a reduction.[30] Some fishers resort to illegal activities, such as evading border controls to fish in other countries' waters, to survive. During the 2011 civil war in Libya, fishers took advantage of domestic unrest by fishing in the country's EEZ.[31] Because ICCAT requires that each boat be equipped with a monitoring system, observers were able to detect an unusually high level of activity in Libyan waters. As civil war disrupted monitoring of fishing ports, observers suspected nonauthorized boats had entered Libya's exclusive fishing zone.

The formation of ICCAT inspired countries situated around other tuna spawning regions to form conservation organizations. In addition to ICCAT covering the Atlantic Ocean, three additional RFMOs now represent different areas where tuna concentrate in the Pacific and Indian Oceans. Although the Inter-American Tropical Tuna Commission did not form to protect a specific region, the organization is an RFMO that manages Atlantic and Pacific fisheries bordering the Americas. Despite efforts by these organizations, management has proven difficult, resulting in diminishing stocks of Atlantic and southern bluefin tuna.

All five RFMOs met for the first time in 2007 at the first meeting of the Kobe Process to better coordinate policies, guidelines, and strategies to preserve endangered varieties of tuna, among other highly migratory fish and bycatch. The IGOs drafted a plan of action to implement steps to issue certificates of origin to prevent illegal fishing and promote greater transparency in setting regional fishing quotas. At the third meeting in 2011, several concerns were raised, with a steering committee formed to address issues such as better data sharing (including a single shared list of authorized active tuna vessels), standardization of procedures, documentation, reporting, and enforcement.[32] The unfortunate reality of this meeting is that, despite four years of collaborative efforts between the first and third meetings, the individual organizations still have a lot of coordinating to do.[33]

In response to difficulties the RFMOs face in effecting policy, the International Seafood Sustainability Foundation formed in 2009 as a coalition of the RFMOs, tuna industry MNCs, scientists, and the World Wildlife Fund for Nature (WWF). Although its mission is tuna conservation, blatantly absent from its scope is any mention of bluefin tuna, even though the Atlantic and southern species are the most critically threatened. The most likely reason for this omission is the difficulty in coming to an agreement about how to protect the species.

Through the United Nations, countries have made efforts to address the common goods issue of the ocean. Although the UN Convention on the Law of the Sea (UNCLOS) was not ratified until 1982, members passed a number of treaties subsequent to the first conference held in 1958, including one recognizing the need to address rights disputes and promote aquatic conservation.[34] The 1982 UNCLOS treaty offered substantial evidence of specific concerns for migratory species, requiring island and coastal states, as well as distant-water fishing countries, to take responsibility for tuna conservation.[35] Because the depletion of fish stocks has a direct effect on world food supplies, particularly in developing countries, the Food and Agriculture Organization (FAO) created the Committee on Fisheries (COFI) in 1965. The committee works with both the RFMOs and NGOs in an attempt to protect tuna.

## Conservation Strategies

Despite the attention paid to tuna by the RFMOs and other IGOs, states' self-interest continues to put the fish at risk. Attempts at conservation through setting quotas have proven ineffective, and monitoring, controlling, and surveillance efforts are plagued by illegal, unreported, and unregulated fishing. Thus far, states have resisted proposals to implement a new strategy of rights-based management. Regulatory cooperation, increased public awareness, and aquaculture offer potential ways to turn the odds in favor of tuna survival.

## Rights-Based Management

States' inability to agree to rights-based management with reasonable sustainability levels is a seemingly immovable barrier to tuna conservation. The problem is that as more vessels with bigger catch capacity fish dwindling stocks, competition increases. Instead of states committing to adopt conservation programs, the fishing industry pushes them to remove restrictions and avoid agreements that set limits. Enforcement efforts are challenged by state interests that outweigh desires to protect an endangered species. Different models can be used for conservation, but the biggest hurdle to implementing any strategy for this common goods dilemma is getting state buy-in. Regulation, thus far, has been through a combination of country-level management and IGOs.

Attempts have been made over the years to manage fish stocks, but RFMOs have largely been limited to an open-access type of management whereby any vessel from anywhere in the world can fish in a given regulated region so long as set catch limits are respected. The primary problem with open-access fishing is a "race to fish," which pits vessel against vessel as each tries to catch as much as possible before the total fishery quota limit has been reached. Glutting the market early on depresses prices, only to cause them to spike later, when shortages occur.[36] Other methods have included asking states to voluntarily freeze fishing activities, fix a number of days fishers are permitted to fish during a season, and establish quotas.[37] For example, when Italy closed its own waters to tuna fishing, it entered into a bilateral agreement with Libya to fish in that country's waters.[38] These approaches only serve to cause hostilities and provoke heavier fishing in nonregulated zones.

A lack of uniform regulations also opens fisheries to vessels flying FOCs. Instituting consistent regional fisheries policies whereby ports refuse to buy fish from FOC vessels gives fishers an incentive to follow the rules. This approach, however, would disadvantage fishers from countries that offer FOC registry.[39] RFMOs would collectively deny these vessels access to ports in order to bar those taking advantage of FOC status. Nonparty states that sell FOCs would thus have an incentive to join RFMOs, which would in turn eliminate the benefits derived from FOC registry.

RFMOs are also in a position to tackle poaching and laundering. Discouraging FOC registry will address these issues in part. Cooperation on data coordination and vessel monitoring will also help to ban violators from entering ports. Cooperation would benefit all parties involved by reducing free riding. Susceptibility to corruption in developing countries, however, will continue to pose a problem as long as poorly paid enforcement agents can be bribed.

Difficulties with the open-access approach have led RFMOs to recognize that rights-based management is the only effective means to implement conservation policies for tuna. RBM offers promise because this approach relies on the market to determine the value of access, whether through a specific number of licenses or catch limits. This easy-to-implement system would offer a sustainable way to guarantee tuna conservation while at the same time allowing the fishing industry to continue to operate. States, however, are at a stalemate over who should manage these rights and how to define, and thus distribute, them.

**Ownership and rights distribution** Because open-access management has only led to a depletion of tuna stocks, finding another means to administer a system of allocation is imperative for preserving this common good. One of the biggest hurdles standing in the way of states adopting a conservation strategy is the dispute over who should manage ownership rights to fish stocks.

An RBM program would need to establish "ownership" (i.e., who manages the rights and the fishery) and how the rights are distributed. Three potential parties could control ownership and manage fish stocks: states, RFMOs, or corporations. Two different means to allocate rights may be used, though licensing is arguably less effective than setting quotas.

**Licenses** A fixed number of licenses would have to be determined by the owner based on the projected harvest numbers for the season, factoring in how many fish could be caught while still leaving a sustainable supply. The number of licenses would be limited by the predicted catch per vessel. Each state, RFMO, or corporation would have a number of licenses to sell. Vessels would need licenses for each region in which they fished. An option might be included so that owners who wanted to sell their boats could transfer licenses to the new owner. As with open-access fishing, one problem is that different vessels have very different catch capabilities. Some vessels' size and equipment give them a greater advantage, increasing the difficulty of predicting the number of fish each vessel might catch. This approach would clearly disadvantage small fishers and favor corporate trawlers.

**Capacity quotas** Limited capacity approaches conservation from the angle of total allowable catch (TAC) by setting quotas. Each year, states, RFMOs, or corporations would sell TAC shares to vessels, setting a limit for each species of regulated fish. A clause could be included allowing fishers to sell their shares with their vessels (called an individual transferrable quota).

The fishery owner would be responsible for fixing a number of catch shares to sell. The maximum possible amount of fish that could be caught while allowing the fish to sustainably replenish would determine the number of shares that could be sold. Each share would permit the vessel to catch a certain number of fish in a particular time frame. Other factors, such as vessel size, type of equipment, number of superfreezers, and so forth, would not factor into the equation because each fisher would be limited to a specified number of pounds for a particular species. Another advantage of the TAC model is that, because anyone can buy shares, environmental interest organizations could contribute to replenishing supplies by buying but not using shares.[40] This strategy would be less effective with the licensing scheme, which does not limit TAC.

**Reservations** GS states that have yet to take advantage of their EEZs, most often to due to insufficient technology and lack of foreign direct investment in their fishing industries, have reservations about RBM. Adopting a licensing scheme would disadvantage developing countries' fishers, whose vessels and equipment are far smaller and less sophisticated than those of the global north. Quotas would certainly offer a better management option, but GS island and coastal countries are reluctant to agree to RBM schemes because they want to develop their fisheries and do not want to sign an agreement that will bind them to catch limits.[41] Developing countries fear that when they do acquire the means to fully take advantage of this resource, they will be limited to less than others will have gotten in the interim.

The unfortunate irony of this position is that by foregoing agreements at a time when they cannot benefit from tuna fishing may mean that the fish will be extinct before they are in a position to tap the resource. Strategies are being considered to bring these countries on board with an RBM program.[42] One example involves setting an initial capacity limit that includes GS countries' access rights, even though they may not immediately opt to utilize them. GN countries would be able to use those rights until GS countries were able to do so, at which point the rights would be transferred back to the developing countries. This strategy offers a way to better manage the fisheries than open access, while allowing GS states to develop their fishers with impunity.

## Public Awareness

NGOs seek to draw attention to the threats facing tuna by educating the public and vendors about the effect of consumption on the future of the fish. Raising public awareness in the 1980s to encourage consumers to boycott non-dolphin-safe canned tuna was phenomenally successful in pressuring the US government to pass and stringently enforce bycatch legislation. Subsequent movements to "Give Swordfish a Break" and stop restaurants from serving Chilean sea bass also drew attention to the plight of these endangered species. To inform the public about the status of tuna, a number of organizations have compiled informational cards, websites, and even phone apps to let consumers know which fish are better or worse choices for the environment.

The Monterey Bay Aquarium Seafood Watch Program is one attempt by a conservation group to inform consumers about fish sustainability. By red-listing endangered fish and green-lighting those at sustainable levels, it helps consumers stay more informed about how their dietary choices affect the environment. The organization regularly updates its "wallet card" available online to consumers who want to know how to minimize their impact on ocean life but still enjoy seafood. With Fishphone, the Blue Ocean Institute will send consumers text messages about their fish choices, letting them know whether a given variety of tuna, for instance, will be one of the last in the sea or instead comes from a healthy stock. To avert disaster, Fishphone offers alternatives of more sustainable options as well as information for those concerned about mercury levels or carcinogens.

NGOs have worked tirelessly to inform the public about the plight of the tuna. Greenpeace ships actively protest pirate fishing. Tuna-org acts as a clearinghouse for the RFMOs. The Pew Foundation conducts independent research to keep governments honest and to pressure legislators. The WWF was integral in founding the International Seafood Sustainability Foundation, a consortium of the RFMOs, governments, the tuna industry, and scientists working to coordinate conservation efforts by pooling research and resources to better manage tuna stocks, reduce bycatch, and promote ecosystem viability.

**Table 7.1  Monterey Bay Aquarium's Seafood Watch "Wallet Card" Excerpt**

| Best Choices | Long-Line | Purse Seine | Troll/Pole | Region |
|---|---|---|---|---|
| Albacore | | | X | Pacific Northwest |
| Bigeye | | | X | US Atlantic |
| Skipjack | | | X | Worldwide |
| Yellowfin | | | X | Pacific, US Atlantic |
| *Alternative Choices* | Long-Line | Purse Seine | Troll/Pole | Region |
| Albacore | X | | | Hawaii |
| Bigeye | X | | | US Atlantic |
| Skipjack | X | | | Hawaii, US Atlantic |
| Yellowfin | | | X | Worldwide except Pacific, US Atlantic |
| *Avoid* | Long-Line | Purse Seine | Troll/Pole | Region |
| Albacore | X | | | All except Hawaii |
| Bigeye | X | | | All except US Atlantic |
| Skipjack | X | X | | Imported |
| Yellowfin | X | X | X | All except Hawaii and US Atlantic |

Table created by author from information from "Buyer's Guide," Monterey Bay Aquarium, http://www.montereybayaquarium.org/cr/seafoodwatch/web/sfw_regional.aspx (accessed July 13, 2013).

> ## Recipe Box
>
> ### Red Fish, Green Fish, Phone a Fish
>
> So, now that you are concerned about tuna conservation, but not so concerned that you intend to stop eating tuna, what do you do? If you want to be sure you are not about to contribute to the extinction of a species when ordering dinner or shopping at the fish counter, print out a copy of the Monterey Bay Aquarium's "Buyer's Guide" or, better yet, install "Fishphone" on your mobile device to get virtually instant information with the Blue Ocean Institute's Guide to Ocean-Friendly Seafood application.
>
> Now that you know something about tuna, how helpful might a chart or a text message be? For example, if you want to eat sashimi, what option will you choose? The disadvantage of these information sources is that it is often necessary to know not only the fish's origin but the means by which it was caught. Will a Japanese menu give this information? How about the chef at your local sushi bar? Despite the best efforts of conservation organizations to raise awareness and inform consumers, effecting change can prove difficult. What do you think might offer a more effective means of tuna conservation?

Although public awareness is important for effecting change, NGOs alone cannot save tuna. The fishing industry and pirate fishers need economic incentives to adhere to conservation practices, which NGOs are not in a position to offer. Governments are better positioned to offer positive incentives and punishments that can promote sustainability. NGOs do contribute a bottom-up approach to conservation by providing information and mobilizing people to pressure governments in their policy decisions. Imagine if consumers effectively lobbied to push the tuna industry to provide tuna-safe tuna, in the way that MNCs were pressured to produce dolphin-safe tuna.

### Is Aquaculture the Answer?

Aquaculture is a type of farming that raises fish in captivity. This alternative has proven very effective in farming shrimp and salmon, making both more widely available without endangering wild populations. Two very different approaches to aquaculture are taken in tuna farming: tuna ranching and tuna breeding. The first, not aquaculture per se, actually undermines tuna conservation, whereas the latter may help to revive depleted stocks. Tuna ranching rounds up juvenile fish and puts them in big, deep pens, where they are raised and fattened before being shipped to market. Ranches need endless supplies of fish food, including sardines, herring, mackerel, and anchovies. Because fish ordinarily require a lot of food anyway, extra food to fatten up them means supplying even more feed than usual.

Operations started in the early 1990s in Australia and a few Mediterranean countries. Farm fishing is very resource intensive, requiring ranchers to catch the tuna, as well as the smaller fish to feed them. Pens require daily maintenance and cleaning. Even when pens are cleaned, farmed tuna are still at greater risk for diseases and parasites. Because farm fishing necessarily restricts their area of movement, tuna are susceptible to "captivation bubbles," which cause harmful lesions.[43] The fish are also at high risk during storms, as they are trapped in pens, where they can drown if debris gets caught in their gills.[44]

Fish farming presents a difficulty when quota systems are in place because monitors have difficulty identifying whether the fish coming to port have originated from a fish farm. The lack of traceability presents problems with calculating countries' compliance with quotas. Another problem associated with tuna ranching is that juveniles are caught and raised in captivity, never having a chance to mature and reproduce. Bluefin have a greater chance of survival in the wild.

Tuna breeding is the result of assiduous research to spawn and raise tuna in captivity. Breeding has proven very difficult since tuna are migratory fish by nature, so successfully raising them in captivity has been challenging. Another problem that has made breeding inefficient thus far is the amount of fish food needed. Even without fattening the tuna, the ratio of twenty pounds of fish feed to one pound of harvested flesh makes breeding economically nonviable.[45] Alternatives such as vegetable-based feed pellets are being tested, and trials are underway to develop fish that do not require fish meal.[46] Until these alternatives are perfected, wild fish sources will continue to be tapped to feed the tuna.

Perhaps because the country is the target of much criticism, Japan has been the leader in researching viable tuna-breeding methods. Since the late 1970s, researchers at Kinki University have worked on "closed-farm" breeding projects, starting with eggs from wild fish to produce fish spawned in captivity. Researchers have been able to successfully reproduce three generations of its Kindai bluefin species and have also released captivite-bred fish into the wild.

In 2011, the university sold the first batch of offspring to a Toyota subsidiary.[47] Tuna Dream Goto will manage feeding operations for the three years it will take for the fish to be ready for market. Similar strides in research have been made in the European Union, where scientists discovered a hormone-free way to successfully spawn Atlantic bluefin in captivity; in blind taste tests, it was found to be as palatable as the wild variety.[48] Although closed-farm tuna are spawned and are not wild juveniles placed in captivity, they are still pen raised and thus subject to the same problems affecting ranched tuna. On the positive side, however, adding spawned tuna to the market should help to take some of the pressure off wild tuna, allowing fish stocks to replenish.

## CONCLUSION

Desire to fill an increasing demand in the market encourages fishers to catch more tuna. Because demand is greater than supply, prices rise, encouraging more fishers to catch more tuna. The immediate reward of payment out-weighs longer-term concerns about exhausting the resource. Even the threat of depletion to the point of extinction has not been enough of an incentive to motivate states to cooperate on conservation policies. States join the RFMOs, abide by UNCLOS, and support planning measures by the FAO's COFI—all indications of their concerns about conservation. Even the fishing industry recognizes the need for conservation, realizing that its own demise lies in its failure to protect tuna, but it lacks the economic incentive to adopt conserva-tion methods if everyone is not bound by the same rules. Convincing states to collectively adopt sustainable measures requires that they set aside immediate self-interest dictated by economic pressures, public opposition, and business interests. Without full cooperation on this common goods issue, cheaters will continue to satisfy their own immediate desires and undermine the possibility of everyone's reaping the benefits of conservation efforts.

Improved fishing techniques have not just threatened the extinction of tuna; sophisticated methods have also endangered the livelihoods and lives of people in developing countries. Demand for tuna ripples down the food chain, so to speak, as consumers in developed countries get the best, most expensive fish, whereas those in developing countries struggle to make ends meet. Fish stocks targeted by traditional fishers are becoming depleted by fleet fishers, who use them as bait for long-line tuna fishing and feed in aquaculture. Diets of people in poorer coastal countries, particularly in the South Pacific, are also suffering. People in fishing villages need to make money, so they have to sell the better fish at market. The dwindling size and availability of fish means the families of fishers rely on even smaller fish in their own meals. The smaller fish that were once the feed for bigger fish are now a dietary staple for poorer people. With fleets taking bigger fish to bait long-lines for tuna, and with tuna ranchers and breeders catching larger fish for tuna farming, coastal people are reduced to eating smaller, less desirable fish as their source of protein. As local economies have fewer fish to sell, small island countries bring in less hard currency from foreign exchange.

Fishing villagers are among those who support fishing restrictions. One such village in Oma, Japan, wants the government to regulate catch limits in its waters, which the same companies pressuring the government not to set limits are rapidly depleting.[49] These villagers depend on tuna fishing for their livelihoods. They recognize humans' symbiotic relationship with the oceans and the need to respect their capacity and not overtap their resources. Tuna fishers, in particular, recognize the need to limit overfishing since the migratory fish take longer to reproduce and mature. If the fish are caught before they can reproduce or are not allowed to grow to a reasonable size, everyone loses, resulting in a tragedy of the commons.

Governments are in a unique position to deal most effectively with fishery-management issues. Administrations can pressure legislators to pass conservation-friendly policies and allocate funding to support MCS. Legislators are also in a position to eliminate fishing industry subsidies, which disrupt supply and demand. Governments have any number of agencies staffed with well-equipped personnel who have the expertise to conduct research into managing fisheries. States are also armed to defend their territories, meaning that they can police their waters. This unilateral approach, however, is much more feasible when dealing with species within the boundaries of one country's territory or maybe even when bordering just one other country. Efforts to revive flagging stocks of swordfish in the United States, mussels in New Zealand, and the *locos abalone* in Chile have proven successful, largely due to their limited movement within each country's EEZ.[50]

Governance of a highly migratory fish, however, requires more than unilateral government attention, as conservation is contingent on the global cooperation of sovereign states. Both the United States and the European Union have attempted to tackle tuna-conservation issues but are constrained by how effective one country or small coalition can be in having a serious impact on a global public goods issue. Their unwillingness to commit to an issue, knowing others will take advantage of their conservation efforts, is discouraging. The US government determined in 2011 that the Atlantic bluefin was not endangered enough to be protected under its Endangered Species Act[51] and is waiting to see whether ICCAT will implement stricter international regulatory measures,[52] despite much evidence that the fish is critically under threat of overfishing. The EU countries, as a coalition, have implemented a different strategy, which may prove effective but is still susceptible to free riders. Better regulation of ports is stopping FOC vessels from selling their tuna. Unfortunately, however, even this strategy can be undermined by registered vessels that buy the catch from FOC fishers and take it to port.

Aquaculture has proven an effective means of farming shrimp and salmon. Whether tuna can be successfully harvested through breeding to provide a sufficient alternative to open-sea tuna remains to be seen. Tuna ranching, or the rounding up of juvenile fish to fatten for market, is currently the more common method of aquaculture, which actually does more harm than good to conservation efforts. Given the fish's increase in popularity, growth in the world population, and improvements in technology, the long-term sustainability of tuna is threatened. Countries need to find a way to compromise in the interest of conserving tuna if extinction is to be avoided.

This two-level game of balancing international and domestic affairs requires a more complex strategy. States need to find a way to cooperate over rights and management issues, working through the IGOs, NGOs, and MNC network that have already emerged to tackle MCS issues. States must tap into the domestic resources already at their disposal, while working to reduce industry subsidies. But these efforts need to be complemented by consumer education and pressure on industries (from restaurants to supermarket chains to fleet operators) to adopt sustainable practices. This multidimensional strategy tackles the problem from different directions, increasing the possibility of saving the tuna from extinction.

## CHAPTER QUESTIONS

1. What changes over time have led to threats of tuna extinction?
2. How do fishers in GN and GS countries view fishing differently?

3. With so many compelling reasons to adopt rights-based management, why do states have yet to implement this type of strategy for tuna conservation?

4. Is aquaculture the answer to meeting the increasing demand for tuna?

# CHAPTER 8

———— ∞∞∞ ————

# FOOD FOR THOUGHT

## *The Export-Driven Global Food System*

Most people are not aware of their part in the global food system. Some unique points separate the food items highlighted in this book, yet they are connected by producers and the issues that arise from being part of the global food system. Governments set trade policies to protect their industries and consumers. Multinational corporations (MNCs) have a profound impact on shaping the global food supply in terms of production, processing, and retailing goods, as well as seeking out labor, land, and commodities to improve their bottom lines. Intergovernmental organizations (IGOs) work to implement regulations that set global standards governing food-production policies. These organizations are positioned to negotiate between states and corporations, yet constrained by the sovereignty of their state members. The collision of these interests has sparked attempts by nongovernmental organizations (NGOs) to hold governments and corporations accountable for their actions by raising public awareness about social and environmental injustices in hopes of drawing enough attention to encourage change.

The risks and rewards of the global food system are best understood in the context of the themes explored throughout the food-item chapters. Desire to control the spice trade first inspired Europeans to seek the source of the fabled Spice Islands, laying the foundation for a global food system. The effects of colonialism and the global economic divide that grew out of it help to explain the consequences of globalization and the related transnational issues. Labor, health, and environmental issues challenge governments. When pressured to address these issues, they may turn to IGOs to facilitate cooperation for policy coordination. NGOs also respond to these issues, putting pressure on countries and IGOs with the hope of actually seeing the problems not only addressed but resolved. NGOs, in turn, keep the pressure on governments and their institutions to respond to transnational problems.

The global food system holds risks but also offers rewards. On one hand, the self-interested nature of states, corporations, and farmers involved in food production results in conflicts of interest that cause transnational economic, political, social, and environmental problems. On the other hand, globalization of the food supply offers the possibility of not only feeding more people but also raising the standard of living of more people through greater integration into the neoliberal economic market. This chapter examines the actors and factors that shape and are shaped by increased involvement in the global food system and the benefits and disadvantages of being part of the international food chain.

## PRODUCTION IN THE GLOBAL FOOD SYSTEM

Production in the global food system involves both risks and rewards. Countries, MNCs, and farmers are involved in feeding the world, though each is driven by self-interests. States, in obligation to their citizens, are concerned about feeding the domestic population. Global north (GN) countries are better positioned in that malnutrition and poverty are much less constraining factors when determining food policy. Corporations are involved in the global food system to find the most efficient way to increase their bottom lines. Farmers are at the whim of governments and corporations as they struggle to earn a living. Dependence on earnings from agriculture exports unfortunately perpetuates global south (GS) countries' and farmers' reliance on cash crops, necessitating that food for domestic production take a back seat to crops grown for export.

## States

Food security is an ongoing challenge for most countries in the world. As reliance on cash crops is so high due to developing countries' struggle to industrialize, GS governments encounter difficulty supporting policies that secure domestic food availability. Developing countries rely heavily on cash crops, using the best land for exports. The UN Food and Agriculture Organization estimates that one in eight people suffer from chronic undernourishment; the overwhelming majority of these people live in developing countries.[1] Without question, the best land in developing countries is designated for growing cash crops over food for domestic consumption.

In the neoliberal economic market, governments seek to promote and protect the interests of their laborers, industries, and consumers. These policies privilege domestic production over imports. In the global food system, these policies are construed as barriers to open trade that give preferential treatment to domestic markets. Government subsidies to farmers are a hotly contested issue in global food politics because they give producers, usually from the GN, an advantage in the global marketplace. Attempts by intergovernmental organizations to compel governments to eliminate supports are met with resistance. In the spice industry, for example, the International Pepper Community (IPC) attempts to coordinate government policies and member countries' production to guarantee a consistent market return on peppercorn sales. When countries feel they benefit from the terms of the agreement, they are more likely to cooperate. By agreeing to sell a certain amount of pepper, member countries can receive a more consistent price. An upswing in the market price might convince them to exercise their sovereignty, perhaps by selling more pepper than they agreed to, in order to reap the short-term benefit of getting the higher price. For the IPC to help stabilize returns over the long run, however, producing countries have to set aside their short-term self-interests and focus on the long-term benefits of cooperation.

✳Many GS countries encountered financial difficulties when transitioning to independent statehood after colonialism. When they had to turn to the International Monetary Fund for money, cuts in government subsidies supporting farmers was one condition for borrowing. Because the mission of the World Trade Organization (WTO) is to open trade between countries, which at times means settling disputes over perceived barriers, GS countries now have recourse for pushing GN countries to also eliminate farmer subsidies. The WTO has repeatedly ruled that these subsidies violate international law and therefore need to be eliminated in order to level the playing field to give GS countries a fairer chance to compete in the world market.

The WTO has the power to fine and to permit retaliatory tariff measures to force states to comply with global trade rules. Although countries reserve the right to decide whether to accept the WTO's decisions, they have compelling reasons to follow the organization's rulings, ranging from maintaining a good international image, succumbing to peer pressure, and minimizing economic losses. Despite these incentives, GN countries find it difficult to eliminate supports. The US Congress struggles to gain a consensus to revise the Farm Bill, dictated by prevailing reelection concerns. And even as the government is required to eliminate direct payments to farmers, funds are shifting to crop insurance, bypassing direct payments. This indirect support offers advantages to American farmers that GS countries can rarely afford. These practices put Brazilian soy farmers, for example, at a comparative disadvantage in relation to US producers.

The European Union has made the most progress in the GN in reducing benefits under the Common Agricultural Policy; yet lack of cooperation between member states forestalls total elimination. Subsidies paid out to European processors in the tomato industry undermine the potential for Ghana to earn profits by processing its own tomatoes. Fishers in developing countries are similarly disadvantaged by EU subsidies going to those in the fishing industry.

The Japanese lag the farthest behind in reducing agricultural subsidies. For decades, high payouts to rice growers, the biggest recipients of subsidies in the world, have confronted Japanese prime ministers. This hot-button political issue remains to be resolved, as the controlling parties have had difficulty gaining consensus to reduce payments.

States enter the neoliberal free market despite these risks. Although GS countries face an uphill battle against the GN, IGOs have made progress toward breaking down trade barriers. Some countries have even been able to take advantage of their agricultural production to support industrialization. China and Brazil have used the increasing demand for agricultural commodities in the global food system to facilitate development. Mass production in food commodities has supported export-led growth. This success has been contingent upon political stability, of which well-fed people are a key component. The expectation is that as more people become exposed to and immersed in the global marketplace, similar progress can be made in their standard of living.

## MNCs

MNCs undisputedly play an integral role in the global food system, which means their actions have a direct impact on people and the planet. The success of MNCs is contingent upon finding new consumers and markets for investment. Corporations have leverage over smaller local businesses. MNCs are able to co-opt them and, in the case of suppliers, to set demand and prices for goods. The global food supply chain offers corporations the chance to capitalize on the improving standard of living in the GS, particularly in emerging economies, to tap into a new customer base. To take advantage of this opportunity, MNCs have to find creative ways to integrate into GS countries. One tactic they use is appealing to local tastes. Indians go for spicier, curried Lays potato chips, Chinese prefer less sugary and more exotic green tea–flavored Oreos, and Thais demand the more intensely flavored Extreme BBQ Doritos.

Another strategy used by MNCs is establishing ties with local producers to secure supply. Connections with cocoa plantations in West Africa, for example, guarantee consistent flavor of the beans as well as a reliable source through investments in those communities. MNCs also open processing plants in developing countries, which has a dual benefit. Having plants where crops are grown allows corporations to streamline the process, as in the case of soy production in Brazil for exports, animal feed, and biofuel. A second effect of investing locally is an increase in the number of paid laborers and thus the potential consumer base.

Conglomerates have an incentive to invest in ventures that offer rewards through economies of scale, whether through ownership of processing operations or provision of multiple products in a supply chain, such as seeds, fertilizer, herbicides, and pesticides. The connection between an agribusiness conglomerate such as Monsanto and homegrown tomatoes might seem distant, but the same scientists developing seeds, soil, and fertilizer for the commercial farmers also develop products for the consumer market.

The legacy of colonialism has facilitated the globalization of the food supply, positioning GN MNCs to dominate, supported by neocolonial policies that reinforce GS disparities. The system's structure perpetuates exploitation and underdevelopment of developing countries in the global food system. Shifting the risks to rewards in the food chain requires GS producers to engage in sustainable agriculture, moving away from dependence on a few cash crops to diversify in a way that encourages foreign direct investment and facilitates industrialization.

The vast majority of corporations in the world come from GN countries, derived from a technological advantage rooted in colonialism. This advantage is evident in the food system, from Mitsubishi's enormous refrigerated tuna-fishing vessels to Monsanto's sophisticated assembly line of soy-processing equipment. MNCs also have the advantage of having long ago established brand-name products, making it difficult for small companies, such as Divine Chocolate, a Ghanaian farmer-owned cocoa cooperative, to compete internationally with chocolate giants like Hershey's, Cadbury, and Nestlé. Spice producers are similarly situated, competing for shelf space with companies, like McCormick's, that have very deep pockets and loyal customers.

MNCs need an economic incentive to address transnational issues, as they are in business to make money and face fierce competition. Regularly blamed for the impact of free market policies on the environment and people in developing countries, MNCs necessarily engage in philanthropic endeavors to show the public how much they care about people and the planet. The bottom line, however, dictates company policies. Unless everyone plays by the same rules, companies will continue to exploit land and labor to make a profit. Only when MNCs uniformly adopt standards, such as pledging to buy only ethically sourced cocoa, do they have an economic incentive to change. With a minority of consumers aware of child labor abuses in the cocoa industry, only a pact between MNCs to play by the same rules will eliminate the abuses. If Hershey's continues to buy the less expensive, uncertified cocoa beans, they would have an unfair advantage over producers who pay more and necessarily increase their product prices to make up the difference. In the tomato industry, only when companies reached a consensus about the penny-per-pound proposal were they willing to take the hit, as all buyers were equally affected. If McDonald's had to raise its prices to compensate for paying more per pound for tomatoes, so did its competitors.

MNCs' business model depends on finding new places to invest their money and find consumers as GN markets become saturated. GS countries benefit as corporations seek out cheaper labor and land sources for production, ensuring job creation. As people's situations in developing countries improve, pressure on the government for political rights and social benefits increases. The increasing number of strikes and protests in authoritarian countries like China and transitioning countries like Brazil is evidence of their governments' willingness to tolerate these demands for better conditions.

## Farmers and Fishers

Farmers and fishers encounter any number of challenges as producers in the global food system. Producers in the GN benefit from stable governments, developed institutions, and social safety nets, putting competitors in the GS at a comparative disadvantage. MNCs have a huge impact on commodity prices as buyers of food and because they are increasingly getting involved in the farming end of agribusiness. Farmers and fishers are also affected by economic trends and natural disasters, though these tend to hit those in the GS harder as developing countries' governments lack the social safety nets available to producers in GN countries.

Farmers are subject to government policies that give an advantage to large-scale farmers and even to small farm owners within the GN over those in the GS. Government subsidies, tariffs, and nontariff policies in developed countries make it difficult for GS farmers to compete on the international market. The WTO's Dispute Settlement Body has given GS countries leverage they lacked prior to its inception, better positioning GS farmers to be globally competitive. But they are increasingly competing with corporate farming that can produce on a considerably larger economy of scale. This disparity is apparent in soybean production, as MNCs can afford to buy huge tracts of land, invest in the most cutting-edge equipment, and rely on the most scientifically advanced seeds and chemicals to produce more plants per acre than traditional farming methods.

Many farmers and fishers rely on MNCs to buy their produce and seafood. In the GN, small family farms are increasingly giving way to big agribusiness. Those who opt to keep the family farm struggle to compete. As international grocers push out local shops in emerging economies, farmers in those countries find themselves on the same treadmill as their GN counterparts. MNC leverage allows corporations to set prices and standards for commodities, forcing farmers to find ways to cut costs to make ends meet. Although not the only contributing factor to the poor work conditions and abuses of tomato pickers and cocoa plantation workers, increasing pressure to accept less per pound complicates addressing human-security issues.

Fishers find themselves in a similar situation. GN owners of small vessels are also on the treadmill as they regularly invest in more sophisticated equipment, taking on more debt in the process. GS fishers are losing ground to megaships capable of catching more than three thousand tons of tuna in a single voyage thousands of miles from land and safely refrigerating it until it reaches port. In one day, a corporate vessel can net about 165 tons of tuna, the equivalent of 165 elephants.[2] That is enough tuna to fill over 10 million cans! The sad reality for all fishers is that unless states, corporations, and fishers come to an agreement on realistic catch limitations, everyone will lose.

With increased global interdependence on crop production, natural disasters have a greater impact on more people because they affect both food availability and prices. Disasters affect those in the GS even more adversely because developing countries are not able to provide farmers and fishers with the same level of price supports—if any—as GN countries. When a tsunami wiped out cinnamon tree groves in Sri Lanka, lack of government support meant a loss of livelihood for not only the farmers but also the peelers who cut the bark from the trees. A beetle infestation in Thailand drove up world prices for coconut oil and coconut milk by 134 percent in 2011.[3] Flooding in West Africa regularly creates food shortages, thereby increasing prices, making Senegal and Burkina Faso, among others, heavily dependent on food imports. Meanwhile, droughts and heat waves in the United States and eastern Europe in the summer of 2012 pushed maize and soybean prices to record highs. Policies in the United States requiring the use of corn for ethanol biofuel production affect world maize prices. Farmers are encouraged to grow corn over other crops, knowing they will have a guaranteed buyer. In addition to a rise in corn prices for staple foods like tortillas in Latin America, which led to food riots, this policy subsequently affected the price of other staple crops. Poor countries in Africa were hit the hardest. In South Sudan, the price of sorghum rose by as much as 220 percent.[4] Increased crop prices in Malawi prompted hawkers to sell mouse kabobs to make money while providing cheap food for hungry people.[5] Spikes in food prices push more people into poverty. Concerns over increased food prices in 2012 prompted the G-20 to consider an international emergency meeting to address food security for people in developing countries.

Price volatility causes a boom-and-bust cycle that undermines development in GS countries by dually affecting the availability and cost of food for consumers and the amount paid to farmers, fishers, and workers. Poor people in developed countries are most affected by price increases because so much of their budget goes toward food costs. A barely noticeable increase in tomato prices in Great Britain would put the staple food out of reach for people in India. Spice and cocoa prices have proved volatile over time. In the cocoa industry, for example, prices shot up in 2010 in response to a coup d'état in Ivory Coast, encouraging farmers in Cameroon to grow cocoa. Once these crops mature, however, the added volume could cause prices to drop if demand does not match the increase in supply.

Being a farmer or fisher is risky business; yet many continue this work because they lack other options to earn a living. GN producers are often so heavily invested financially that they are discouraged from changing jobs. People in the GS are particularly limited due to the lack of social safety nets. Governments lack the capital to invest in job-training programs and unemployment benefits that might otherwise encourage a change of occupation. Because developing countries depend so heavily on agriculture as a source of income, they face similar challenges. Without the support to industrialize, they also continue to rely on farming and fishing, with little incentive to diversify.

## SUSTAINABLE DEVELOPMENT IN THE GLOBAL FOOD SYSTEM

Sustainable development is an approach to economic growth that does not compromise the planet and its population. Finding ways to improve the economic situation for people in the GS requires promoting human and environmental security. Although the GS tends to be the focus of sustainable development discussions, GN corporations and consumers have a considerable impact on production practices in developing countries. For instance, competition between corporations to offer the best-tasting, least expensive candy bars impacts the price of cocoa beans. Plantation owners, in response, may have to resort to farming and labor practices that are detrimental to the planet and workers.

Production of any of the food items discussed in the book threatens either deforestation or overfishing because farmers and fishers are driven by the insatiable demands of the consumer market. Increased competition forces producers to make cuts to be more competitive, which in the cocoa and tomato industries results in labor abuses. As the global standard of living rises and consumers have more disposable income, a sustainable approach to supplying the world's food is even more important, yet more difficult to achieve. The biggest threat to sustainable development comes from the growing demand for meat. Increasing production in the livestock and aquaculture sectors threatens the planet with higher methane levels, deforestation to meet feed requirements, and pollution that threatens water supplies.

The simplest solution to saving the planet is for people to forgo meat. If more people in the world opted for a vegan diet, exclusively eating plant-based foods and eschewing meat, dairy, and egg products, the population would be better positioned to address any number of global issues, ranging from food shortages to climate change, from chronic disease to water scarcity. The impact of an animal-product-based diet is staggering:[6]

- Thirty percent of land in the world is used to raise livestock.
- Seventy percent of all agricultural land supports feeding livestock.
- Livestock production is a major contributor to freshwater pollution, freshwater shortage, increased runoff, and decreased water tables.
- More greenhouse gases are emitted from livestock production than are produced by transportation.
- Raising livestock contributes to deforestation, land degradation, and loss of biodiversity (e.g., livestock grazing reduced previously forested land in the Amazon by 70 percent).
- Protein from meat requires eleven times more fossil fuels and one hundred times more water to produce than vegetable-based protein.
- Factory farming of animals in the United States uses 80 percent of the total supply of antibiotics administered in the country.[7]
- Production of one Quarter Pounder is responsible for emitting as much carbon dioxide into the atmosphere as driving a very fuel-efficient car ninety-two miles.[8]

Not only does eating a plant-based diet help the planet, but vegans suffer from far fewer diseases and are less likely to be obese. Think back to Chapter

1 and the statistics on rising rates of obesity and other diseases. Consumers in the GN would benefit from eating less meat and put fewer demands on the health-care system. People in the GS are better off not increasing meat consumption as they are already tackling developed-country-related health issues.

Sustainable development is often considered a GS concern as countries seek to improve their economic opportunities. GN countries, however, must also adopt planet- and people-friendly policies, especially because these countries are at an economic advantage as they have already industrialized and diversified their economies. Development disparities induced by colonization perpetuate global food-system norms that favor the GN, particularly its MNCs. Without an economic incentive to push for a sustainable-development approach in food production, human security and environmental conservation remain at risk.

Because GN countries are just as self-interested as GS countries when it comes to long-term strategies for human and environmental rights protections, countries form IGOs in an attempt to find a way to address global issues. The most fledgling of these serve as a forum for discussion with the hope of coming to a consensus on how to address the issues, but they often

---

## Recipe Box

### Take the "Meatless Monday" Challenge

The Johns Hopkins Bloomberg School of Public Health's Center for a Livable Future started the "Meatless Monday" campaign in 2003 in response to the rise in public health problems in the United States. The organization posed the challenge of going one day a week without eating any meat products. Cities, companies, and even schools have risen to the challenge to encourage citizens, employees, and students to give up meat for a day. Celebrities and politicos have taken up the cause including Ellen DeGeneres, Bill Clinton, and Bill Gates, though their motivations differ—love of animals, health, and sustainable development concerns, respectively. The campaign has since gained popularity in other GN countries, such as with Paul McCartney's MeatFreeMondays.org challenge in the United Kingdom. So, the next time you think about eating a bacon cheeseburger, consider the impact your dietary choice is having on your health and on the planet.

lack the means to compel members to act. Few IGOs hold the power that the WTO has to push countries into following the rules agreed on in the forum. The regional fishing management organizations are a perfect example of this dilemma because the short-term benefits continue to outweigh the potential long-term gains that accompany tuna conservation. They struggle to find a solution that countries can agree on, as the clock ticks toward Atlantic and southern bluefin extinction.

Sustainable development is contingent upon human security. As the standard of living improves, so does the likelihood that people will work to protect the environment. When people struggle to make ends meet, their first concern will always be self-preservation, and they will use the resources at their disposal to provide for their families. Ensuring human security requires minimizing labor abuses, improving health conditions, and ensuring food availability. The dilemma lies in finding a way to improve human security without irrevocably damaging the planet.

## Labor

Disparities between GN and GS countries facilitate the capitalist desire to exploit cheap labor that, at times, results in abuse and even human trafficking. From child slave labor in cocoa-producing West African states to immigrant worker abuses in tomato farming in GN countries, people around the world rely on the cheapest labor available to make ends meet. This situation is evident in the tomato and cocoa industries, where owners resort to exploiting and abusing laborers, in some cases going so far as to enslave them. Workers in developing countries and immigrant laborers in developed countries are willing to accept poor employment and living conditions in return for greater earning potential to support their families.

Where governments have the authority to act—for instance, in eliminating Worst Forms of Child Labor (WFCL) in Ghana and Ivory Coast or immigrant abuses in tomato farming in the United States and Italy—numerous factors affect their ability to address a domestic situation. For developing countries, lack of funding, trained personnel, and the effect of eliminating a cheap labor supply on rural families have a huge impact on states' effectiveness in implementing and enforcing policies. In the GN, immigrants' fear of deportation, the lack of rights for heavily relied-on migrant workers, and threats from employers interfere with well-developed legal systems' abilities to protect laborers. The lack of social services to provide education and training in skilled labor pushes workers to emigrate abroad for better pay. Workers consequently see GN countries as a better option for earning more money to support their families. The remittances sent home offer an incentive to risk migration.

Although committed to regulating labor standards, the International Labor Organization (ILO) is limited in its power to enforce international labor laws, as countries regularly disagree on minimum pay and work-condition guarantees. To address abuses in the cocoa industry, the ILO is working with governments, corporations, and NGOs through the International Cocoa Initiative, created by the Harkin-Engel Protocol. Government and public pressure to push MNCs to buy ethically sourced cocoa better positions the ILO to enforce international WFCL laws than is the case in the tomato industry, where migrant labor issues in the United States and Italy are regarded as domestic issues.

Although IGOs have the backing of governments, power for NGOs comes from public support. These organizations are often behind the public pressure that pushes countries and IGOs to act. In the case of migrant workers in Florida, an NGO grew out of grassroots efforts to raise public awareness about their work conditions. Language barriers prevented tomato pickers in Italy from starting their own organization. Instead, an Italian labor union pushed the government for rights for migrant workers.

## Food Availability

Food prices affect a population's ability to afford food, which is often directly tied to the price paid to farmers for their goods. In the case of spices, when spice restrictions were eliminated between Sri Lanka and India, Indian cinnamon farmers received less per pound, which meant they had less money to spend on food to feed their families. Even if the going rate for the commodity rises, earning producers more for their goods, the rising demand that led to the price increase will also affect domestic prices, making that item and others more expensive. People in fishing villages are dually affected by increased demand for tuna and loss of smaller fish used for bait and aquaculture feed.

Governments run the risk of political instability if people take to the streets to protest shortages and inflated prices, as they did across North Africa and the Middle East during the Arab Spring, demanding better food access.

Accounts of the uprisings rarely focused on the food-security concerns that drove people to protest. Rather, GN media tended to focus on the more abstract issues of democracy and rights. In reality, people were trying to draw attention to the concrete issues of food-price inflation, food shortages, and corruption affecting the food supply.

Food riots are not a new phenomenon. Cicero documented protests in ancient Rome.[9] Food rioting is a common reaction to both rising food prices and government policies. When a Texan attempted to control regional salt lakes in 1877, the indigenous people of the Guadalupe Mountains rioted. A similar episode occurred in British-controlled India in 1930 when Gandhi led the Salt March to protest the British salt tax. Rising corn prices due to the increased use of biofuels in the United States sparked the Mexican "tortilla riots" between 2007 and 2010. The public rioted to push the government to intervene in the tortilla industry to keep prices at an affordable level.[10] The "onion riots" in India in 2011 were a reaction to the high inflation that doubled prices for the staple food, pushing it beyond the reach of many households.[11]

People also take to the streets when governments are subjected to austerity programs as part of structural adjustment plans. Food protests were common in Latin America during the economic transition of the 1980s, which led

## Recipe Box

### Le Pain de la Révolution

Perhaps the most notable food riot recorded in history is remembered with the line "Qu'ils mangent du gateau s'ils n'ont pas de pain" ("Let them eat cake if they have no bread").

The phrase prompts images of French peasants demanding food from the monarch.

Although scholars aver that Marie Antoinette never actually said these words, they live on as evidence of the harsh times that sparked the bread riots and, ultimately, the French Revolution. Food shortages not only contributed to massive political upheaval but also led to the Reign of Terror, with its mass executions and beheadings, including those of Louis XVI and his wife, Marie Antoinette. Food riots continue today as a means to draw attention to food shortages and to demand political change and governmental accountability.

many families to combine their food through soup kitchens to stretch the little they had. The lack of foodstuffs is considered a contributing factor to the fall of the Soviet Empire, as bread riots turned out not to be a thing of the past. As recently as 2012, in a different twist on food riots, the Greeks took to the streets throwing yogurt as a way to demonstrate against what they deemed harsh conditions in exchange for economic bailout funds. That same year, people flooded the streets of Iran to protest the increased price of chicken, a direct result of economic sanctions against the country.

More food riots are expected to occur in the coming years as global warming increasingly affects food production, making staple foods less affordable to people in developing countries. The Indian government is trying to forestall unrest with its plan to provide cheap food through increased subsidies. Although criticized as a scheme by the ruling party to win election seats, a food-security ordinance was enacted to provide cheap grain to poor people. Each month about 800 million people in both rural and urban areas will receive subsidized wheat and millet.[12] Some argue, however, that the costs to the government are too high, raising the question of whether the effort to prevent food riots will inevitably cause them.

## Health

Human security in both the GN and the GS is tied to the global food system. As the standard of living improves worldwide, people have greater access to meat and processed foods. The livelihood of MNCs depends on selling more products at competitive prices while incurring the lowest possible costs. Consumers are addicted to, susceptible to, and reliant on processed foods for a variety of reasons. MNCs create an array of processed foods that offer new taste sensations, ready-made meals, and on-the-go snacks. They cater to affluent adults and people struggling to make ends meet. The growing global obesity problem is in no small way the result of brilliant advertising campaigns and willingness to send sales representatives to shops in remote villages to secure customers. Even countries with populations suffering from malnutrition struggle to deal with increasing rates of heart disease, cancer, and type 2 diabetes associated with obesity. The global food system is heavily influenced by MNCs that simultaneously increase the possibility of feeding more people on the planet and threaten the health of those same people with value-added, calorie-dense foods that increase the risk of disease.

## The Environment

Concerns about sustainable development have given rise to a battle between those who want to take advantage of the economies of scale a globalized food system has to offer and those who fear the environmental and human toll of such a system. Critics point to the less-than-green impact of the technology behind food production. In order to increase yields of staple foods such as wheat, rice, and corn, seeds had to be genetically engineered to withstand the conditions of nonnative environments and to increase resistance to weeds and pests.

Genetically modified organisms (GMOs), also referred to as transgenic plants, are developed in laboratories using sophisticated techniques to create plants to better tolerate droughts, monsoons, and other extreme conditions. These seeds differ from the products of crossbreeding, which farmers have been doing since plants were domesticated. Soybeans developed to thrive in the very different soil and climate conditions of nonnative Brazil are considered a success story. The increasing demand for livestock feed certainly benefits from GMO seeds that produce higher yields and are less taxing on the land and water supplies. People question the long-term effects of consuming transgenic plants; yet modified seeds are far more productive and less environmentally destructive. Choosing locally grown organic food over imported supplies gives consumers peace of mind but endangers the livelihoods of farmers in developing countries.

Tomato production introduces two environmental challenges. The steady stream of tomatoes coming from southern Florida during the winter months to stock grocery store shelves and restaurants provides Americans with fresh tomatoes year-round. The sheer volume of chemicals needed to induce growth is an environmental trade-off, not to mention a threat to the health of tomato pickers. Hothouse production might seem like a better option, due to controlled conditions, but this method is not a green alternative, since producers in Canada, the Netherlands, and Turkey burn fossil fuels to power the hothouses.

Concerns abound that conventional farming will poison people and pollute the planet through the use of GMOs and agricultural chemicals. The locavore movement and organic farming, which have arisen in reaction to concerns about the environment, are in direct opposition to the efficiency of the globalized food system, as discussed in the soy chapter. Food-sovereignty movements in developing countries similarly seek to make farmers independent of corporate control by relying on organic, local foods. Although this is possible on a small scale to support pockets of communities in developing countries, considerably more land would be necessary to feed a world population relying exclusively on organic production. The current locavore trend in GN countries actually undermines access to food and development opportunities for people in the GS. These same practices also further contribute to the rise in obesity in the global north by increasing fresh food and meat prices. More land is necessary to yield comparable amounts of these products, which means dedicating more acreage to organic food (as well as grass-fed cows), thereby pushing up land prices. As a result, the price for conventional food will also increase, denying more consumers wholesome foods and driving them toward cheaper, processed foods.

Revisiting crops that are native to various climates and conditions would help to address environmental concerns. The rise of quinoa as a superfood has facilitated production in the Andean countries where it originates. Huge demand in the United States and rising demand in Europe give farmers an incentive to grow this indigenous crop, which is much better for the environment. Yet its global popularity might end up causing issues endemic to nonindigenous cash crops, including monocropping, deforestation, and switching to chemical fertilizers. Any number of plants native to Africa, including teff and sorghum, far better withstand the droughts and flooding that plague the continent than those imported to grow as cash crops. Sorghum and cassava, while staple foods for many people living in sub-Saharan Africa, have little export value. Although teff is also rising in popularity as a healthful ancient grain, these commodities are in less demand than nonindigenous moneymakers like wheat and cotton, which are far more taxing on the land. But if teff takes off, farmers run the same risk as those in the Andean region growing quinoa. Focusing on indigenous plants to grow as cash crops introduces environmental hazards that were not present when the crops were raised through polycropping on a smaller scale.

As a common good, tuna draws the attention of environmentalists concerned about the impact production has on the ecosystem. Overfishing limits reproduction, which threatens extinction. Taking tuna out of the food chain leads to increases in the number of jellyfish and other fish eaten by tuna. Global demand also impacts fishing communities' livelihoods. Tuna fishers in developing countries face the reality of depleted sources of not only tuna

## New-to-You Food: Quinoa

Quinoa (pronounced KEE-nwah) is touted as a superfood for being packed with nutrition, including protein, numerous vitamins and minerals, and antioxidants with anti-inflammatory compounds. Even though the yellowish-white variety resembles millet, a staple grain in many developing countries, quinoa is actually a pseudocereal. Unlike wheat and corn, the plant is a chenopod rather than a grass and is actually genetically closer to beets and spinach. Although the seeds are of primary interest, the leaves are also edible. Quinoa, however, easily substitutes for grains because its characteristics are similar. The seeds are also very versatile, as they can be sprouted and eaten raw, ground into flour for pasta and baking, cooked and used in salads, soups, and desserts, and even eaten as a dry cereal. Before use, quinoa must be thoroughly rinsed to remove the saponin, which would otherwise leave a very bitter taste. The saponin, however, can be used as a detergent and antiseptic.

The plant's name comes from the Quechua language, as quinoa originated in the Andes and remains a dietary staple there. People in the central Andes domesticated the plant and had been using it for thousands of years before the Spanish conquered the Incas. Quinoa was to the Incas what cocoa was to the Aztecs, because when mixed with fat, these "war balls" fueled Incan warriors, in the same way that cocoa sustained Aztec soldiers. When the conquistadors encountered quinoa, however, not only did the Spaniards not take it back to Europe with them, but their cultural influence also helped diminished the importance of the crop. For many centuries after colonization, quinoa was a food grown and eaten primarily by peasants.

Interest by the Bolivian government to change the image of quinoa as a poor person's food, coupled with increased demand for its export, has led to a resurgence in cultivation. Peru has also picked up on production, increasing by sixfold what was grown before quinoa became a valuable export crop.[1] The UN Food and Agriculture Organization declared 2013 the "International Year of the Quinoa" because of the grain-like seed's superfood qualities and because it is deemed a key to food security. The plant is easy to grow in climates with hot days and cool nights, requires very little processing, and is even endorsed by the World Health Organization for its nutritional value.

Although increased GN interest has been a boon for some farmers in the Andes, demand for quinoa has also caused problems, including rising domestic

but the smaller fish that tuna feed on, which is used as bait and harvested for tuna ranches. The traditional ranching method relies on rounding up the smaller fish to fatten the captive tuna. The new method taps the environment in a different way because it relies on vegetable-based fish pellets. A shift to "vegetarian" tuna introduces the same issue as livestock production by increasing agricultural demands.

prices and land rights disputes. Some reports have appeared in the news indicating that since peasants want to export the crop to earn cash, domestic prices have skyrocketed, forcing poorer people for whom quinoa has been a nutritional dietary staple to turn to less healthful foods.[2] Others counter this assertion by arguing that farmers are actually benefiting from the rising global demand for quinoa. Increasing demand improves their buying power, which offers a wider variety of foods and a move away from this staple food, even drawing some urban migrants back to their farmlands to grow quinoa to take advantage of higher earnings.[3] In the same way that obesity rates are on the rise in India and Mexico, increased buying power for Andean peasants is resulting in increased consumption of processed foods.

Andean farmers struggle to keep pace with global demand for the latest superfood. Increased production has raised concerns about overtaxing the fragile ecosystem as more crops are planted. Limited production on minimally treated soil, polycropping with other indigenous foods, and the traditional practice of grazing llamas to supply fertilizer for crops resulted in reliable harvests. In an effort to cash in on the higher prices being offered, farmers are escalating output but moving away from these methods. Attempts to grow the plant in the Rocky Mountains, an area offering the same climate conditions as the Andes, began in the 1980s. Although domestic production in the United States will help meet growing demand and reduce strain on the Andean ecosystem, as long as global interest continues to rise, Peruvians and Bolivians farming quinoa will suffer the same maladies as other cash crop farmers, unless they can find a way to sustainably increase yields.

1. "The Andes' New Cash Crop," *Economist*, May 12, 2012, http://www.economist.com/node/21554570.

2. "Quinoa's Global Success Creates Quandary at Home," *New York Times*, March 19, 2011, http://www.nytimes.com/2011/03/20/world/americas/20bolivia.html; "Can Vegans Stomach the Unpalatable Truth about Quinoa," *Guardian*, January 16, 2013, http://www.theguardian.com/commentisfree/2013/jan/16/vegans-stomach-unpalatable-truth-quinoa.

3. "Quinoa Should Be Taking Over the World. This Is Why It Isn't," *Washington Post*, July 11, 2013, http://www.washingtonpost.com/blogs/wonkblog/wp/2013/07/11/quinoa-should-be-taking-over -the-world-this-is-why-it-isnt; "Quinoa Boom Puts Stress on Bolivian Economics, Environment," *Huffington Post*, February 20, 2013, http://www.huffingtonpost.com/2013/02/20/quinoa-boom -bolivian_n_2724251.html.

As with cocoa and tomato labor issues, tuna conservation is a transnational issue that requires international cooperation to address. Meeting demand for tuna depends almost exclusively on open-sea fishing due to migration patterns of tuna, raising questions as to who can or should regulate international waters. Although everyone involved recognizes that without cooperation the tuna industry itself faces extinction, countries continually fail to reach agreement.

Concerns about the environment have also spurred NGOs to act. Resistance to transgenic modification of plants has led to increased consumer demand for locally produced and organic foods. Despite its increased dependence on agricultural exports such as soybeans, a movement to protect the rain forests of Brazil has rallied citizens both domestically and globally to push the government to adopt policies to reduce deforestation in the Amazon Basin. Citizen awareness also sparked the Monterey Bay Aquarium Seafood Watch Program to inform consumers about the threatened extinction of tuna. NGOs alone cannot effect change, so these organizations push governments to coordinate their policies, monitor progress, and endlessly work to increase public awareness about environmental injustices.

## CONCLUSION

The world is increasingly becoming more interdependent. Food is no exception. The global food system is so heavily dependent upon livestock, crops for animal feed, processed foods, and seasonable produce being available year-round that consumer habits would need to change radically to reduce interdependence. This model raises concern for humans and the environment and the forces that shape food trends. The choices consumers in the global north make have an impact on the global food supply and world food prices. Think about the way your own food choices are connected to the different issues raised throughout the book. Will you make different choices now that you have a better understanding of the global political economy of food production and supply? The next time you put a dash of cinnamon in your coffee, will you be more aware of how weather conditions in countries in the Indian Ocean might affect availability or price? The next time you eat a tuna salad sandwich or sushi, will you wonder where your tuna came from and how it was caught? When you go out for dinner, will you order steak or pasta? Cocoa issues in many ways mirror those for coffee, bananas, and sugar because they are all predominately produced on plantations. Whaling concerns parallel tuna fishing, consumption, and conservation efforts, whereas understanding the demand and uses for soybeans sheds light on the corn industry. This book has offered a starting point for understanding the basics of the global economy and the foods that feed the world's population, with the hope of imparting the knowledge to make further connections.

What does the future hold? The risks and rewards of a global food supply are plenty. The number of people suffering from malnutrition has dropped by 8 percent over the last decade, reducing those suffering from chronic hunger to 15 percent; at the same time, global obesity rates are at an all-time high and rising.[13] The public cringes at stories of abusive labor conditions; yet GN consumers benefit from having tomatoes year-round, and immigrants earn much-needed cash. More people around the globe now enjoy chocolate, but at the cost of a reliance on child slave labor. The growing middle classes in emerging economies have more disposable income, allowing them greater variety in their diets, but increased demands for meat put pressure on the land that produces soybeans for animal feed. Public pressure, protocol cooperation, and consumer willingness to pay fair trade prices are all necessary to guarantee human and environmental security.

If more consumers opted to decrease the amount of animal protein in their diets—not to mention the endangered tuna—tuna stocks might stabilize, and organic food production might be a more realistic option for global food supply. Associated health risks would also decrease, and an increased reliance on a plant-based diet would reduce environment costs. As an increasing percentage of the world's growing population eats meat and processed foods, conventional farming will continue to be necessary to meet the world's food demands, putting human security and the environment at risk.

## CHAPTER QUESTIONS

1. How do conflicting interests among producers affect the global food supply chain?
2. How does the colonial legacy continue to affect food production in former colonies?
3. How do consumers' food choices affect human security?
4. Why does a plant-based diet offer increased human security and environmental protection?

# NOTES

## CHAPTER 1

1. Paul Roberts, *The End of Food* (New York: Houghton Mifflin Company, 2008).

2. Eastern countries employed the same policies during the Cold War. Due to their command economies, they did not experience the same oversupply problem that resulted in the Western, capitalist countries where farmers received subsidies. See Chapter 5's discussion on agricultural subsidies for more information.

3. "Trends in U.S. Agriculture," National Agricultural Statistics Service, US Department of Agriculture, August 11, 2009, http://www.nass.usda.gov/Publications/ Trends_in_U.S. _Agriculture (accessed July 27, 2010).

4. "Demographics," US Environmental Protection Agency, Agriculture Newsroom, http://www.epa.gov/agriculture/ag101/demographics.html (accessed August 8, 2010).

5. Roberts, *The End of Food*.

6. Robert A. Hoppe and David E. Banker, "Structure and Finances of U.S. Farms: 2005 Family Farm Report," Economic Information Bulletin No. EIB-12, May 2006, USDA Economic Research Service, http://www.ers.usda.gov/publications/eib-economic -information-bulletin/eib12.aspx#.Uyn36YVKN8o (accessed March 19, 2014).

7. "Where the Trough Is Overflowing," *New York Times*, June 3, 2012, http://www .nytimes.com/2012/06/03/opinion/sunday/where-the-trough-is-overflowing.html.

8. "Structure and Finances of U.S. Farms: Family Farm Report, 2010 Edition," USDA Economic Research Service, July 2010, http://www.ers.usda.gov/publications /eib-economic-information-bulletin/eib66.aspx#.Uyn2OYVKN8o (accessed March 19, 2014), iv.

9. See Roberts, *The End of Food*, ch. 3, for a greater discussion of the impact of Walmart on the grocery retail.

10. Roberts, *The End of Food*, 78.

11. "Do Increased Portion Sizes Affect How Much We Eat," Centers for Disease Control and Prevention (CDC), http://www.cdc.gov/nccdphp/dnpa/nutrition/pdf/portion _size_research.pdf (accessed August 2, 2010).

12. "Controlling the Global Obesity Epidemic," World Health Organization, http:// www.who.int/nutrition/topics/obesity/en (accessed July 29, 2010).

13. The categories "overweight" and "obese" are determined by the Body Mass Index (BMI), which measures body fat. This scale was developed to differentiate body types, but, generally, those thirty pounds over average body weight for height are also considered obese. As defined by the CDC, a healthy BMI ranges from 18.5 to 24.9, the overweight range is 25 to 29.9, and anyone with a BMI over 30 is considered obese.

14. "Obesity and Overweight" (US data), CDC, http://www.cdc.gov/nchs/fastats/ overwt.htm (accessed July 29/2).

15. "Prevalence of Obesity among Children and Adolescents: United States, Trends 1963–1965 through 2007–2008," CDC, http://www.cdc.gov/nchs/data/hestat/obesity _child_07_08/obesity_child_07_08.pdf (accessed July 29, 2010).

16. "Adult Obesity Facts," CDC, http://www.cdc.gov/obesity/data/trends.html#State (accessed August 2, 2012).

17. "F as in Fat: How Obesity Threatens America's Future 2010," Trust for America's Health, http://healthyamericans.org/reports/obesity2010 (accessed August 2, 2010).

18. "Obesity Hits Lower Income Households Harder," *Twin Cities Daily Planet*, July 10, 2010, http://www.tcdailyplanet.net/blog/hindsight/ obesity-hits-lower-income-households-harder.

19. "Causes and Consequences: What Causes Overweight and Obesity?" CDC, http://www.cdc.gov/obesity/adult/causes/index.html (accessed August 14, 2013). "Study: American Taxes Pay for Most Obesity-Tied Health Ills," *USA Today*, January 21, 2004, http://usatoday30.usatoday.com/news/health/2004-01-21-taxes-obesity_x.htm (Accessed March 19, 2014).

20. "Is It Fair to Fine Fat People for Not Dieting?" *BBC World News*, http://www.bbc .co.uk/news/world-us-canada-13397306 (accessed May 17, 2011).

21. "Japan, Seeking Trim Waists, Measures Millions," *New York Times*, June 13, 2008, http://www.nytimes.com/2008/06/13/world/asia/13fat.html.

22. David R. Bassett et al. "Walking, Cycling, and Obesity Rates in Europe, North America, and Australia," *Journal of Physical Activity and Health* 5 (2008): 795–814.

23. WHO European Ministerial Conference on Counteracting Obesity, "European Charter on Counteracting Obesity," WHO, 2006, http://www.euro.who.int/__data/assets /pdf_file/0009/87462/E89567.pdf (accessed December 28, 2013), 1.

24. WHO European Ministerial Conference on Counteracting Obesity, "European Charter on Counteracting Obesity."

25. "Health Statistics: Obesity (Most Recent) by Country," NationMaster.com, http:// www.nationmaster.com/graph/hea_obe-health-obesity (accessed August 2, 2010).

26. "Controlling the Global Obesity Epidemic," WHO.

27. "Health Statistics: Obesity (Most Recent) by Country."

28. "As Indian Growth Soars, Child Hunger Persists," *New York Times*, March 12, 2009, http://www.nytimes.com/2009/03/13/world/asia/13malnutrition.html.

29. "Feast and Famine," *Economist*, March 3, 2012, http://www.economist.com/node /21549018.

30. "Small, Rich, and Overweight," *Economist*, December 15, 2012, http://www .economist.com/news/special-report/21568075-how-abu-dhabi-tackling-its-obesity -problem-small-rich-and-overweight.

31. "The Last Course," *Economist*, December 15, 2012, http://www.economist.com /news/special-report/21568067-what-will-it-take-make-world-less-round-last-course.

32. Adam Drewnowski, "Fat and Sugar in the Global Diet: Dietary Diversity in the Nutrition Transition," in *Food in Global History*, edited by Raymond Grew (Boulder, CO: Westview Press, 2000), 194–206.

33. Drewnowski, "Fat and Sugar," 204.

34. Yangfeng Wu, "Overweight and Obesity in China," *BMJ* 333 (2006): 362.

## CHAPTER 2

1. Jeffrey M. Pilcher, "Industrial Tortillas and Folkloric Pepsi: The Nutritional Consequences of Hybrid Cuisine in Mexico," in *The Cultural Politics of Food and Eating*, edited by Melissa Caldwell and James L. Watson (Boston, MA: Blackwell Publishing, 2005), 230.

2. Paul Roberts, *The End of Food* (New York: Houghton Mifflin Company, 2008).

## CHAPTER 3

1. Tom Standage, *An Edible History of Humanity* (New York: Walker and Company, 2010), 102; William J. Bernstein, *A Splendid Exchange: How Trade Shaped the World* (New York: Atlantic Monthly Press, 2008), 211; "A Taste of Adventure: The History of Spices Is the History of Trade," *Economist*, December 17, 1998, www.economist.com/node /179810.

2. Author calculation based on "List of Prices of Medieval Items" (http://whitebard .tripod.com/prices.htm) and Reginald Robinson Sharpe, City of London (England), Court of Common Council, Library Committee, *Calendar of Coroners Rolls of the City of London, A.D. 1300–1378* (N.p.: R. Clay and Sons, 1913), 109. Available at http://books .google.com/books?id=yWdMAAAAMAAJ&pg=PA109&lpg=PA109&dq=4+shillings +in+1300+AD+was+worth&source=bl&ots=nGRqS75DGm&sig =ZA5d5IF8c8KhvhVLlIkD04RxSms &hl=en&sa=X&ei=ZantUbbBFrbI4APA6oD wCA&ved=0CC0Q6AEwAA#v=onepage &q=4%20shillings%20in%201300%20AD %20was%20worth&f=false (accessed July 22, 2013).

3. "History of Spices," McCormick Science Institute, http://www .mccormickscienceinstitute.com/Spice-Landing/History-of-Spices.aspx (accessed July 22, 2013).

4. "36 Records in Indonesia," Good News from Indonesia, January 19, 2011, http:// goodnewsfromindonesia.org/2011/01/19/36-records-in-indonesia-part-3 (accessed February 24, 2011).

5. Listing for WTO Case DS409 at "Chronological List of Disputes Cases," WTO, http://www.wto.org/english/tratop_e/dispu_e/dispu_status_e.htm.

6. "WTO Ruling Is Blow to U.S. Anti-Smoking Effort," *Wall Street Journal*, April 24, 2012, http://online.wsj.com/article/SB10001424052702303302504577323892583458740.html.

7. "To Bake Beef like Red Deer," 17th Century English Recipes, Gode Cookery, http://www.godecookery.com/engrec/engrec87.html (accessed May 20, 2011).

8. "A Taste of Adventure."

9. Bernstein, *A Splendid Exchange*, 111.

10. "A Taste of Adventure."

11. Standage, *An Edible History of Humanity*, 98.

12. Jack Turner, *Spice* (New York: Alfred A. Knopf, 2004), 27.

13. Jeffrey M. Pilcher, *Food in World History* (New York: Routledge, 2006).

14. Pilcher, *Food in World History*, 30.

15. Murray Rothbard, *A History of Money and Banking in the United States: The Colonial Era to World War II* (Auburn, AL: Ludwig von Mises Institute, 2002).

16. Bernstein, *A Splendid Exchange*, 211–12.

17. Paul Temperton, *The UK and the Euro* (London: Wiley and Sons, 2001), 6.

18. CIA World Factbook country profile data for 2012 (https://www.cia.gov/library /publications/the-world-factbook).

19. *Pepper News and Review*, January 2012, http://www.ipcnet.org/admin/data/news /1332295452.pdf (accessed March 12, 2012).

20. "Misery of India's Spice Farmers," *BBC World News*, May 17, 2005, http://news .bbc.co.uk/2/hi/south_asia/4536961.stm.

21. "India: Making Insurance Markets Work for Farmers," World Bank News and Broadcast, 2010, http://web.worldbank.org/WBSITE/EXTERNAL/NEWS/0 „contentMDK:22892134~menuPK:141310~pagePK:34370~piPK:34424~theSitePK :4607,00.html (accessed July 26, 2013).

22. "Nutmeg Prices Soar," *Gleaner*, October 6, 2010, http://jamaica-gleaner.com / gleaner/20101006/business/business92.html.

23. "Private Sector Trade Note Vol. 18: CARICOM's Nutmeg Trade," Office of Trade Negotiations, March 2, 2011, http://www.crnm.org/index.php?option=com_content &view=article&id=515:private-sector-trade-note-vol-18-caricoms-nutmeg-trade&catid =91:trade-publications&Itemid=106 (accessed March 12, 2012).

24. "New Roots," *Lanka Business Online*, June 8, 2006, http://www .lankabusinessonline.com/fullstory.php?nid=640124071.

25. *Pepper News and Review*.

26. *Pepper News and Review.*

27. "Report on Peppercorn Sector in Vietnam," ASEAN-Korea Centre, 2007, http://www.aseankorea.org/files/upload/board/120/6/Vietnam%20Pepper%202007.pdf (accessed January 27, 2011).

28. "Boosting Pepper Cultivation," *Viet Nam News,* January 7, 2009, http://vietnamnews.vn/agriculture/189498/boosting-pepper-cultivation.html.

# CHAPTER 4

1. Pauline Tiffen, "A Chocolate-Coated Case for Alternative International Business Models," *Development in Practice* 12, no. 3/4: (2002): 393.

2. "Report: $19.5 Billion in U.S. Chocolate Sales—and 20% Growth in Organic," Candy Industry, May 30, 2012, http://www.candyindustry.com/articles/85215-report —-19-5-billion-in-chocolate-sales-and-20—growth-in-organic (accessed July 13, 2013).

3. "Who Consumes the Most Chocolate?" CNN Freedom Project, January 17, 2012, http://thecnnfreedomproject.blogs.cnn.com/2012/01/17/who-consumes-the-most-chocolate (accessed July 13, 2013).

4. China data from Yu Tianyu, "Love like a Chocolate Box for Sweethearts," *China Daily,* February 14, 2011, http://usa.chinadaily.com.cn/epaper/2011-02/14/content _12004341_2.htm; Europe data from "Cocoa," Food and Agriculture Organization of the United Nations (FAO), http://www.fao.org/docrep/006/y5143e/y5143e0x.htm (accessed July 13, 2013).

5. China figures from "The Bitter and the Sweet: How Five Companies Competed to Bring Chocolate to China," Knowledge@Wharton, January 12, 2011, http://knowledge .wharton.upenn.edu/article.cfm?articleid=2512; Swiss figures from Ellen Kuwana, "Discovering the Sweet Mysteries of Chocolate," Neuroscience for Kids, October 1, 2010, http://faculty.washington.edu/chudler/choco.html (accessed July 13, 2013).

6. "Barry Callebaut Buys Petra Foods Cocoa Unit," *Bloomberg News,* December 12, 2012, http://www.bloomberg.com/news/2012-12-12/petra-foods-sells-cocoa-unit-to-barry -callebaut-for-950-million.html.

7. "Cocoa Farming: An Overview," CocoaFarming.org.uk, http://www .cocoafarming.org.uk/cocoa_farming_bw_v8_uk.pdf (accessed July 13, 2013).

8. "Cocoa: Crop," UNCTAD, http://r0.unctad.org/infocomm/anglais/cocoa/crop .htm (accessed July 13, 2013).

9. This is an industry term and the same term used to describe the pressed solids in soybean processing.

10. For real chocolate aficionados, some fine chocolate makers and fair trade cooperatives have begun listing the "conche time" on their bars, which indicates how long the mix is heated and agitated in the conche vats. The time indicates how smooth the chocolate should be, with three days marking the smoothest chocolate.

11. Sophie D. Coe and Michael D. Coe, *The True History of Chocolate,* 2nd ed. (New York: Thames and Hudson, 2007), 100–101.

12. Carol Off, *Bitter Chocolate: The Dark Side of the World's Most Seductive Sweet* (Toronto: New Press, 2006), 42.

13. Allen M. Young, *The Chocolate Tree: A Natural History of Cacao* (Gainesville, FL: University Press of Florida, 2007), 35.

14. "Cameroon's Cocoa Production Rises 20% in 2010–11 to 236,690 Metric Tons," *Bloomberg News*, August 15, 2011, http://www.bloomberg.com/news/2011-08-15 /cameroon-s-cocoa-production-rises-20-in-2010-11-to-236-690-metric-tons.html.

15. "Origins," Nestlé Cocoa Plan, http://www.nestlecocoaplan.com/cocoa-origins (accessed July 13, 2013).

16. Global North data from "Cocoa," FAO; cocoa production calculation from "Production—Latest Figures from the *Quarterly Bulletin of Cocoa Statistics*," International Cocoa Organization, http://www.icco.org/about-us/international-cocoa-agreements/cat _view/30-related-documents/46-statistics-production.html (accessed July 13, 2013).

17. "Cocoa: Trade Issues for the ACP," Agritrade, October 1, 2009, http:// agritrade.cta.int/en/Resources/Agritrade-documents/Agriculture-Executive-briefs/ Cocoa-Trade-issues-for-the-ACP#31.

18. Ivory Coast figures based on author calculations from Olivier Monnier and Baudelaire Mieu, "Ivory Coast Cocoa Bean Shippers Declare 911,497 Metric Tons for Export," *Bloomberg News*, June 17, 2011, http://www.bloomberg.com/news/2011-06-17 /ivory-coast-cocoa-shippers-declare-911-497-metric-tons-table-.html; average price of cocoa from October 2010 to June 2011 based on data from http://www.indexmundi .com/commodities/?commodity=cocoa-beans&months=12; Barry Callebaut data is for the previous fiscal year, with sales increases in the first half of the 2010–2011 fiscal year indicating a projected increase in profit of 10 percent ("Barry Callebaut—Half-Year Results, Fiscal Year 2010/11: Growing Twice as Fast as the Market," Barry Callebaut, April 1, 2011, http://www.barry-callebaut.com/51?release=6713).

19. Ivory Coast, Ghana, and Cameroon, based on author's calculations from World Bank data. Although Nigeria is a bigger producer than Cameroon, its GDP is skewed by oil revenues. Nestlé data is from "Global 500," *CNN Money*, http://money.cnn.com /magazines/fortune/global500/2010/full_list/index.html (accessed July 13, 2013).

20. Author calculations are based on http://faostat.fao.org/site/342/default.aspx from 2000 to 2010.

21. "Cocoa," FAO.

22. "Low Fertilizer Use Drives Deforestation in West Africa's Tropical Forest Area, Study Suggests," *Science News*, April 7, 2011, http://www.sciencedaily.com /releases/2011/04/110407092031.htm.

23. Nigeria is the only country with no age minimum. *Rooting Out Child Labour from Cocoa Farms: A Manual for Training Education Practitioners: Ghana* (Geneva: International Labour Office, 2007), 3:14.

24. "Critics: Chocolate Financing Ivory Coast's Gbagbo," *Seattle Times*, February 14, 2011, http://seattletimes.nwsource.com/html/businesstechnology/2014219729 _apafafricabittersweetchocolate.html.

25. "Chocolate's Bittersweet Economy," *CNN Money*, January 24, 2008, http://money.cnn.com/2008/01/24/news/international/chocolate_bittersweet.fortune.

26. INTERPOL, http://www.interpol.int/Public/News/2009/CotedIvoire20090803.asp (accessed July 13, 2013).

27. "Oversight of Public and Private Initiatives to Eliminate the Worst Forms of Child Labor in the Cocoa Sector in Côte d'Ivoire and Ghana," Tulane University Report, Tulane University, Payson Center Oversight Project, March 31, 2011, http://www.childlabor-payson.org/Tulane%20Final%20Report.pdf (accessed July 13, 2013).

28. "List of Goods Produced by Child Labor or Forced Labor," US Department of Labor, 2010, http://www.dol.gov/ilab/programs/ocft/pdf/2010TVPRA.pdf (accessed July 13, 2013), 31.

29. "NGOs Slam Industry Inaction over Child Labour," International Service of the Swiss Broadcasting Corporation, September 20, 2011, http://www.swissinfo.ch/eng/business/NGOs_slam_industry_inaction_over_child_labour_.html.

30. "Critics: Chocolate Financing Ivory Coast's Gbagbo."

31. "Oversight of Public and Private Initiatives," Tulane University Report, 7.

32. "Oversight of Public and Private Initiatives," Tulane University Report, 9.

33. "Oversight of Public and Private Initiatives," Tulane University Report, 16.

34. "Critics: Chocolate Financing Ivory Coast's Gbagbo." In other news around the same time as the boycott, Hershey's was exposed for underpaying foreign exchange students it employs in its Pennsylvania factory ("Blank Rome Signs to Lobby for Hershey Co. on Labor Issues," *BLT: The Blog of Legal Times*, September 12, 2011, http://legaltimes.typepad.com/blt/2011/09/blank-rome-signs-to-lobby-for-hershey-co-on-labor-issues.html (accessed July 13, 2013).

35. "Chocolate's Bittersweet Economy."

36. "The Market for Organic and Fair-Trade Cocoa," FAO, September 2009, http://www.fao.org/fileadmin/templates/organicexports/docs/Market_Organic_FT_Cocoa.pdf (accessed July 13, 2013), 1.1.

37. FLO-Cert Impact Assessment Report, November 29, 2013, http://www.kuapakokoo.com/docs/2013ImpactReport.pdf

38. "The Market for Organic and Fair-Trade Cocoa," 11.

39. "Armajaro Targets 85,000 Tonnes of Cocoa Next Season," GhanaWeb, September 1, 2011, http://www.ghanaweb.com/GhanaHomePage/NewsArchive/artikel.php?ID=217631.

## CHAPTER 5

1. Throughout the book, the term "meat" is used to denote animal protein derived from livestock (beef, buffalo, and the like), poultry, sheep, goats, pigs, and aquaculture.

2. "Brazil Expects a 90 Million Tons Soybean Crop, Making It the World's Top Producer," *MercoPress*, December 12, 2013, http://en.mercopress.com/2013/12/12/brazil

-expects-a-90-million-tons-soybean-crop-making-it-the-world-s-top-producer (accessed January 17, 2014).

3. Data from "FDI in Figures," OECD, April 2013, http://www.oecd.org/daf/inv /FDI%20in%20figures.pdf (accessed December 29, 2013).

4. "A Taste Test for Hunger," *New York Times*, July 10, 2011, http://www.nytimes .com/2011/07/10/opinion/sunday/10gray.html.

5. "It's Corn vs. Soybeans in a Biofuels Debate," *New York Times*, January 13, 2006, http://www.nytimes.com/2006/07/13/business/13ethanol.html.

6. "Diesel from Soy Sparks $560 Million Investment by ADM, Cargill," *Bloomberg News*, May 6, 2011, http://www.bloomberg.com/news/2011-05-06/diesel-from-soybeans -sparks-560-million-investment-by-adm-cargill.html.

7. Data from "Share of World Soybean Exports Going to China, 1964–2010" (March 23, 2011) and "Grain Production, Consumption, Imports and Exports in China, 1960–2010" (March 09, 2011), Earth Policy Institute, http://www.earth-policy.org/data _center/C24 (accessed March 17, 2013).

8. "Soybeans and Oil Crops: Trade," US Department of Agriculture, March 2011, http://www.ers.usda.gov/Briefing/Soybeansoilcrops/trade.htm#foreign (accessed July 21, 2011).

9. "Soybeans and Oil Crops."

10. "Common Agricultural Policy Factsheet," Civitas, http://www.civitas.org.uk /eufacts/FSPOL/AG3.php (accessed July 21, 2011).

11. "The Key to a Successful Return on Your Investment in Brazil," Brazil Access Investment and Trade, http://www.brazilaccess.com (accessed July 21, 2011).

12. "Soybeans and Oil Crops."

13. "How Brazil Outfarmed the American Farmer," *CNN Money*, January 16, 2009, http://money.cnn.com/2008/01/16/news/international/brazil_soy.fortune/index.htm (accessed December 29, 2013), 4.

14. "The Key to a Successful Return on Your Investment in Brazil."

15. "Attractiveness for MNC in Brazil," Scribd, http://www.scribd.com/doc /45579711/Attraction-for-MNC-in-Brazil (accessed March 17, 2013).

16. "Executive Summary," InvestorsInsight.com, http://www.investorsinsight.com /blogs/global_emerging_markets_gems/archive/2009/08/07/brazil-investment-case.aspx (accessed March 17, 2013).

17. "Latam FDI Soars 40% in 2010, Mainly Natural Resources and Services," *MercoPress*, May 4, 2011, http://en.mercopress.com/2011/05/04/latam-fdi-soars-40-in -2010-mainly-natural-resources-and-services.

18. "Foreign Direct Investment in Latin American and the Caribbean," ECLAC, 2010, http://www.eclac.org/publicaciones/xml/0/43290/2011-138-LIEI_2010-WEB _INGLES.pdf (accessed March 17, 2013), 29.

19. "Investments by Chinese Companies in Brazil Total over US$29.5 Billion in 2010," Macauhub, March 31, 2011, http://www.macauhub.com.mo/en/2011/03/31 /investments-by-chinese-companies-in-brazil-total-over-us29-5-billion-in-2010.

20. Paul Roberts, *The End of Food* (New York: Houghton Mifflin Company, 2008), 132.

21. "World's Top 10 Food Exporters," Gateway to South America, http://www.gatewaytosouthamerica.com/en/index.php (accessed March 17, 2011).

22. "Invest in Brazilian Farmland," Gateway to South America, http://www.gatewaytosouthamerica.com/en/index.php (accessed March 17, 2011).

23. "Saudis to Invest $500 Million in Brazil Agriculture," *Peninsula*, October 5, 2010, http://www.thepeninsulaqatar.com/latest-news/128199-saudis-to-invest-500-million-in-brazil-agriculture.html.

24. These companies were American-owned Monsanto, DuPont, and Dow, Swiss-owned Novartis, Sakata of Japan, the French-German corporation Aventis, and Mexican-owned Savia. "Sustainability Assessment of Export-Led Growth in Soy Production in Brazil," World Wildlife Fund, 2003, http://awsassets.panda.org/downloads/soylongeng.pdf (accessed March 17, 2011), 33.

25. "Brazil Creates Seeds of New Life," Monsanto, August 4, 2010, http://www.monsanto.com/newsviews/Pages/brazil-creates-seeds-of-new-life.aspx.

26. Interestingly, Nestlé opened the world's most advanced infant formula plant in Brazil in 2007, perhaps in retaliation for the heavy criticism it received in the late 1970s for promoting formula over breast milk in Brazil and other developing countries.

27. "Archer Daniels Midland Company to Invest in Sustainable Palm Production in Brazil," Invest in Brazil, February 10, 2011, http://www.investinbrazil.biz/investmentbrazil/2011/02/archer-daniels-midland-company-to-invest-in-sustainable-palm-production-in-brazil.

28. Author calculations based on data at "The GATT Years: From Havana to Marrakesh," WTO, http://www.wto.org/english/thewto_e/whatis_e/tif_e/fact4_e.htm#rounds (accessed March 17, 2011).

29. Roberts, *The End of Food*, 136.

30. "Agricultural Subsidies," *Economist*, September 4, 2011, http://www.economist.com/node/21530130.

31. "At the Trough," *Economist*, June 1, 2013, http://www.economist.com/news/united-states/21578688-awful-farm-bill-faces-opposition-trough.

32. See Roberts, *The End of Food*, ch. 1, for more on MNCs and agribusiness.

33. Roberts, *The End of Food*, 122–23.

34. See DS 265, DS 266, and DS 267 at "Chronological List of Disputes Cases," WTO, http://www.wto.org/english/tratop_e/dispu_e/dispu_status_e.htm.

35. "News Release: U.S., Brazil Agree upon Path toward Negotiated Solution of Cotton Dispute Would Avoid Imposition of Countermeasures against U.S. Exports, U.S. Intellectual Property Rights," USDA, April 6, 2010, http://www.usda.gov/wps/portal/usda/usdahome?contentidonly=true&contentid=2010/04/0168.xml.

36. "Stuffed," *Economist*, June 26, 2013, http://www.economist.com/news/united-states/21580158-house-rejects-farm-bill-stuffed.

37. "Where the Trough Is Overflowing," *New York Times*, June 3, 2012, http://www.nytimes.com/2012/06/03/opinion/sunday/where-the-trough-is-overflowing.html.

38. See European Court of Justice Case C-59/10 at http://curia.europa.eu/juris /recherche.jsf?cid=174810.

39. "Brazil's Huge New Port Highlights China's Drive into South America," *Guardian*, September 15, 2010, http://www.guardian.co.uk/world/2010/sep/15/brazil -port-china-drive.

40. "China's Interest in Farmland Makes Brazil Uneasy," *New York Times*, May 26, 2011, http://www.nytimes.com/2011/05/27/world/americas/27brazil.html.

41. "Looking Ahead, Brazil's Farmers Take Up Reforestation," *Washington Post*, November 23, 2009, http://www.washingtonpost.com/wp-dyn/content/article /2009/11/22/AR2009112201845.html.

42. Jan Suszkiw, "USDA Scientists, Cooperators Sequence Soy Genome," USDA, January 13, 2010, http://www.ars.usda.gov/is/pr/2010/100113.2.htm (accessed March 17, 2011).

43. "South Korea to Expand Overseas Farming on Rising Food Costs," *Bloomberg News*, July 9, 2011, http://www.bloomberg.com/news/2011-07-10/south-korea-to-expand -overseas-farming-on-rising-food-costs.html.

44. "Sojitz to Produce Soybeans, Other Crops in Argentina for Export to Asia," *Bloomberg News*, November 17, 2010, http://www.bloomberg.com/news/2010-11-17/sojitz -to-produce-soybeans-other-crops-in-argentina-for-export-to-asia.html.

45. "China's Interest in Farmland Makes Brazil Uneasy."

46. "China's Interest in Farmland Makes Brazil Uneasy."

47. "China Invests $12.67 Billion in Brazil," *Economic Times*, July 5, 2011, http://articles.economictimes.indiatimes.com/2011-07-05/ news/29738779_1_brazil-accounts-chinese-investment-brazil-s-ministry.

48. "Sustainability Assessment of Export-Led Growth in Soy Production in Brazil," 9.

49. Data from "Explore. Create. Share: Development Data," World Bank Databank, http://databank.worldbank.org/data/views/reports/tableview.aspx.

50. Roberts, *The End of Food*, 236.

51. "JBS" is an acronym based on the initials of founder José Batista Sobrinho; "SA" is an abbreviation for used for corporations, in the same way that "Ltd." is used to denote "limited."

52. "All You Can Eat," *Forbes*, April 20, 2011, http://www.forbes.com/forbes/2011 /0509/global-2000-11-americas-brazil-jbs-mendonca-batista-eat.html.

53. "Marfrig Alimentos Will Conclude Acquisition of Keystone for $1.26 Billion," *Bloomberg News*, September 30, 2010, http://www.bloomberg.com/news/2010-10-01 /marfrig-alimentos-will-conclude-acquisition-of-keystone-for-1-26-billion.html.

# CHAPTER 6

1. "Table 102," ERS, http://usda.mannlib.cornell.edu/MannUsda /viewDocumentInfo.do?documentID=1210 (accessed May 15, 2012); 2007 data based on fresh and processed consumption.

2. "Tomatoes," ERS, http://www.ers.usda.gov/briefing/vegetables/tomatoes.htm (accessed May 15, 2012).

3. "Fresh vs. Processed Tomato Consumption (2)," Tomatoland Information Services, July/August 2011 Report, http://staging.corpuspro.com/tomatoland/documents/2259.pdf (accessed May 15, 2012).

4. "Fresh vs. Processed Tomato Consumption (2)."

5. "Egyptians Still Await Economic Change," *BBC World News*, September 15, 2011, http://www.bbc.co.uk/news/business-14907631.

6. "Retailers Driving Rise in Veggie Prices?" *Times of India*, April 17, 2012, http:// articles.timesofindia.indiatimes.com/2012-04-17/delhi/31355121_1_wholesale-rates -tomato-prices-vegetable.

7. 2011 IMF data at "World Economic Outlook Databases," IMF, http://www.imf .org/external/ns/cs.aspx?id=28 (accessed May 15, 2012).

8. "Vegetable Prices Soar in Metros, Other Cities," *Times of India*, April 4, 2012, http://articles.timesofindia.indiatimes.com/2012-04-04/india/31286778_1_vegetable -prices-potato-wholesale-fruits-vegetables-market.

9. Based on author's calculation using 2012 US GDP per capita of $48,112.

10. "E.U. Offers Farmers $300 Million for *E. coli* Crisis," *Lubbock Avalanche-Journal*, June 11, 2011, http://lubbockonline.com/agriculture/2011-06-11/eu-offers-farmers-300 -million-e-coli-crisis#.URvs6GcWjP0.

11. "Top Production: Tomatoes," FAOSTAT, 2010, http://faostat.fao.org/site/339 /default.aspx (accessed May 15, 2012).

12. "Top Exports: Tomatoes," FAOSTAT, 2009, http://faostat.fao.org/site/342 /default.aspx (accessed May 15, 2012). Note that domestic demand in Italy is so high that despite its being the top producer in the EU, the Netherlands is a bigger exporter).

13. Roberts, *The End of Food*, 125.

14. "Italy: Tomatoes Annual Report," Foreign Agricultural Service Report, USDA, December 16, 2011, http://gain.fas.usda.gov/Recent%20GAIN%20Publications /Tomatoes%20Annual%20Report_Rome_Italy_6-4-2009.pdf (accessed May 15, 2012).

15. "Top Exports: Tomato Peeled," FAOSTAT, 2009, http://faostat.fao.org/site/339 /default.aspx (accessed May 15, 2012).

16. "Trivia," Heinz, http://www.heinz.com/our-company/press-room/trivia.aspx (accessed June 19, 2012).

17. Roberta Cook and Linda Calvin, "Greenhouse Tomatoes Change the Dynamics of the North American Fresh Tomato Industry," Economic Research Service, April 2005, http://www.ers.usda.gov/publications/err2/err2fm.pdf.

18. Cook and Calvin, "Greenhouse Tomatoes," 57.

19. Paul Roberts, *The End of Food* (New York: Houghton Mifflin Company, 2008), 17.

20. "China—People's Republic of: Annual Report: Tomatoes and Products," Foreign Agricultural Service, USDA, May 21, 2009, http://gain.fas.usda.gov/Recent%20GAIN %20Publications/Annual%20Report_Beijing_China%20-%20Peoples%20Republic %20of_2009-5-21.pdf (accessed May 15, 2012).

21. These terms will be used interchangeably. Although methods vary among them, these types of production are all done in an enclosed, controlled environment.

22. "Kenya Starts Greenhouse Tomato Farming," Fresh Plaza, October 5, 2007, http://www.freshplaza.com/news_detail.asp?id=8859.

23. "Tomatoes," ERS.

24. Roberts, *The End of Food*, 78.

25. "India's Rural Poor Battle with Price Rises," *BBC World News*, November 6, 2011, http://www.bbc.co.uk/news/business-15327271.

26. "Tomato Production," FAOSTAT, http://faostat.fao.org/site/339/default.aspx (accessed May 15, 2012).

27. "Agricultural Dimensions of the WTO EU Trade Policy Review," Agritrade, August 30, 2011, http://agritrade.cta.int/en/layout/set/print/Agriculture/Topics/WTO /Agricultural-dimensions-of-the-WTO-EU-trade-policy-review (accessed May 15, 2012).

28. Nicholas Minot, "Smart Fertilizer Subsidies in Sub-Saharan Africa: New Wine or Just New Bottles?" International Food Policy Research Institute, July 24, 2009, http:// www.ifpri.org/sites/default/files/20090724Minotppt.pdf (accessed May 15, 2012).

29. "Insurance Debate Heats Up as Farm Bill Votes Near," FB Insider, June 1, 2012, http://www.fbactinsider.org/insurance-debate-heats-up-as-farm-bill-votes-near.

30. "Canned: Why Local Tomatoes Cop a Pasting," *Age*, May 27, 2012, http://www .theage.com.au/national/canned-why-local-tomatoes-cop-a-pasting-20120526-1zc2q.html.

31. "Ghanaian Tomato," *BBC News*, http://news.bbc.co.uk/2/hi/programmes /panorama/2823015.stm.

32. "Obama, Africa, and Food Insecurity," Third World Network, July 13, 2009, http://www.twnside.org.sg/title2/gtrends/gtrends258.htm.

33. "Transforming Agriculture: The Case of Tomato in Ghana," International Food Policy Research Institute, April 11, 2010, http://www.ifpri.org/pressrelease /transforming-agriculture-case-tomato-ghana.

34. "Ghanaian Tomato."

35. Branden Born and Mark Purcell, "Avoiding the Local Trap: Scale and Food Systems in Planning Research," *Journal of Planning Education and Research* 26 (2006): 195–207.

36. Charles Kenny, "Got Cheap Milk? Why Ditching Your Fancy, Organic, Locavore Lifestyle Is Good for the World's Poor," *Foreign Policy*, September 12, 2011, http://www .foreignpolicy.com/articles/2011/09/12/got_cheap_milk.

37. Christopher L. Weber and H. Scott Matthews, "Food-Miles and the Relative Climate Impacts of Food Choices in the United States," *Environmental Science Technology* 42, no. 10 (2008): 3508–13.

38. Michael Barratt Brown, "'Fair Trade' with Africa," *Review of African Political Economy* 34, no. 112 (2007): 276.

39. "Can Organic Food Feed the World? New Study Sheds Light on Debate over Organic vs. Conventional Agriculture," *Science News*, http://www.sciencedaily.com /releases/2012/04/120425140114.htm (accessed April 22, 2012).

40. From Ronald Bailey, "Norman Borlaug, Happy 95th Birthday!" Reason.com, March 26, 2009, http://reason.com/blog/2009/03/26/norman-borlaug-happy-95th-birt.

41. Kenny, "Got Cheap Milk?"

42. "Flavour Changer: Genome Could Enhance Tomato Taste," *BBC News*, May 30, 2012, http://www.bbc.co.uk/news/science-environment-18253577.

43. Barry Estabrook, *Tomatoland* (Kansas City, MO: Andrews McMeel Publishing, 2011), 41.

44. Estabrook, *Tomatoland*, 20.

45. "This Terrifying Chart Shows We're Not Growing Enough Food to Feed the World," *Washington Post*, http://www.washingtonpost.com/blogs/wonkblog/wp/2013 /07/01/this-unsettling-chart-shows-were-not-growing-enough-food-to-feed-the-world /7/1/13.

46. "Frankenfoods Reduce Global Warming," *Economist*, http://www.economist.com /blogs/feastandfamine/2013/03/gm-crops-and-carbon-emissions (accessed March 4, 2013).

47. "Stephen Colbert, UFW's Rodriguez Ask U.S. Citizens to Take Farm Jobs, Urge Congress to Pass Immigration Reform and AgJOBS," United Farm Workers, September 23, 2010, http://ufw.org/_board.php?mode=view&b_code=news_press&b_no=7811 &page=1&field=&key=8,600&n=1.

48. "Immigrant Farm Workers," CSPN Video Library, September 24, 2010, http:// www.c-spanvideo.org/program/295639-1.

49. "Immigrant Workers in the U.S. Labor Force," Brookings Institute, March 15, 2012, http://www.brookings.edu/~/media/Research/Files/Papers/2012/3/15 %20immigrant%20workers%20singer/0315_immigrant_workers_appendix.PDF.

50. Estabrook, *Tomatoland*, 99–100.

51. "About CIW," Coalition of Immokalee Workers, http://ciw-online.org/about.html (accessed June 27, 2012).

52. For the standard US commercial bushel size, see "U.S. Commercial Bushel Sizes," University of North Carolina, Chapel Hill, http://www.unc.edu/~rowlett/units/scales /bushels.html.

53. "Labor: U.S. Fruits and Vegetables," *Rural Migration News*, 17, no. 1 (2011), http://migration.ucdavis.edu/rmn/more.php?id=1596_0_5_0.

54. "Migrant Workers Journey-Basilicata," *Ecologist*, September 1, 2011, http://www. theecologist.org/News/news_analysis/1033179/scandal_of_the_tomato_slaves _harvesting_crop_exported_to_uk.html (accessed May 15, 2012).

55. No connection to the US tomato company.

56. "Italian Senate Introduces Bill to Stop 'CAPORALATO,'" BWI Connect, August 31, 2011, http://connect.bwint.org/?p=342 (accessed May 15, 2012).

57. "Canned: Why Local Tomatoes Cop a Pasting."

58. "Indagine sulle condizioni dei braccianti immigrati in alcune regioni del Mezzogiorno," FLAI-CGIL, June 27, 2012, http://www.flai.it/index.php?option=com _content&view=article&id=625:indagine-sulle-condizioni-dei-braccianti-immigrati-in -alcune-regioni-del-mezzogiorno&catid=1:comunicati (accessed May 15, 2012).

59. "Trade and Labor Standards: Subject of Intense Debate," WTO, http://www.wto .org/english/thewto_e/minist_e/min99_e/english/about_e/18lab_e.htm (accessed May 15, 2012).

60. See Chapter 3 for a more in-depth explanation of the history of, verification process for, and issues with labeling.

61. "About Food Alliance," Food Alliance, http://foodalliance.org/about (accessed July 3, 2012).

# CHAPTER 7

1. "Bluefin Tuna Fetches Record $736K," *ABC News*, January 5, 2012, http:// abcnews.go.com/blogs/headlines/2012/01/bluefin-tuna-fetches-record-736k.

2. Although often sold as a canned tuna variety, skipjack is only a tuna-like species. Stock levels for skipjack are not currently under threat.

3. "Tuna Fished 'Illegally' during Libya Conflict," *BBC World News*, November 6, 2011, http://www.bbc.co.uk/news/science-environment-15597675.

4. "E.U. Confirms Support for Bluefin Tuna Trade Ban," EurActiv.com, March 11, 2010, http://www.euractiv.com/sustainability/ eu-confirms-support-bluefin-tuna-trade-ban-news-329139.

5. "The IUCN Red List of Threatened Species," IUCN Red List, http://www .iucnredlist.org/apps/redlist/details/170341/0 (accessed June 5, 2012).

6. "Greece Jellyfish Warning for U.K. Tourists," *BBC World News*, July 12, 2013, http://www.bbc.co.uk/news/science-environment-23243759.

7. "Bycatch" is the term used for fish unintentionally caught when another fish is targeted. Quantities of marine life end up as bycatch in tuna fishing, particularly when the long-line fishing technique is used.

8. Maria José Juan-Jordá et al., "Global Population Trajectories of Tunas and Their Relatives," *PNAS* 108, no. 51 (2011): 20651.

9. Paul Greenberg, *Four Fish: The Future of the Last Wild Food* (London: Penguin, 2010), 200–201.

10. United Nations Convention on the Law of the Sea (UNCLOS), Art. 56, 1982, http://www.un.org/depts/los/convention_agreements/texts/unclos/closindx.htm (accessed June 5, 2012).

11. "Global Tuna Catches by Stock," FAO Fisheries and Aquaculture Department, http://www.fao.org/fishery/statistics/tuna-catches/en.

12. "The Bitter Battle over Bluefin Tuna," *BBC World News*, March 19, 2010, http:// news.bbc.co.uk/2/hi/europe/8577538.stm.

13. Sovereignty over territory and resources raises the issue of ownership and global responsibility, particularly in regard to preservation of biospecies and rainforests.

14. "Tuna Hits Highest Price in Nine Years at Tokyo Auction," *BBC World News*, January 5, 2010, http://news.bbc.co.uk/2/hi/asia-pacific/8440758.stm; nonedible parts are factored out of the weight per pound.

15. "Giant Bluefin Tuna Fetches Record $396,000 in Tokyo Auction," *Huffington Post*, January 5, 2011, http://www.huffingtonpost.com/2011/01/05/bluefin-tuna-record -tokyo-auction_n_804553.html.

16. "Bluefin Tuna Fetches Record $736K."

17. Kathryn J. Mengerink, Harry N. Scheiber, and Yann-Huei Song, "Japanese Policies, Ocean Law, and the Tuna Fisheries: Sustainability Goals, the IUU, Issue, and Overcapacity," in *Conservation and Management of Transnational Tuna Fisheries*, edited by Robin Allen, James Joseph, and Dale Squires (Ames, IA: Blackwell Publishing, 2010), 283–320.

18. "East Africa: U.S. and E.U. Officials on Pirates' Pillaging of the Ocean's' Bounty," IIP Digital, September 8, 2011, http://iipdigital.usembassy.gov/st/english/article /2011/09/20110908173319su0.8142756.html#axzz2g0dVaJW4.

19. "Revealed: The Bid to Corner World's Bluefin Tuna Market," *Independent*, June 3, 2009, http://www.independent.co.uk/environment/nature/revealed-the-bid-to-corner -worlds-bluefin-tuna-market-1695479.html.

20. Elizabeth R. DeSombre, "Flags of Convenience and Property Rights on the High Seas," in *Conservation and Management of Transnational Tuna Fisheries*, edited by Robin Allen, James Joseph, and Dale Squires (Ames, IA: Blackwell Publishing, 2010), 270.

21. DeSombre, "Flags of Convenience," 271.

22. DeSombre, "Flags of Convenience," 2010.

23. "East Africa: U.S. and E.U. Officials on Pirates' Pillaging of the Ocean's' Bounty."

24. Michael Scott Moore, "Fish: Poached and Laundered," *Miller-McCune* (January/ February 2012): 17.

25. Renée Sharp and U. Rashid Sumaila, "Quantification of U.S. Marine Fisheries Subsidies," North American Journal of Fisheries Management 29, no. 1 (2009): 18–32. These subsidies were designated specifically for nonfishing management expenses, such as surplus fish purchases, fishing access payments, and disaster aid (pp. 25, 27; amount in 2007 dollars).

26. "Subsidies: Public Funds for Public Services," Briefing Paper 6, Ocean12.eu, June 2010. For a comparison of the amount spent on fisheries support versus subsidies, the EU puts $1.05 billion toward industry support, whereas only $61.9 million is received for conservation management (figures given for 2000 to 2008).

27. Sharpe and Sumaila, "Quantification of U.S. Marine Fisheries Subsidies."

28. Because they cannot be broken down by species, estimates for fuel subsidies on all fishing amounted to $2.825 million from 1996 to 2004 (Sharpe and Sumaila, "Quantification of U.S. Marine Fisheries Subsidies," 25).

29. "Bluefin Tuna Ban Proposal Meets Rejection," *BBC World News*, March 18, 2010, http://news.bbc.co.uk/2/hi/8574775.stm.

30. "E.U. Changes Mind on Bluefin Tuna Being Over-Fished," *BBC World News*, November 19, 2010, http://www.bbc.co.uk/news/world-europe-11793880.

31. "Tuna Fished 'Illegally' during Libya Conflict."

32. Fisheries and Oceans Canada, http://www.dfo-mpo.gc.ca/international/tuna -thon/Kobe-eng.htm (accessed June 5, 2012).

33. As of early 2014, when this book went to press, there was no indication of a fourth round of meetings, which questions the level of commitment to the process and reinforces the difficulties of protecting global common goods.

34. Convention on Fishing and Conservation of Living Resources of the High Seas.

35. UNCLOS Art. 64, 1982, http://www.un.org/depts/los/convention_agreements /texts/unclos/closindx.htm (accessed June 5, 2012).

36. James Joseph et al. 2010. "Addressing the Problem of Excess Fishing Capacity in Tuna Fisheries," in *Conservation and Management of Transnational Tuna Fisheries*, edited by Robin Allen, James Joseph, and Dale Squires (Ames, IA: Blackwell Publishing, 2010), 11–38.

37. Robin Allen, James Joseph, and Dale Squires. 2010. *Conservation and Management of Transnational Tuna Fisheries*, edited by Robin Allen, James Joseph, and Dale Squires (Ames, IA: Blackwell Publishing, 2010), xiii–xiv.

38. "Tuna Fished 'Illegally' during Libya Conflict."

39. DeSombre, "Flags of Convenience," 270.

40. Joseph et al., "Addressing the Problem of Excess Fishing Capacity," 32.

41. Joseph et al., "Addressing the Problem of Excess Fishing Capacity," 19.

42. Joseph et al., "Addressing the Problem of Excess Fishing Capacity," 22.

43. Daniel Pauly, "Aquacalypse Now," *New Republic*, September 28, 2009, http://www.tnr.com/article/environment-energy/aquacalypse-now.

44. Richard Ellis, *Tuna: A Love Story* (New York: Random House, 2008), 10.

45. Greenberg, *Four Fish*, 229.

46. "Taming the Wild Tuna," *New York Times*, September 5, 2010, http://www .nytimes.com/2010/09/05/weekinreview/05greenberg.html.

47. "Bump in Farmed Bluefin Due in 2015," Seafood Source, May 10, 2012, http://www.seafoodsource.com/newsarticledetail.aspx?id=15560.

48. "True Bluefin: The Breeding Scheme Promising a Future for Tuna," European Commission, http://ec.europa.eu/research/infocentre/article_en.cfm?id=/research/star /index_en.cfm?p=326&item=Infocentre&artid=23633 (accessed May 17, 2012).

49. "Tuna Town in Japan Sees Falloff of Its Fish" *New York Times*, September 19, 2009, http://www.nytimes.com/2009/09/20/world/asia/20tuna.html.

50. Dale Squires, "Property and Use Rights in Fisheries," in *Conservation and Management of Transnational Tuna Fisheries*, edited by Robin Allen, James Joseph, and Dale Squires (Ames, IA: Blackwell Publishing, 2010), 50.

51. "U.S. Declines to Protect the Overfished Bluefin Tuna," *New York Times*, May 27, 2011, http://www.nytimes.com/2011/05/28/science/earth/28tuna.html.

52. Stephanie Hedlund, "U.S. Rejects Listing Bluefin as Endangered," Seafood Source, May 26, 2011, http://www.seafoodsource.com/newsarticledetail.aspx?id=10394 (accessed May 17, 2012).

## CHAPTER 8

1. "The State of Food Insecurity in the World," FAO, 2012, http://www.fao.org/docrep/016/i3027e/i3027e00.htm.

2. "Only Commercial Fishers Can Exploit Benham Rise," *Manila Standard Today*, May 31, 2013, http://manilastandardtoday.com/2013/05/31/only-commercial-fishers-can-exploit-benham-rise.

3. "Food Prices," *Economist*, June 2, 2011, http://www.economist.com/node/18775171.

4. "Press Release: Severe Droughts Drive Food Prices Higher, Threatening the Poor," World Bank, August 30, 2012, http://www.worldbank.org/en/news/2012/08/30/severe-droughts-drive-food-prices-higher-threatening-poor.

5. "Selling Mouse Kebabs on Malawi's Roads," *BBC News*, September 3, 2012, http://www.bbc.co.uk/news/world-africa-19466229.

6. Unless otherwise noted, all statistics are from Andrew Joyce et al., "Reducing the Environmental Impact of Dietary Choice: Perspectives from a Behavioural and Social Change Approach," *Journal of Environmental and Public Health*, 2012, http://www.hindawi.com/journals/jeph/2012/978672.

7. "Factory Farms Use 80% of the United States' Antibiotic Supply," *Atlantic Wire*, February 8, 2013, http://www.theatlanticwire.com/technology/2013/02/factory-farms-use-80-united-states-antibiotic-supply/61963/#.URWcW9UDX2M.mailto.

8. Author's calculation based on data from "Rethinking the Meat-Guzzler," *New York Times*, January 27, 2008, http://www.nytimes.com/2008/01/27/weekinreview/27bittman.html.

9. Raj Patel and Philip McMichael, "A Political Economy of the Food Riot," *Review: A Journal of the Fernand Braudel Center* 33, no. 1 (2009): 9–35.

10. "'Tortilla Riots' Give Foretaste of Food Challenge," *Financial Times*, October 12, 2010, http://www.ft.com/cms/s/0/a0aa9ef0-d618-11df-81f0-00144feabdc0.html#axzz2Icy0QTO7.

11. "Food Inflation Soars to 18.32%," *Business Standard*, January 7, 2011, http://www.business-standard.com/india/news/food-inflation-soars-to-1832/421036.

12. "India Launches Huge Cheap Food Programme ahead of Election," *BBC World News*, July 3, 2013, http://www.bbc.co.uk/news/world-asia-india-23164697.

13. "The State of Food Insecurity in the World."

# Selected Bibliography

Allen, Robin, James Joseph, Dale Squires, and Elizabeth Stryjewski. 2010. "Introduction." In *Conservation and Management of Transnational Tuna Fisheries*, edited by Robin Allen, James Joseph, and Dale Squires, 3–10. Ames, IA: Blackwell Publishing.

Bassett, David R., et al. 2008. "Walking, Cycling, and Obesity Rates in Europe, North America, and Australia." *Journal of Physical Activity and Health* 5: 795–814. http://policy.rutgers.edu/faculty/pucher/JPAH08.pdf (accessed December 27, 2013).

Bernstein, William J. 2008. *A Splendid Exchange: How Trade Shaped the World*. New York: Atlantic Monthly Press.

Coe, Sophie D., and Michael D. Coe. 2007. *The True History of Chocolate*. 2nd ed. New York: Thames and Hudson.

DeSombre, Elizabeth R. 2010. "Flags of Convenience and Property Rights on the High Seas." In *Conservation and Management of Transnational Tuna Fisheries*, edited by Robin Allen, James Joseph, and Dale Squires, 269–282. Ames, IA: Blackwell Publishing.

Drewnowski, Adam. 2000. "Fat and Sugar in the Global Diet: Dietary Diversity in the Nutrition Transition." In *Food in Global History*, edited by Raymond Grew, 194–206. Boulder, CO: Westview Press.

Estabrook, Barry. 2011. *Tomatoland*. Kansas City, MO: Andrews McMeel Publishing.

Greenberg, Paul. 2010. *Four Fish: The Future of the Last Wild Food*. London: Penguin.

Joseph, James, Dale Squires, William Bayliff, and Theodore Groves. 2010. "Addressing the Problem of Excess Fishing Capacity in Tuna Fisheries." In *Conservation and Management of Transnational Tuna Fisheries*, edited by Robin Allen, James Joseph, and Dale Squires, 11–38. Ames, IA: Blackwell Publishing.

Kolavalli, Shashi, and Marcella Vigneri. 2011. "Cocoa in Ghana: Shaping the Success of an Economy." In *Yes, Africa Can: Success Stories from a Dynamic Continent*, edited by Punam Chuhan-Pole and Manka Angwafo, 201–218. Washington, DC: World Bank.

MacClean, Rachel. 2010. *Informal Institutions and Citizenship in Rural Africa: Risk and Reciprocity in Ghana and Côte d'Ivoire*. Cambridge: Cambridge University Press.

Mengerink, Kathryn J., Harry N. Scheiber, and Yann-Huei Song. 2010. "Japanese Policies, Ocean Law, and the Tuna Fisheries: Sustainability Goals, the IUU Issue, and Overcapacity." In *Conservation and Management of Transnational Tuna Fisheries*, edited by Robin Allen, James Joseph, and Dale Squires, 283–320. Ames, IA: Blackwell Publishing.

Off, Carol. 2006. *Bitter Chocolate: The Dark Side of the World's Most Seductive Sweet*. Toronto: New Press.

Pilcher, Jeffrey M. 2005. "Industrial Tortillas and Folkloric Pepsi: The Nutritional Consequences of Hybrid Cuisines in Mexico." In *The Cultural Politics of Food and Eating*, edited by Melissa Caldwell and James L. Watson, 222–239. Boston: Blackwell Publishing.

———. 2006. *Food in World History*. New York: Routledge.

Roberts, Paul. 2008. *The End of Food*. New York: Houghton Mifflin Company.

Rothbard, Murray. 2002. *A History of Money and Banking in the United States: The Colonial Era to World War II*. Auburn, AL: Ludwig von Mises Institute.

Sharp, Renée, and U. Rashid Sumaila. 2009. "Quantification of U.S. Marine Fisheries Subsidies." *North American Journal of Fisheries Management* 29, no. 1: 18–32.

Sharpe, Reginald Robinson, City of London (England), Court of Common Council, Library Committee. 1913. *Calendar of Coroners Rolls of the City of London, A.D. 1300–1378*. N.p.: R. Clay and Sons. http://books.google.com /books?id=yWdMAAAAMAAJ&pg=PA109&lpg=PA109&dq=4+shillings +in+1300+AD+was+worth&source=bl&ots=nGRqS75DGm&sig =ZA5d5IF8c8KhvhVLlIkD04RxSms&hl=en&sa=X&ei =ZantUbbBFrbI4APA6oDwCA&ved=0CC0Q6AEwAA#v=onepage&q=4 %20shillings%20in%201300%20AD%20was%20worth&f=false (accessed July 22, 2013).

Shurtleff, William, and Akiki Aoyagi. 2007. "History of World Soybean Production and Trade—Part 1: A Special Report on History of Soybean Production and Trade around the World: A Chapter from the Unpublished Manuscript, *History of Soybeans and Soyfoods: 1100 B.C. to the 1980s*." SoyInfo Center. http://www.soyinfocenter.com/HSS/production_and_trade1.php (accessed September 22, 2013).

Squires, Dale. 2010. "Property and Use Rights in Fisheries." In *Conservation and Management of Transnational Tuna Fisheries*, edited by Robin Allen, James Joseph, and Dale Squires, 39–64. Ames, IA: Blackwell Publishing.

Standage, Tom. 2010. *An Edible History of Humanity*. New York: Walker and Company.

Temperton, Paul. 2001. *The UK and the Euro*. London: Wiley and Sons.

Turner, Jack. 2004. *Spice*. New York: Alfred A. Knopf.

Young, Allen M. 2007. *The Chocolate Tree: A Natural History of Cacao*. Gainesville: University Press of Florida.

# INDEX

# About the Author

Kimberly A. Weir is associate professor at Northern Kentucky University. This book developed out of a desire to raise awareness among students of their individual relationships with the global food system. In addition to food politics, her research interests include pedagogy, gender issues, and the fair trade movement. Given the opportunity, she will travel just about anywhere in the world, where, invariably, she will discover yet another food issue to explore.